Religion and the Authority of the Past

RATIO
INSTITUTE FOR THE HUMANITIES

Edited by Tobin Siebers

To take the measure of things and their mismeasure, to reason unto unreason, to suffer to count and to be accountable—such is the ratio of that form of life called the human.

Discourses of Sexuality: From Aristotle to AIDS
Edited by Domna C. Stanton

Religion and the Authority of the Past
Edited by Tobin Siebers

RELIGION AND THE AUTHORITY OF THE PAST

Edited by Tobin Siebers

With an Introduction by Wendy Doniger

Ann Arbor

THE UNIVERSITY OF MICHIGAN PRESS

ISBN 0-472-10489-6 (cloth)
ISBN 0-472-08259-0 (paper)
Published in the United States of America by
The University of Michigan Press
Manufactured in the United States of America

1996 1995 1994 1993 4 3 2 1

Library of Congress Cataloging-in-Publication Data
Religion and the authority of the past / edited by Tobin Siebers;
with an introduction by Wendy Doniger.
p. cm. — (Ratio)
Includes bibliographical references.
ISBN 0-472-10489-6 (alk. paper). — ISBN 0-472-08259-0 (pbk. : alk. paper)
1. Authority—Religious aspects. I. Siebers, Tobin. II. Series.
BL105.R45 1993
291.6'5—dc20 93-39931
CIP

Permissions

"Imagining Idolatry" by Judith Laikin Elkin first appeared in 1993 as a pamphlet published jointly by the Touro National Heritage Trust, the Program in Judaic Studies at Brown University, and the John Carter Brown Library.

"Seeking the Meridian" by Sidra DeKoven Ezrahi first appeared as "'The Grave in the Air': Unbound Metaphors in Post-Holocaust Poetry" in 1992 in *Probing the Limits of Representation* edited by Saul Friedlander and is reprinted in a substantially revised form with the kind permission of Harvard University Press.

"*Todesfuge*" by Paul Celan, trans. John Felstiner, is reprinted by permission of the publishers from *Probing the Limits of Representation* edited by Saul Friedlander, Cambridge, Mass.: Harvard University Press, Copyright © 1992 by the President and Fellows of Harvard College.

Dein aschenes Haar, Sulamit (1981), *Dein goldenes Haar, Margarethe* (1981), and *Margarethe* (1982) by Anselm Kiefer have been reproduced courtesy of the artist from Mark Rosenthal, *Anselm Kiefer*, published in 1987 by the Art Institute of Chicago and the Philadelphia Museum of Art.

The Attic red-figured kalyx-crater by Euxitheos and Euphronios, Death and Sleep carry away the corpse of Sarpedon as Hermes presides, is reproduced through the permission of the Metropolitan Museum of Art, Bequest of Joseph H. Durkee, Gift of Darius Ogden Mills, and Gift of C. Ruxton Love, by Exchange, 1972 (1972.11.10).

Acknowledgments

Religion and the Authority of the Past is the second volume in *Ratio,* the publication series of the Institute for the Humanities at the University of Michigan. It attests to the fact of *Ratio's* existence as a series, and with this sense of continuity comes an added dimension of gratitude to those people whose sustained efforts have made the series possible. The staff members of the Institute welcome the visitors from whom our contributors are selected, and it is in good part to the atmosphere that they create that our volumes owe their character and quality. They bear from day to day the added work and stress created by the series. To Eliza Woodford, above all, I owe a debt of gratitude. She has worked tirelessly and happily on every aspect of production: contacting authors, securing permissions, converting text to disk, creating new fonts for our character array, and typesetting. I also thank Mary Beecher Price for her good advice, resourcefulness, and sense of humor. James Winn, the Director of the Institute, has supported the series from the beginning both financially and spiritually. Every summer he sets aside his own work to help with the typesetting of the final pages, bringing to each volume his sense of taste and untiring demand for perfection. Our copyeditor, Mary Dearborn, has been notable for her patience and meticulous work. Special thanks for advice about Docutech printing also go to M. J. Wright at the Xerox Corporation, and to Ralph E. Maten, Shereen Sauer, and Brenda Lynn Snyder of the University of Michigan Law School Copy Center.

This volume, of course, would not exist without the cooperation and generosity of our eleven contributors. Editing their work has been a pleasure. Wendy Doniger, especially, deserves my thanks for agreeing to write the introduction. Finally, I would like to acknowledge the last efforts of Barbara Stoler Miller. Her death saddened everyone at the Institute. She remained in the last weeks of her life an exemplary spirit, responding to requests and queries that we felt timid about making but that were for her part of the lifetime of work to which she had dedicated herself with passion, good cheer, and intelligence.

—Tobin Siebers

Contents

Introduction: The Authority of the Parental Metaphor 1
Wendy Doniger

1. Clean Hands and Shining Helmets: Heroic Action in Early Chinese and Greek Culture 13
David N. Keightley

2. The Authority of the Hindu Epics: Genealogy, Authenticity, and Authorship 52
Barbara Stoler Miller

3. Imagining Idolatry: Missionaries, Indians, and Jews 75
Judith Laikin Elkin

4. Empire to Commonwealth: Consequences of Monotheism in Late Antiquity 100
Garth Fowden

5. Current Arab Paradigms for an Islamic Future 119
Yvonne Yazbeck Haddad

6. Carving for the Saints 161
Michael R. Kapetan

7. Modernizing Tradition: Some Catholic Neo-Scholastics and the Genealogy of Natural Rights 184
Robert E. Sullivan

8. Puritans in Babylon: The Ancient Near East and the Revolution in Intellectual Life, 1888–1938 209
Bruce Kuklick

9. The Search for Authority in Twentieth-Century Judaism 222
Arnold Eisen

10. Seeking the Meridian: The Reconstitution of Space and Audience in the Poetry of Paul Celan and Dan Pagis 253
Sidra DeKoven Ezrahi

Epilogue: Nietzsche's Lion 285
Tobin Siebers

Notes on Contributors 293

INTRODUCTION: The Authority of the Parental Metaphor

Wendy Doniger

It is appropriate, I think, that the task of introduction (or synthesis) should fall to a comparativist, whose job it is to find commonalities among cultural phenomena on all levels. But since, whatever cognitive pen I might manage to construct, one or more of my sheep would escape, I think it is best to settle for a kind of cognitive Venn diagram. I have tried to select not the central line of each essay but rather those aspects of each one that contribute to a line of my own casting, and in this way to comment not on what each of our contributors has made of the relevant data but, rather, on what someone looking at the collection as a whole (i.e., me) can make of the data.

I have looked first for the thread of human meaning in intimate personal relationships; for if these various worlds of archæology and epic, Catholic and Muslim, Hellenistic and Jewish, Chinese and Hindu traditions are joined anywhere, they are joined at the hip. I propose, therefore, to discuss the authority of the past in terms of parental metaphors, to focus attention on the *author* in authority: the Author of the world (G/god), of each of us (father), and of the text (the tradition). When we undertake the sort of regressive reappropriation of the past that Bruce Kuklick has illuminated (in "Puritans in Babylon: The Ancient Near East and the Revolution in Intellectual Life, 1880–1930"), our attitude to that past and to its authority will be tempered, if not determined, by our attitude to the first and most basic authority that we encounter, the authority of our parents. Parental authority is, in short, the bottom line. As Michael Kapetan remarked (in "Carving for the Saints"), when asked what was Macedonian about a carving he had made, "The only thing that I am sure is Macedonian about this carving is that my grandmother was born there."

Polytheistic Parents and Fragmented Children in Greece, China, and India

In many of these essays, parents are not only authorities (which we might expect) but antiauthorities (which is more surprising); the parental model of God is the problem as often as it is the solution. For instance, when David N. Keightley (in "Clean Hands and Shining Helmets: Heroic Action in Early Chinese and Greek Culture") contrasts the ancient Greek and Chinese attitudes to fathers, he cites Achilles' lament over Patroclus in Homer's *Iliad*: "There is no more shattering blow that I could suffer, not even if I should learn of my own father's death ... or the death of my dear son." And Keightley remarks, "The degree of Achilles' anguish and alienation, as well as the non-Chineseness of his response, is to be found in his willingness to put his love for his friend Patroclus above his love for his nearest kin, his father!"

These fathers can be frightening to their sons, as Keightley notes. Hector in his battle helmet frightens his son and Hector prays that the child will be "a better man than his father," a wish that would have made Freud's day. Chinese fathers, by contrast, are seldom if ever depicted in opposition to their sons, a contrast that surely correlates with the fact that, as Keightley remarks, "Early Chinese mythology, thus, does not present malevolent gods who resented human success or conspired to destroy man. The Chinese knew neither a Prometheus nor a Zeus." And he concludes that "The problems, including that of theodicy, that the Greeks had treated as 'mythological issues,' had been resolved by the Chinese creation of ancestors, who, following Fortes's definition, were ancestors precisely because they were *not* comprehensive or detailed representations of personality and social roles. The concern with unstructured and potentially adversarial personality—in both religion and art—had been displaced by harmonious order and design." Thus familial disharmony is banished or denied, and the resulting familial harmony is the cause (or effect, or, most likely, both cause and effect) of religious harmony.

The Hindu epics, so closely related to Homer's epics in language and in other, more subtle structures, present a model of relationships with both parents and deities not unlike Homer's. Beyond that, however, as Barbara Stoler Miller demonstrates (in "The Authority of the Hindu Epics: Genealogy, Authenticity, and Authorship"), the Indian epics present the author as father. Vālmīki, the author of the text of the *Rāmāyaṇa*, is also the stepfather of the heroes' sons, the literary surrogate parent. But the parentage of the hero of the *Rāmāyaṇa*, Rāma himself, and of his brothers is highly problematic: the joint embryology is strangely fragmented (for the consecrated pot of rice that impregnates the mothers is divided into highly irregular fractions), resulting in competition among the mothers; and the failure of Rāma's father to resolve these competing claims to succession results in the tragedy of the *Rāmāyaṇa*—the death of Rāma's father and the suffering of Rāma and Sītā.

So, too, in the other great Sanskrit epic, the *Mahābhārata*, Vyāsa, the "author" of the text, is the "author" (the grandfather) of the heroes, but a most problematic grandfather, an unsatisfactory substitute for the true parent, and so he produces unsatisfactory offspring (one pale, one blind, one a servant). Bhīṣma, too, the other grandfather, is a problematic father, to put it mildly. And Karṇa, the son rejected by his mother and father, is one of the great tragic figures of the *Mahābhārata*. Beneath these impotent fathers lie angry women, and behind the whole epic myth lies the earlier, Vedic story of the unsatisfactory substitute mother, the Shadow (Chāyā) of the true mother, who mistreats her stepchildren, the ancestors of the human race, so that death comes into the world.[1] These tragically flawed, rejecting fathers (and mothers) go a long way to explain the violence and malevolence of the Hindu gods. For if, as Freud argued, God is our father, what does it mean for our theology (more precisely, for our theodicy) to discover that he is a false and impotent father? Or even (a thought that never occurred to Freud) a false and sterile mother? How does this qualify our attitude to the authority of the parental deity? The inadequacy of human parents is, in this view, an inevitable reflection of the inadequacy of the divine parents; as Woody Allen put it, in his reply to Leibniz's theodicy, "God isn't evil; he's just an underachiever."

---

[1]On the Vedic Shadow mother, see Wendy Doniger O'Flaherty, *Women, Androgynes, and Other Mythical Beasts* (Chicago: University of Chicago Press, 1981).

Monotheistic versus Polytheistic Fathers in Catholic and Muslim Encounters with Others

The Malinowskian anthropologists who argued that savages didn't know who their daddies were might have assumed that monotheisms would present a parental model of divinity while polytheisms would not. But the materials presented by Keightley and Miller reveal a greater complexity: polytheistic religions still have mothers and fathers, but they fragment them, to correspond to the fragmentation of the pantheon. Thus we may recall the antiparental revolt in Greek polytheism—Zeus castrating Kronos—and the revolt of the younger gods against the older gods in the Babylonian *Enuma Elish.* Whether it is Zeus against his one father, or a group of younger gods against a group of older gods, it still happens, just as Freud (in *Totem and Taboo*) said it happened.

What happens, then, when the parental model of monotheism encounters, historically, the parental models of polytheism? Judith Elkin (in "Imagining Idolatry: Missionaries, Indians, and Jews") analyzes a meeting of three religious currents, two monotheistic (Catholic and Jewish) and one polytheistic (Native American). She portrays the paradoxical situation in which the church persecuted Jews, and not Native Americans, for idolatry, although the Native Americans were idolatrous and the Jews (what few Jews there were at all) were staunchly anti-idolatrous. (In fact, as Margalit and Halbertal have pointed out, the anti-idolatrous stance in ancient Judaism is often expressed in metaphors of relationships between parents and children, husbands and wives.[2]) Elkin sees this as an example of what Rolena Adorno has called "the process of fixing 'otherness' by grasping onto similarities," and she points out what the Spanish had to gain by emphasizing the "similarities" between idolatrous Jews and Native Americans: "Most Native Americans living under Spanish rule 'understood' what was required of them, at least in part because they were required to attend the periodic burnings of those other New Christians, those who descended from Jews. The sight of presumed idolaters being burned alive must have con-

[2]Avishai Margalit and Moshe Halbertal, *Idolatry*, trans. Naomi Goldblum (Cambridge, Mass.: Harvard University Press, 1992).

centrated their minds wonderfully." But there may have been another explanation for the sideways displacement of the accusation of idolatry, stemming from a paternal heritage: Don Carlos had been accused of idolatry by his nephew. "One aspect of the matter that the bishops failed to investigate was whether there might have been an ulterior motive for the denunciation. In fact, the nephew was a rival claimant to the estate of his late father, Don Carlos's brother." Might we not replicate this insight on the outer frame of the analysis, and suggest that since the Jews were the rival claimants (against the Christians) to the estate, as it were, of the Hebrew Bible, they were more hated than the Native Americans who were not yet, as it were (again), part of the family at all? In a similar vein, the early Christians claimed Rachel, the younger and more beloved daughter, as a symbol of their tradition, while Leah, the older but rejected sister, represented the Jews. And Garth Fowden (in "Empire to Commonwealth: Consequences of Monotheism in Late Antiquity") presents a dispute about the true son of the father in the Ethiopian epic, stated in parental terms: the text argues that the Ethiopians were the true inheritors of the biblical authority, descendants of the first-born son of Solomon, while the Byzantine emperor was descended merely from a younger son.

The other sibling in this monotheistic family circle, Islam, is in itself a family within which there are sibling rivalries and similar squabbles about inheritance, which provide the argument at the heart of (or at least the excuse for, the metaphor for) the Sunnī/Shī'īte split: who is the true son of Muḥamad? Or, to shift from fathers to mothers, still within Islam, we might note the problem of Hagar, the mother of the Arabs, who is just a substitute mother (like the Vedic Shadow mother). Some have solved this problem by arguing that Sarah rather than Hagar was in fact the mother of the Arabs.

This pattern suggests that fragmented claims to authority within monotheisms are not between rival fathers (as in polytheism) but between the rival sons of the one father (or the one mother). Garth Fowden details the workings of such sibling disputes within two different "missionary monotheisms" in late antiquity, Christianity, and Islam. He notes that polytheistic Hellenism lacked the power of penetration and the appeal to the illiterate that Christianity had; it could not reach the level on which polytheism actually functioned. The combination of polyarchy and polytheism in Rome gave way to the monarchy and monotheism of Constantine. But "monotheism is a less effective friend of monarchy" than might be supposed. The unity of monotheism was undercut both by its Trinitarian nature and by its dual nature (Christ as both human and divine), leading to schisms. For monotheism itself is divisive: while polytheism diffuses the natural tendency to human diversity, monotheism, when it is too rigid, ignites debate. Intolerance leads to heresy. In other words, where the parental yoke is too heavy, it leads to rebellion; the children won't go to church. Where there are more contradictions, there are more exits. Yvonne Yazbeck Haddad told a striking anecdote to this effect during the conference that produced some of these essays, though she did not include it here: a woman she knew was raised by a strict churchgoing Christian mother and rebelled against her; not wanting her children to be like her mother (and perhaps recalling the old adage that the reason that children and their grandparents get along so well is that they share a common enemy), she forced her children to accompany her to church, hoping that when they grew up they would rebel against her and hate the church—as she did. It worked. Thus, to return to our historical instance, Christianity was *more* successful in areas where Rome was *less* successful. The humble image of suppliant women prevailed where the macho image of Christian soldiers failed.

Contrariwise, Fowden notes that a flexible relationship between religion and empire was the key to Islam's success in conversion. The Muslims were inflexible in doctrine but flexible in their actual dealings with other monotheisms. In striking contrast to the Spanish policy that favored Native Americans over Jews, the Muslims in late antiquity banned polytheistic religions but were tolerant toward other monotheisms. In this way, they allowed revolutions within in order to forestall revolutions from without. Significantly for our unifying paradigm, Fowden characterizes Baghdad as the "senescent or dead parent." This senescence apparently made it possible for the brothers to dwell in relative harmony, like the harmony of the Chinese descendants of the vague and distant ancestors. Empires, like religions, have parents, and live within parental metaphors.

Yvonne Yazbeck Haddad (in "Current Arab Paradigms for an Islamic Future") comments on the importance of "family values" in the contemporary Islamic critique of the West: "Continued emulation of the West can only lead to a moral, cultural, and intellectual bankruptcy and to a replication of its ills, represented, these critics say, by the breakdown of the family, pornography, drugs and AIDS." These four "social diseases" from the West, which Islam wishes to reject, culminate in AIDS, an acronym laden with irony in the context of the aid program of American imperialism. For Islam today, the West is a paradoxical combination of a "senescent or dead parent" and an unacceptably rebellious child. An even more telling, if implicit, parental metaphor is reflected in the stark contrast that Haddad draws between the way in which European philosophers tend to deny their Muslim intellectual parents and acknowledge only their Greek lineage, while Muslims explicitly reject certain Greek ideas in favor of their own orthodox code of law.

Loss of Monotheistic Parent, Loss of Author, Loss of Faith, in the Christian Encounter with the Pagan Past

Thus we have seen ways in which fragmented claims to authority within monotheisms produce shifting patterns in the confrontations with polytheism. Other sorts of fragmentations take place within the monotheisms themselves. Robert E. Sullivan (in "Modernizing Tradition: Some Catholic Neo-Scholastics and the Genealogy of Natural Rights") describes a diffusion of authority in the resurrection of Aquinas in neo-Scholasticism. Pio Nono asserts his own authority in the notorious phrase, "*La tradizione son'io*" (which might be translated as, "*L'état, c'est moi*," or, even, "I am the authority; I am the father; I am the author"—that is, he claimed authority over church and state, but also over the family). This centralization of authorities made it necessary to interpret medieval pluralism as a kind of a unity, and to do this Pio Nono picked a staunchly unitary author (Aquinas) to support his own claims. Yet at the same time, in order to make modern pluralism possible, it was necessary to make Aquinas more flexible, more vague, and less rigid. The inspiration to do this by appropriating, of all people, John Locke, a heretic on the proscribed list, is truly stunning. When Locke is used without being cited, and Aquinas is cited without any actual statement of what he said (in part because what he said would not make the arguments that are wanted, and in part because people no longer know what he said), who is the author? The pope, of course, the Holy Father; and, by implication, God. We know all about Whig history, but it can't hold a candle to Whig theology.

We might go on to note still other sorts of fragmentations of parental authority in the Catholic church, such as the visualization of the earth as mother and the church as father, with God on top (in the missionary position, of course), and Mary and all those female saints on the bottom. This is, in effect, a division between authority (the father, single) and power (the mother, multiple), and it requires a polygamous model, rather than a polyandrous model: one male, with many females.[3] But therein lies another tale.

Within the monotheistic traditions, parental authority was eroded in various ways. Bruce Kuklick shows us how a generation of archæologists became progressively less religiously committed: that is, the ones who started out on the later expeditions started out with less religious ideas and motivations, and, in addition, some of them lost some of their faith in the course of the expedition. What they took back with them, in place of that lost faith, was the basis of some sort of comparative religion (this is also the era in which F. Max Müller was establishing that discipline): "Ours is not the only road, but, still, ours may be a road." Yet, though the scholars on the digs became less religious, they did not, apparently, become less racist, less Eurocentric ("Ours is not the only race, the only civilization"). The valuing of the disembodied objects over the embodied human beings who guarded them and in fact owned them (the racism of the pith helmet movies: "We of the enlightened West must save these objects, which contain the soul of our own civilization, from the barbarians who do not understand them") implied that *we* are authoritative, and the people who had the custodianship of these objects are not. For racism and Eurocentrism are not ideas, like monotheisms; they are practices, felt in the gut rather than in

---

[3]For the relationship between power and authority, see O'Flaherty, and for the relationship between polygamy/polyandry and images of divine power, see Margalit and Halbertal.

the mind, and they hang on long after the ideas have been modified.

There were other, more subtle ways in which the authority of the Christian past was eroded in the trenches of Babylon. First of all, the scholars on the expeditions encountered the impermanence of empire, the death of the parents: at first, it was just the death of their parents and not ours ("Babylon is in ruins, but Christianity lives"). Ultimately, however, the powerful images of the mighty fallen cast their shadow on the scholars' confidence in their own impermanence as well: "We are all orphans." This loss of faith in the authority of the past is reflected in both Nietzsche (God is dead) and Dostoyevski (whose Grand Inquisitor pointed out that, if God is dead, *anything is possible*).

What was left for these archæologists? In their Enlightened minds, the authority of the past lay in the authority of time and space, particularly in the way that time and space could be precisely tabulated with numbers and laid out on a grid. Stratigraphy and seriation laid down the law: lower=older. But this model, too, soon began to crumble, leading to an experience of the impermanence of time and space. The fact that the excavators did not respect their own codes in taking the tablets out of the mound, and hence did *not* have any seriation or even horizontal variables, suggests that they had loss faith in the Enlightenment authority as well as the authority of the church.

Bad-Enough Fathers, Bad-Enough Deities, in Contemporary Judaism

To relax authority in order to remain flexible may solve the problem of conversion (as Fowden has shown), but it does not solve the problem of *de*-conversion, of loss of faith (as Kuklick has shown). Sullivan notes that the Vatican worried about "the confusion of liberty with license." For the Jews, too, as Arnold Eisen has demonstrated (in "The Search for Authority in Twentieth-Century Judaism"), emancipation led, for some, to the fear of freedom: anything is possible (as the Grand Inquisitor noted in another, but not unrelated, context). The idea that lack of authority leads to chaos is in itself a parental idea: what *child* ever conceived of freedom as a problem? Total freedom means that we ourselves are the authors of our lives, as Sartre pointed out, or that we are in search of the author, as Pirandello pointed out and Eisen recalls: "The drama is in us and we are the drama."

From Kant on, the Enlightenment was a rebellion against the Father, against "irrational" obedience to God. Does God favor one child over another? The idea of being "chosen" becomes very problematic indeed if there are siblings; it is fine if you regard yourself as God's only child. As Eisen suggests, we need communities, but we also need to find ways to keep them from killing one another in sibling rivalry. We need Jerusalem as a place, a center of parental religious authority, but the brothers (and sisters) will fight over it, as they fight over all parental inheritances. Did God die intestate?

What is the authority of the human father in Judaism? As Eisen notes of contemporary Jews: "Their decision concerning faith, like their ambivalence concerning Judaism, forms part of the larger process of identity formation through which they become the children of their parents, indebted but separate. Because Judaism, like Christianity, is permeated with imagery of fathers (and, increasingly, mothers) and children, because one cannot hear 'chosen people' or similar phrases without the love of a parent coming to mind, the link is all the stronger." Abraham, the model father, was a terrible father, and hence a very *good* example for modern parents; he teaches us that we, too, are bound to be terrible parents (or, if we allow Bettelheim to get us off the hook, good-enough mothers). Moses Mendelssohn argued that belief, as such, was not so important; you have to internalize it and hand it on. But then two of his three children converted to Christianity (and his grandson, Wach, "invented" the history of religions). To rationalize religion is to remove the parental authority, which is, I think, to remove the authority. The following story (a variant of Eisen's story of the river flowing upstream) makes my point. Ten rabbis debated whether a certain oven was sufficiently purified to be kosher for a special occasion. Nine of them said that it was, but the tenth said that it wasn't. Finally, the tenth rabbi invoked God. "If I am right about this oven," he said, "let the Almighty send a sign from heaven." Suddenly, the sky grew dark, a single, terrible bolt of lightning struck the synagogue, and a voice boomed out: "The oven is not purified." Then it became light again. After a considerable silence, one of the nine rabbis cleared his throat and said, "Okay, now the vote is nine to two." God may not be dead, but he has certainly lost his veto power—which is a very precious parental prerogative.

Religious arguments can be usefully classified according to two groups: "because" arguments (which are explicit dogmas, or appeals to authority) and "this is why" arguments (which are implicit rationalizations, or appeals to persuasion). The "because" arguments are like the nonarguments that every parent uses when he or she cannot, or will not, explain something to a child who asks "why" something should be done as the parent says it should be done: "I am bigger than you and I run this show and I tell you it *is* this way and that is all I am going to tell you." Franz Rosenzweig, as Eisen reveals him to us, is arguing with, and on behalf of, the "because" arguments. These are arguments not about logic ("why") but about affect and habit (as Weber, James, and Freud have demonstrated). There is an experiential basis to the parental argument: "You had to have been there" translates into "I have been there, and you haven't, and so I invoke the authority of *my* past (which I equate with *your* future) to tell you not to do this."

If experiential parental authority vanishes, what can take its place? Sidra DeKoven Ezrahi (in "Seeking the Meridian: The Reconstitution of Space and Audience in the Poetry of Paul Celan and Dan Pagis") holds out the fragile hope that language might, in various ways, provide a new kind of authority for contemporary Judaism, replacing not only parents but the parental land. Both of the poets who concern her incorporated into their art, into their linguistic constructions, their grief for their lost parents and their lost homeland (Bukovina in Romania).

Paul Celan's parents were deported in 1942 to a Nazi internment camp in Transnistria. The following year he learned that his mother was shot to death. She was to become a haunting presence in his subsequent poetry. As Ezrahi comments, "The poet's native ground had become a grave, but only set loose, ungrounded—only as a 'grave in the air'—could it become truly portable: the locus of a poetry that hovers over the earth, that frees (or *compels*) the survivor to become a wanderer." To assimilate this understanding to our central argument, it might be said that only when you break away from the mother land do you possess it/her. It might well be that this image of a lost mother lurks behind the famous image of "black milk," a maternal oxymoron that resonates with the strange *molu* plant that Homer speaks of in the *Odyssey* (10:305), which had a black root and a white flower and protected men from an evil goddess.

Dan Pagis lost his mother to disease and his father through emigration to Palestine in 1934 (when Pagis was four). In "Written in Pencil..." as elsewhere, Pagis "replaces the archetypal victim, Isaac, with a composite figure, a fraternity of murder, Cain *and* Abel." Again, as in so many of the essays collected here, we see a religion wrestling with its own traditions: the threatening parental figure of the Bible is passed over in favor of an equally troubled but more equal image of rival brothers.

Sidra Ezrahi points out a telling difference between the ways in which Celan and Pagis dealt with the loss of their parents and their parental lands: "The first [Celan] remained lost at sea, as it were, or stranded on a desert island, positing his poetry as a message sent out in a bottle.... The second [Pagis] washed ashore, in Palestine, on a language and a clearly defined audience engaged in a collective act of reparation." It seems to me that the essays in this volume cumulatively speak a warning against the solution found by Pagis, the replacement of one lost authority with another, leading to the inevitable replication of rebellion and the equally inevitable reassertion of the new authority. Celan's solution, though tragically lonely, seems better to represent the genuine option of our age—we find ourselves on a desert island, cut off forever from the religious authority of the past.

CLEAN HANDS AND SHINING HELMETS: Heroic Action in Early Chinese and Greek Culture

David N. Keightley

For large periods of time in both the West and China the authority of a "classical" past had a paramount importance in shaping the conception of what it was to be human. It is true that between the fall of the Roman Empire and the fall of Constantinople, knowledge of Greece had been lost to Christendom for the better part of a millennium,[1] but a renewed interest in the traditions of Greece and Rome was a central feature of the great cultural and humanistic revolution that we call the Renaissance. It is evident, furthermore, as Frank M. Turner has written, that "extensive ... concern with ancient Greece" became an important and "novel factor in modern European intellectual life" as "the values, ideas, and institutions inherited from the Roman and Christian past became problematical." Europeans turned to the Greeks, accordingly, "for new cultural roots and alternative cultural patterns ... in the wake of the Enlightenment and of revolution." This led to a situation in which "to no small extent knowledge of the classical world and acquaintance with the values communicated through the vehicle of classical education informed the mind and provided much of the intellectual confidence of the ruling political classes of Europe."[2]

What had become true of England and late modern Europe had, more or less, been true of China for a period of some two thousand years. The degree to which Chinese elites, down to the intellectual and political revolutions of the late nineteenth and the twentieth centuries, found their power in the authority of tradition is well known. This tradition had been institutionalized in a system of education and recruitment based on an orthodox classical curriculum that took as its core a series of so-called Confucian texts, some of which dated to the first part of the first millennium *B.C.* Just as late modern Europe had accepted "the centuries-old belief that a

---

[1]Bernard Knox, "Introduction" to *The Iliad*, trans. Robert Fagles (New York: Viking, 1990) 5–6.

[2]Frank M. Turner, *The Greek Heritage in Victorian Britain* (New Haven: Yale, 1981) 1–2, 5.

man had only to know Greek and Latin to be educated—to be a cut above humanity,"[3] so had the Chinese accepted the millennia-old belief that knowledge of the Classics and the rather arcane language in which those hallowed texts were written gave a man the right, as well as the duty, to rule his fellow men.

Certain early texts served in Greece and China, at roughly comparable stages of development, to exemplify what it was to be human in terms of past heroic action. In what follows, I shall look primarily at epics and histories, not at philosophical or other texts, though I suspect that many of the distinctions I identify could be found in those materials as well. For Greece, I rely primarily upon the epic traditions, represented by Homer's *Iliad* (and to a lesser extent, his *Odyssey*) and by Hesiod's *Theogony*; these texts were compiled and recorded, give or take a century, around 700 *B.C.* but had their roots in the oral compositions of the previous centuries. For China, I rely primarily upon the closest equivalents we have: the *Book of Songs (Shi)*, the pronouncements of the *Book of Documents (Shu)*, and the extensive historical anecdotes recorded in *Zuozhuan*; the material in these texts is of varying date, running from the early part of the first millennium to about the fourth century *B.C.*[4]

These Chinese and Greek materials are not, strictly speaking, comparable documents. Indeed, if I wanted to reduce the burden of my essay to one idea, it would be that the early Chinese did not produce—or at least did not preserve—the kind of epics that the early Greeks did.[5] This does not

---

[3]Ved Mehta, "Personal History: The Classics at Oxford, A Lasting Impression," *The New Yorker*, 11 November 1991, 92. Mehta's fascinating memoir is an account of Jasper Griffin's education and career as a classicist in the mid-twentieth century.

[4]A useful introduction to these and related texts is provided by Burton Watson, *Early Chinese Literature* (New York: Columbia University Press, 1962). For a more technical introduction to the dating and authenticity of the Chinese texts referred to in this essay, see Michael Loewe, ed., *Early Chinese Texts: A Bibliographical Guide* (Berkeley: Society for the Study of Early China, forthcoming).

[5]The point is well argued by C. H. Wang, "Towards Defining a Chinese Heroism," *Journal of the American Oriental Society* 95, 1 (January-March 1975): 25–35.

mean that we cannot compare the two cultures in a fruitful way. It means, rather, that we need to consider what kinds of representations of the human condition the Chinese did produce and preserve in the place of such epics, why they produced and preserved them, and what kinds of humanity were portrayed and venerated in those representations. If the works of Homer and Hesiod helped to define what it was to be Greek, the *Songs*, *Documents*, and *Zuozhuan* played a similar role in China, particularly in the long imperial period that followed the Han dynasty (206 *B.C.-A.D.* 220).

The traditional Chinese, in fact, invested so much philosophical and literary effort in their classical tradition that when China was faced with the onslaught of the West and with the social upheavals accompanying the end of the Qing dynasty (1644–1911), it did not—unlike the Europeans of the eighteenth century—have its own Greece to turn to for *fresh* inspiration. The attempt was certainly made, in the forced and even tragic exertions of the *jinwen* ("modern text") thinkers and late Qing political reformers, but China had already, as it were, exhausted that inspiration. It could not be made fresh and new. Whether in the Marxism of Mao Zedong or the yearnings for democracy of student dissidents after him, the West has, for better or worse, now become, to a significant degree, China's Greece and Rome.

The Asian Games, recently held in Beijing, like the Olympics that the Chinese hope to host in the year 2000, can thus be seen as the descendants of the games that Achilles held for Patroclus's funeral, games that the Greeks felt lay at the origin of their own Olympic and other pan-Hellenic competitions. They serve as one example of China's attempt to appropriate part of the West's classical and now international heritage into China's modern culture. The modernization of China—including the modernization of its artistic as well as its political culture—will inevitably involve a reconsideration of classical representations of the human condition, whether in China or the West.

Representations of the Hero

I define the hero in broad terms as a protagonist of exceptional courage and fortitude who engages in bold and significant actions. I do not insist in a comparative essay of this sort on the hero's most fundamental Homeric aspect, "that the hero must experience death" and be associated with religious cult.[6] The nature of religious belief and practice has a fundamental influence in such matters (see the discussion of ritual and worship below), but here I would simply note that my instinctive preference for using, in an essay about humanity, a basic analytical category derived from the Greek *heros* suggests the degree to which my concerns are shaped—even misshaped—by Western assumptions. I shall return to this point in my conclusion.

Let me start with a specific example: the legendary theme of Achilles and Penthesileia, the Amazon queen. The theme, which was popular in both Greek and Roman culture, expresses significant views about the individual and society that would have been entirely foreign to Chinese contemporaries. It provides an excellent example of the way in which Chinese and Greek conceptions of man and hero may be distinguished.

If we consider the theme as treated by the Attic black-figure potter and painter Exekias on an amphora from around 540 *B.C.* (fig. 1), we can note a variety of characteristic features. The two protagonists are heroic in size, seeming to burst the confines of the bowl. Achilles is naked from the waist down. His face is concealed by his helmet so that only his eye glares forth; his victim's face, by contrast, is exposed and vulnerable.[7]

---

[6]Gregory Nagy, *The Best of the Achæans: Concepts of the Hero in Archaic Greek Poetry* (Baltimore: Johns Hopkins University Press, 1979) 9.

[7]My discussion of the Greek vase and the of the Chinese *hu* (below) is largely taken from David N. Keightley, "Early Civilization in China: Reflections on How It Became Chinese," in *Heritage of China: Contemporary Perspectives on Chinese Civilization*, ed. Paul S. Ropp (Berkeley: University of California Press, 1990) 16–19.

Figure 1. Detail from black-figure amphora by Exekias, ca. 540. B.C., depicting Achilles fighting Penthesileia at Troy. London: British Museum B210. Photo: Max Hirmer.

The painting is characterized by the particularity of both its subject and author. We can identify the two figures, Achilles and Penthesileia, and we can identify the individual, Exekias, who made the vase; all three names are actually painted on the vase. And, most importantly, there is the irony of the tale itself. At the moment when Achilles plunges his sword into the breast of his swooning victim, their eyes meet and he desires her! The artist has captured precisely this moment of dramatic and fatal pathos. The painting and the legend express in powerful, individual, and supposedly historical terms one of the major assumptions of the heroic tradition in the West, namely, that man's condition is tragic and poignant, that the best and most valorous deeds may lead to undesired consequences, and that heroic virtue must be its own reward. Man lives in a quirky, unpredictable, and ironic world that is, by its very nature, unresponsive to human values and desires.

The gods of the *Iliad* are unpredictable in precisely this way and they are frequently hostile to certain men. "Hera, the wife of Zeus, and Athena, his daughter," for example, "hate Troy and the Trojans with a bitter, merciless hatred."[8] As Apollo says in Book 24 of the *Iliad*, "Hard-hearted are you, you gods. You live for cruelty" (24:39).[9] Like Homer, Hesiod in his *Theogony* and *Works and Days* portrays the gods as "changeable, irresponsible, and frequently hostile to individuals or groups of men."[10]

We may consider, by contrast, the decoration found on an Eastern Zhou bronze *hu*-vase (fig. 2), probably about one hundred years later in date.[11] The differences are striking: the Chinese artisans depicted stereotypical silhouettes rather than individuals (see note 7). We know the names of none of

---

[8]Knox, "Introduction" 41.

[9]All translations of the *Iliad* are from Fagles; the line citations are those of his English text.

[10]Robert Lamberton, *Hesiod* (New Haven: Yale University Press, 1988) 90–91; see also 113, 115, 120.

[11]Similar scenes have been found on at least three other bronze *hu*. See Jenny F. So, "The Inlaid Bronzes of the Warring States Period," in *The Great Bronze Age of China*, ed. Wen Fong (New York: Metropolitan Museum and Knopf, 1980) 316, and Esther Jacobson, "The Structure of Narrative on Early Chinese Pictorial Vessels," *Representations* 8 (Fall 1984): 77–80.

Figure 2. Decor on an Eastern Zhou *hu.* From *Wenwu* 1977.11:86. Among the scenes depicted are a battle (bottom); archers, a banquet, and an orchestra (middle); and more archery and the plucking of branches (top).

the people represented or of the master craftsmen and artisans who cast the vessel. Whatever is being represented, the viewer receives a strong impression of regimented mass activity. An anonymous master-designer has subordinated the small and anonymous individuals to a larger, impersonal order. Indeed, they cannot really be called "individuals" at all. Such art expresses the bureaucratic ideals of impersonal administration that Chinese social theorists and ministers were applying during the Warring States period (453–221 *B.C.*).

To be sure, one can see superficial similarities between these orderly soldiers who fought in the Eastern Zhou ranks and the Greek hoplites who, from around 700 to 550 *B.C.* "fought in close-packed phalanxes, their round, emblazoned shields interlocked, their safety depending on the steadfastness of the next man in line, their individual prowess less important than the integrity of the whole."[12] But major differences separate the two experiences. In terms of artistic representation, the painting on the Late Protocorinthian *olpe* (ca. 640 *B.C.*; fig. 3) depicts the ranged bodies of the hoplites with a perceptual realism and individual detail (including the attention lavished on the shield emblems) lacking in the Chinese case.[13] That realism, it should be noted, is also not emphasized in the Eastern Zhou battle literature, which in fourth and third century *B.C.* texts like *Zuozhuan* and *Discourses of the States* (*Guoyu*) tends to minimize the actual details of the shock and blood of combat in favor of moralizing speeches and stratagems.[14]

Several points, in fact, distinguish the accounts of fighting in Homer and in *Zuozhuan*. First, the Chinese accounts are of battle, in that they usually involve the fate of armies; the protagonist is not alone, but is fighting in the company of, and talking to, companions; Homer's accounts are more frequently of individual combat as hero meets hero. Second, the

---

[12]Jeffrey M. Hurwit, *The Art and Culture of Early Greece, 1100–480 B.C.* (Ithaca: Cornell University Press, 1985) 143, 160; fig. 67.

[13]For an introduction to the Chigi vase, see Tom Rasmussen, "Corinth and the Orientalising Phenomenon," in *Looking at Greek Vases*, ed. Tom Rasmussen and Nigel Spivey (Cambridge: Cambridge University Press, 1991) 57–62.

[14]See, in particular, Wang, "Towards Defining a Chinese Heroism."

Figure 3. Detail from the Late Protocorinthian *olpe* known as the Chigi vase. Rome, Villa Giulia. Photo: Max Hirmer.

Zuozhuan accounts provide little or no reference to the immediate adversary. Chinese protagonists suffer wounds but we often do not know who administered them. Third, there is no reference in the Chinese accounts to the presence of gods on the field of battle who stimulate the warriors or who influence the outcome; no goddess like Pallas Athena feeds nectar and ambrosia, the food of the gods, to a Chinese Achilles to take the field with his energy refreshed; no goddess like Pallas Athena dons mortal form to trick a Chinese Hector into fatal combat (as happens in the *Iliad*, Book 22). Fourth, the Chinese concern is less with the fighting than with the morale and willpower of the fighters, less with the details of the combat and more with the larger issues of strategy and morality.

In short, early Chinese representations of conflict reveal no interest in depicting hands-on experience with all its harsh and disorderly detail (see 25). The Chinese representations, to anticipate the argument to come, were more concerned with conception than perception, for the hero was increasingly not the fighter, as Achilles had been, but the statesman and general who planned and directed the fighting of others. This "bureaucratization" of action, moreover, is implicit both in the decor of our Chinese bronze (fig. 2)—for somebody was presumably overseeing these stereotypical soldiers and orchestra players—and in its manufacture—for somebody had surely directed the numerous artisans involved in the industrial-scale casting that such a vessel required. Once again, we see reinforcement and similarities: the manufacturing process contrasts sharply with the practices of the early Greeks, who both admired the individual and who tended to organize their workshops, like their battle accounts, around a series of acts performed by a small number of protagonists.[15]

---

[15]"Typically, Greek [pottery] workshops employed between ten and fifty potters and painters"; see John Onians, "Idea and Product: Potter and Philosopher in Classical Athens," *Journal of Design History* 4, 2 (1991): 66. According to Andrew Stewart, sculpture workshops employed no more than a dozen workers; see *Greek Sculpture: An Exploration* (New Haven: Yale University Press, 1990) 33–34. For the industrial scale of Chinese bronze production, see Ursula Martius Franklin, "On Bronze and Other Metals in Early China," in *The Origins of Chinese Civilization*, ed. Keightley (Berkeley: University of California Press, 1983) 279–96; "The Beginnings of Metallurgy in China: A Comparative Approach," in *The Great Bronze Age of China: A Symposium*, ed. George Ku-

Turning to representations of the human figure, military or otherwise, it is significant that we have no large, identifiable human figures from Shang or Zhou bronzes or vases, and certainly not from statuary, comparable to those made in contemporary Greece. Geometric Greek art, like the designs found on Shang and Western Zhou bronzes, had been "overwhelmingly abstract," but the human figure had begun to emerge in the last half of the ninth century. A historian of Greek art refers to "a mighty confrontation between the pictorial and the abstract" during the Middle Geometric period (ca. 800 *B.C.*), a confrontation that was eventually won by the advocates of pictorial representation who placed man and the human figure at the center of classical art.[16] No such "confrontation" can be discerned in the art found on Shang or Zhou bronzes; the figures on the Eastern Zhou *hu* (fig. 2), for example, evolved from and continued to express older conceptions of linear and symmetrical order. In this respect, accordingly, Zhou culture remained closer to the culture of the Greek Geometric than to that of the Greek classical age.

Heroic Types—A Choice

It is difficult to generalize about early Greek views of heroism because the subsequent elite culture appears to have been more pluralistic, more given to the preservation and transmission of conflicting views than the elite culture of early China was (at least as that culture has been represented and transmitted to us). Homer's quintessential hero presented in the *Iliad* is Achilles, "best of the Achæans," who will sacrifice his life for *kleos* ("glory"). Homer and Hesiod both lay great stress on *eris* ("strife") as an essential theme. It is significant, however, that even at this early stage, other visions of the hero

---

wayama (Seattle: University of Washington Press, 1983) 94–99. As Robert J. Poor notes, a typical set of molds for making a Shang *gu* beaker, a relatively simple shape, "might consist of twelve interlocking parts"; see "The Master of the 'Metropolis'-Emblem Ku," *Archives of Asian Art* 41 (1988): 74. There was, as he notes, no "eccentric" Shang notion of "personal or individual style" (77).

[16] Hurwit, *Art and Culture* 61–70, 94–95.

were present. Hector, the defender of the civilized, urban Troy, is—to use the terms of this account—represented as far more "Chinese" than the dreadful Achilles. He is, to be sure, a great warrior:

> "War—I know it well, and the butchery of men ...
> I know it all,
> How to charge in the rush of plunging horses—
> I know how to stand and fight to the finish,
> twist and lunge in the War-god's deadly dance."
>
> (7:275–81)

But Hector is also presented as a domestic figure with wife and child; he is a filial son, a defender not just of his selfish honor but of his people.[17] Homer's other epic, the *Odyssey*, also qualifies Achilles' "all-or-nothing" view of heroic action quite radically. In the *Iliad*, Achilles had taken "unfailing glory" as compensation for his impending, deliberately chosen, death. In the *Odyssey* (Book 11), by contrast, his shade tells Odysseus in a famous passage that he, Achilles, "would rather be another's hired hand,/ working for some poor man who owns no land ... / than to rule over all whom death has crushed."[18] The Achilles of the *Odyssey*, in short, had found glory less attractive than the Achilles of the *Iliad* had hoped. Indeed, the disruption of good order portrayed by the *Iliad* is challenged by the restoration of order that forms the main theme of the *Odyssey*.

It is striking to find this tension between martial glory and destruction, on the one hand, and well-ordered domesticity and governance, on the other, in Homer's two epics, the works that were, for Late Geometric Greeks, not just artistic masterpieces, but also, as one modern Western historian has called them, "storehouses of values and ethics and textbooks of conduct ... full of information detailing what it was to be Greek."[19] The Zhou Chinese, by contrast, appear to have resolved the tension between martial heroism and administra-

---

[17]Knox, "Introduction" 56.

[18]*The Odyssey of Homer: A New Verse Translation*, trans. Allen Mandelbaum (Berkeley: University of California Press, 1990) 234.

[19]Hurwit, *Art and Culture* 83, 85, citing Eric A. Havelock, *The Greek Concept of Justice* (Cambridge: Harvard University Press, 1978) 106–14.

tive domesticity unambiguously in favor of civilian rule—in favor, one might say, of the cities rather than the marauders—so that the texts that have been transmitted to us give little attention to matters of glory, killing, and, as we shall see, death. There were at least two Greek views of the heroic enshrined in the major tradition, that represented by Achilles and that represented by Ulysses or Hector. For the Chinese of much of the Eastern Zhou, as we see them in the transmitted record that was to form the Classics, there was only one view. The pluralism of the Greek views and the greater unanimity of the Chinese view is itself significant. This is not to say that alternate models of action, excluded from the orthodox classical canon, were not available in early China. By the late Eastern Zhou and Han dynasties, the eremitic ideal—best exemplified in the Taoist teachings of the *Zhuangzi* (ca. 300 *B.C.*)—had become increasingly attractive.[20] Characteristically, however, the contemplative recluse rejected most forms of cultural engagement, removing himself from the arena of action; he did not, in contrast with, say, Odysseus, provide an alternate model for social, political, and military action in the world. His ideal, rather, was that of *wuwei*, spontaneous action through "nonpurposive action."[21]

Hands—Dirty and Clean

The role of hero and protagonist was represented, as I have suggested, in radically different ways in Greece and China. Achilles, whether in the *Iliad* of the late eighth century, or on the painted vases of the sixth and fifth centuries, acts and speaks for himself. He feels the thrust of the blade as it pierces Penthesileia's breast (fig. 1); he is directly responsible; he has "dirty hands." The "terrible, man-killing hands" of Achilles are, in fact, one of the standard tropes that identify

---

[20]Aat Vervoorn, *Men of the Cliffs and Caves: The Development of the Chinese Eremitic Tradition to the End of the Han Dynasty* (Hong Kong: Chinese University Press, 1990).

[21]For an introduction to this complex idea, see Herrlee G. Creel, *What Is Taoism? And Other Studies in Chinese Cultural History* (Chicago: University of Chicago Press, 1970).

him.[22] (When, one wonders, does an early Chinese text, transmitted to us, ever emphasize any part of the anatomy in this way?) Hector too who, as we have seen, knows "how to charge in the rush of plunging horses," admits to dirty hands when his mother urges him, fresh from the field of battle, to make an offering to Zeus:

> "I'd be ashamed to pour a glistening cup to Zeus
> with unwashed hands. I'm splattered with blood and filth."
> (6:315–16)

Zeus, too, speaks of his power to subdue Poseidon in struggle in terms of "my mighty hands" (15:270). Such bodily engagement and physical prowess were part of the Greek hero's qualities. The valiant and wise Nestor in Book 23 of the *Iliad* can reminisce in detail about his athletic feats—in running, boxing, wrestling, the javelin throw, and charioteering—and can give the names of the particular individuals he defeated: Klytomedes, Angkaios, Phyleus, Polydorus. In the classical age, too, the tragic heroes (and heroines) of Athenian drama, such as Oedipus, Antigone, and Cleon, continued to act for themselves and to take personal responsibility for their deeds.

One assumes that the Bronze Age Shang kings may have done the same, though our sources provide little direct representation of the royal emotions and perceptions. By the late Eastern Zhou, there were stories of notable feats of strength performed by political leaders. King Wu of Qin (310–307 *B.C.*), for example, loved to lift heavy tripods; the incident has given rise to a cautionary phrase, *ju ding jue bin* ("lift the tripod and wrench the knee"), which cautions against overestimating one's strength. The dynastic claimant Xiang Yu lifted tripods too, but such feats do not seem to have been regarded with favor; the strong men who joined with King Wu in tripod-lifting, for instance, were put to death after he died.[23] Feats of strength, it is worth remarking—along with prodigies, disor-

---

[22]For example, *Iliad* 24:561. Achilles' hands, ominous but now gentle, play a large role in his meeting with Priam: see 24:591, 593, 602, 789, 790.

[23]Edouard Chavannes, *Les mémoires historiques de Se-ma Ts'ien*, vol. 2 (Paris: Adrien-Maisonneuve, 1967) 76. Burton Watson, trans., *Records of the Grand Historian of China: Translated from the* Shi chi *of Ssu-ma Ch'ien*, vol. 1 (New York: Columbia University Press, 1961) 38.

ders, and spirits—was one of the four topics about which Confucius (ca. 551–479 *B.C.*) chose not to speak (*Lunyu*, 7:20; *Zi bu yu guai li luan shen*). Homer, by contrast, sang of them all.

In Zhou China, heroic action, at least as it is reflected in our elite texts, increasingly involved delegation and planning. The hero was the clean-handed leader, the exhorter, the strategist; he was not the doer. The *Zuozhuan* contains numerous accounts of moral judgment, moral prophecy, and discussions of statecraft, but, as we have already seen in the case of accounts of battle, the focus tends to be on strategies and justifications, on deciding how other people should act, rather than on the leader's personal action.

Sima Qian, in his early first century *B.C.* history, *Records of the Grand Historian* (*Shiji*), presents a series of biographies of Eastern Zhou figures that confirm this emphasis. One may discern in his account of Wu Zixu of the fifth century *B.C.* some remnants of direct, hands-on action, but these appear to have been increasingly edited out of the later texts. At the start of the story, for example, Wu Zixu "drew his bow, snatched an arrow, and stood facing" those who had come to arrest him.[24] He does not actually shoot the arrow. The rest of the tale involves his wanderings, stratagems, and counsels, but it is only when he eventually cuts his own throat—as a loyal servitor and bureaucrat must do when the king requests it—that he puts his hands on a weapon again.

Sima Qian's biography of the general Tian Dan (first half of the third century *B.C.*), who saved the state of Qi after Yan had occupied most of its territory, is equally "clean-handed." At one point, Tian Dan "took up trowel and mortarboard and personally joined [his officers and men] in their work on the fortifications," but at no point is he described as having fought

---

[24]Burton Watson, trans., *Records of the Historian: Chapters from the* Shi Chi *of Ssu-ma Ch'ien* (New York: Columbia University Press, 1969) 18, 26. David Johnson, "Epic and History in Early China: The Matter of Wu Tzu-hsü," *Journal of Asian Studies* 40, 2 (February 1981): 265, deduces the existence of a longer Wu Zixu narrative from which the didactic anecdotes that now form its core were extracted. The *Zuozhuan*, he concludes is "highly processed.... Its subject matter is 'epic,' but nothing else in it is" (268). And he discerns a general Confucianizing trend in which "narrative drive was subordinated to generic classification and intense focus on a few great heroes was replaced by a multitude of short biographies of the merely eminent or exemplary" (271).

in the ranks; he is the director, the coordinator, devising such stratagems as the flaming torches tied to the tails of a thousand-plus oxen. His role was to furnish, as Sima Qian remarks, "an inexhaustible supply of surprise moves."[25] There is little doubt that the Zhou Chinese tradition had chosen to emphasize the Odysseus-like rather than the Achilles-like hero and to emphasize the hero's intellectual and moral, rather than martial, qualities.

Sima Qian also presents five Zhou and Qin case histories in his chapter, "Biographies of the Assassin-Retainers."[26] Unlike most Greek heroes, these protagonists act at the behest of a lord, not for monetary gain but to repay the tremendous honor conferred by the lord's request that they perform the deed on his behalf. "The lord in these accounts delegates what, in the Greek case, would have been the heroic, the personal, and thus the tragic, task. His hand is clean; it is not on the sword; he is not even near when the deed is undertaken."[27] A bureaucratic chain of command protects the initiator—who, in the Greek view, would have been no hero, but merely an administrator—from the shock and consequences of his deeds. The true hero in these accounts is the delegate, the subordinate, who does his lord's bidding.

Representations of Death

The early Chinese interest in conceived pattern and general order rather than in perceived, particular detail (see 22), may also be seen in representations of death. No early Chinese text provides vivid, unflinching details like the description of brains bursting and covering a spearhead that is found in Book 17 of the *Iliad*. No Chinese text follows the *Iliad* in presenting "the harsh realities of the work of killing ..., the pain and degradation of death."[28] Consider how the demise of one minor combatant, Harpalion, is vividly and precisely—even anatomically—described:

---

[25]Watson, trans., *Records of the Historian* 32, 33.

[26]Watson, trans., *Records of the Historian* 45–67.

[27]Keightley, "Early Civilization in China" 19.

[28]Knox, "Introduction" 26.

with a bronze-tipped arrow, hitting his right buttock
up under the pelvic bone so the lance pierced the bladder.
He sank on the spot, hunched in his dear companion's arms,
gasping out his life as he writhed along the ground
like an earthworm stretched out in death, blood pooling,
soaking the earth dark red.... (13:749–55)

No early Chinese text portrays a mortal blow in this realistic way; no early Chinese text *sees* the physical details with such precision. In terms of the visual arts, there is no early Chinese representation of death or dying to match the numerous mourners and mortal thrusts portrayed on Geometric and Archaic Greek vases or to match the late sixth-century *B.C.* vase painting of Sarpedon's corpse, its wounds gushing blood (fig. 4).

Achilles' lament over the body of Patroclus in Book 19 of the *Iliad* is particularly informative about death and heroism. He says to his departed friend:

There is no more shattering blow that I could suffer.
Not even if I should learn of my own father's death ...
or the death of my dear son ...
if Prince Neoptolemus is still among the living.
(19:382–89)

The degree of Achilles' anguish and alienation, as well as the distinctly non-Chinese quality of his response, is to be found in his willingness to put his love for his friend Patroclus above his love for his nearest kin, his father. The hero's kin ties have been displaced by his personal and transcendingly selfish emotions.

One finds a similar displacement of normal—or should I say, of Chinese?—familial and political relationships in Book 24 of the *Iliad*, when Priam, whose son, Hector—the filial, Chinese-style son—has just been killed by Achilles, comes to Achilles' camp by night and begs for his son's body:

Figure 4. Attic red-figured kalyx-crater by Euxitheos and Euphronios, ca. 515 B.C. Death and Sleep carry away the corpse of Sarpedon as Hermes presides. New York, Metropolitan Museum of Art, 1972. 11.10.

Pity me in my own right,
remember your own father! I deserve more pity ...
I have endured what no one on earth has ever done before—
I put to my lips the hands of the man who killed my son.
(24:588–91)

As Schein notes, the two enemies, Trojan and Achæan, "virtually adopt one another as father and son."[29] No early Chinese text plays on such fundamental themes of death and kinship and with such paradoxical, ironic complexity.

Not only is the *Iliad* filled with accounts of death, but it seems likely that the earliest forms of Geometric pictorial art in Greece were created precisely "to exalt the dead and preserve ritual."[30] Given the importance of death ritual and ancestor worship in Neolithic and Bronze Age China, the virtual absence of representations of death in Chinese art and text is all the more striking. It is true that some of the falling figures in the battle depicted on the Eastern Zhou *hu* (fig. 2) may be dead, but they are given no emphasis, and their silhouettes differ in no way from those of the living. It would be interesting to determine, in fact, when the first Chinese representation of a dead or dying person appeared. Death was evidently reserved for the ritual texts, such as the *Book of Etiquette and Ceremonial* (*Yili*; ca. third to first centuries *B.C.*), which contain remarkably detailed recipes for dealing not so much with a particular death but with the dead in general.[31] We are told much about how to mourn, little about what it was like to mourn.[32] The ritualists, like the artists, were ordering, controlling, and impersonalizing experience, rather than describing or dramatizing it. Death in Zhou China was not rep-

---

[29]Seth L. Schein, *The Mortal Hero: an Introduction to Homer's* Iliad (Berkeley: University of California Press, 1984) 159.

[30]Hurwit, *Art and Culture* 64, 66; figs. 29, 30.

[31]John Steele, trans., *The I-Li or Book of Etiquette and Ceremonial* (1917; reprint, Taipei: Ch'eng-wen, 1966).

[32]As Marcel Granet noted, the gestures of grief stipulated in early Chinese ritual texts could not be simple and spontaneous physiological and psychological reflexes. They were regulated, ceremonial acts that used the words and formulas of a systemic language. See "Le language de la douleur d'après le rituel funeraire de la Chine classique," in Granet, *Etudes sociologiques sur la Chine* (Paris: Presses Universitaires de France, 1953) 235.

resented as a cathartic experience. It was a subject for ritual, not a subject for art. Or, to put the matter another way, what art was to the early Greeks, ritual was to the early Chinese.

Shining Helmets

This Chinese concern with essential generalizations or standard recipes for behavior, whether about death or other topics, stands in sharp contrast to the passionate Archaic Greek attention to individual detail, the joy in existential reality. Auerbach has identified the "Homeric need for an externalization of phenomena in terms perceptible to the senses."[33] Finley has referred to this Archaic Greek attitude as that of "the heroic mind," arguing for "a natural bond between the heroic temper and a gaze that sees the world with sharp and bright particularity."[34] He refers in particular to a passage so striking that I would like to consider it in full. A series of conversations in Book 6 of the *Iliad* first shows us Hector approaching his family. Paris speaks with him, but "Hector, helmet flashing, answered nothing." Helen speaks to him, and "turning to go,/ his helmet flashing, tall Hector answered." And then, "a flash of his helmet/ and off he strode and quickly reached his sturdy/ well-built house." He then finds his wife and child on the ramparts, where she urges caution upon him; "and tall Hector nodded, his helmet flashing." And, after all this preparation—on my part, and Homer's—we come to the passage that Finley refers to:

> In the same breath, shining Hector reached down
> for his son—but the boy recoiled,
> cringing against his nurse's full breast,
> screaming out at the sight of his own father,
> terrified by the flashing bronze, the horsehair crest,
> the great ridge of the helmet nodding, bristling terror—
> so it struck his eyes. And his loving father laughed,

[33]Erich Auerbach, *Mimesis: The Representation of Reality in Western Literature* (Princeton: Princeton University Press, 1953) 3–4.

[34]John H. Finley, Jr., *Four Stages of Greek Thought* (Stanford: Stanford University Press, 1966) 28.

his mother laughed as well, and glorious Hector,
quickly lifting the helmet from his head,
set it down on the ground, fiery in the sunlight,
and raising his son he kissed him, tossed him in his arms,
lifting a prayer to Zeus and the other deathless gods.
(6:556–67)

Hector's prayer is the famous one that the child will one day return from battle himself, "a better man than his father," having killed a mortal enemy in war, and thus be "a joy to his mother's heart."

The shining helmet serves a complex rhetorical and dramatic function. As Fagles notes, it

> not only makes Hector's own career appear meteoric and abruptly snuffed out, but it also supports a chain of tragic ironies throughout the epic. For the flashing helmet—Hector's own at first—is soon replaced by the one he strips from Patroclus when he kills him: the helmet of Achilles. Thus ... when Achilles destroys Hector in revenge he must destroy himself.[35]

I would also note the ominous foreshadowing with which Hector's child (who will presumably be killed or enslaved when Troy falls) reacts to the helmet in terror—just as other Achæan warriors, who fell before the shining Hector, must have reacted as they died. The child will become one with the warriors in this. I would note too that the child is perceiving the helmet—"so it struck his eyes," says Homer. But above all, I would agree with Finley that the flashing helmet—which has been so frequently referred to in the preceding passages—takes on a life of its own in this scene. From a mere formulaic epithet used to identify Hector it becomes a presence, "the flashing bronze, the horsehair crest,/ the great ridge of the helmet nodding, bristling terror" and "fiery in the sunlight."

Its presence is powerful precisely because of the way that, at this critical point in the story, Homer particularizes and vivifies it. As Finley has said,

---

[35]Fagles, trans., "Translator's Preface" x.

> In so deeply felt a scene surely no one but Homer would have paused to note that helmet still shining beside the human figures. It is as if in whatever circumstances it too keeps its particular being, which does not change because people are sad or happy but remains what it is, one of the innumerable fixed entities that comprise the world.[36]

There are no comparable "shining helmets" in early Chinese literature. In no text do we find this sustained interest in a thing, perceived in itself, that reappears in its own right in different situations and contexts. Even in the *Book of Songs*, where early Chinese lyricism is most prominent, the general supersedes the particular and natural objects are present because they are pregnant with allegorical or symbolic meaning, usually moral. Nature in the *Songs* does change, to use Finley's words, "because people are sad or happy"; it takes its meaning from the humans for whom it serves as background. The opening lines of Mao 1 do not call attention to the bird for its own sake—for it disappears, in fact, from the rest of the song:

> "Guan-guan" calls the osprey
> residing on a river isle.

The next two lines imply by their proximity some symbolic connection between the bird and a maid:

> A pure maid, so alluring,
> a good mate for a Lord.[37]

---

[36]Finley, *Four Stages* 4.

[37]Jeffrey K. Riegel, "*Shih*: A Translation and Interpretation of the Ancient Chinese Book of Songs" (unpublished manuscript) "Song 1." As Riegel notes, "the osprey ... symbolized both ferocious tenacity and chastity.... Having the osprey rest upon an island in a river serves to emphasize not only its isolation but perhaps its chasteness as well." On how Chinese commentators have understood such metaphorical allusions, see Pauline Yu, "Imagery in the Classic of Poetry," in her *The Reading of Imagery in the Chinese Poetic Tradition* (Princeton: Princeton University Press, 1987) 44–83, which includes a discussion of this song.

The general result of this allusive, generalized, symbolic approach is that there are love poems in the *Book of Songs*, but these poems express metaphorical connections; they do not portray great or famous lovers. There are heroic actions and emotions, but there are no personalized heroes who, in their particularity and "shiningness" would have been recognizable as heroes to the early Greeks. There are "things" in the *Songs*, but they have come to be appreciated because they mean something else.

To put the matter another way, Zhou texts, like Shang and Western Zhou bronze designs, reveal evidence of what to a Geometric Greek poet or artist would have seemed like severe "editing" (see note 24), in which the particular—the shining helmets and the brains covering spearheads—no matter how formulaically expressed, had been sacrificed to the general, to a concern with rules and order—as in the Chinese case. Either there was no Chinese equivalent of Finley's "heroic mind," or it left no reflection; in either case, its absence in China constitutes one of the important contrasts between the transmitted cultures of classical China and classical Greece. Early Greek art, as we have seen, was one of percepts; early Chinese art was one of concepts.

Homeric and Zhou Passages Compared

The different artistic and cultural approaches to heroism can be seen in a consideration of two passages from Homer and some Chinese analogs. The first passage, from the *Iliad*, describes the last moments of the chariot race that formed part of Patroclus's funeral games:

> In the same breath
> Diomedes came on storming toward them—closer, look,
> closing—lashing his team nonstop, full-shoulder strokes,
> making them kick high as they hurtled toward the goal.
> Constant sprays of dust kept pelting back on the driver,
> the chariot sheathed in gold and tin careering on
> in the plunging stallions' wake, its spinning rims
> hardly leaving a rut behind in the thin dust
> as the team thundered in—a whirlwind finish!

He reined them back in the ring with drenching sweat,
lather streaming down to the ground from necks and chests.
Their master leapt down from the bright burnished car,
propped his whip on the yoke. (23:555–67)

There is to my knowledge no comparable Chinese text of Zhou date that apprehends with such vividness the experience of chariot riding—the laying on of the whip, the high-kicking horses, the shallowness of the ruts, the dust pelting back on the charioteer, the drenching sweat and lather. This was evidently a passage composed by somebody who knew what it was to race a chariot, who took joy in recapturing the experience, and who assumed that his audience would do so too. I am particularly struck by Homer's noting the absence of deep wheel marks; such a perception has the effect of telling the audience, "this event was even more special, more particular, than you might have conceived; there were no deep wheel marks, even though there generally would have been." The long whip propped against the yoke is another "shining helmet"—a small, insignificant detail, recorded primarily, it would seem, to enhance the sense of reality, the sense of perception, the sense of having been there.

What follows is an account of chariots from the Chinese *Book of Songs* written at roughly the same time:

Our chariots are strong,
Our horses well matched.
Teams of stallions lusty
We yoke and go to the east.

Our hunting chariots are splendid,
Our teams very sturdy.
In the east are wide grasslands;
We yoke, and a-hunting we go.

My lord follows the chase
With picked footmen so noisy,

Sets up his banners, his standards,
Far afield he hunts in Ao.[38]

Five more stanzas follow. Certainly some visual details are presented: mention is made of "the tortoise-and-snake banner and the oxtail flag" and the "red knee-covers and gold-adorned slippers" of the riders. There is even a note of something deficient:

If footmen and riders are not orderly
The great kitchen will not be filled.

But that deficiency is prospective, and it is one of behavior, of disorder, not of perception, of keen observation; it derives from the expectations of administrators and diviners, of people responsible for filling kitchens, not from the expectations of chariot riders. Indeed, the poem—with its account of the size, color, and condition of the horses, the direction and geography of travel, the banners displayed, the amount of the catch, the need for proper order—suggests the report of a groom or steward. The intent and the perception of reality are radically different in the Chinese and Greek texts. The tradition of Homer attempts to particularize and to vivify; the composers of the *Songs* tend to generalize and to catalog.

Similar distinctions hold for a second passage from Homer. Book 24, the moving climax of the *Iliad*, describes Priam's night-time visit to Achilles' camp to redeem the corpse of his slain son, Hector. The scene shifts from 1) Achilles' quarters, to 2) Mount Olympus, the home of the gods, to 3) Troy, as Priam is emboldened to undertake the perilous journey and instructs his still living sons (whom he despises for still being alive, now that Hector is dead) to ready a conveyance. Homer then shifts from Priam's viewpoint to 4) that of his sons, of whom he says:

Terrified by their father's rough commands
the sons trundled a mule-wagon out at once,
a good smooth-running one,
newly finished, balanced and bolted tight,

---

[38]Mao no. 179; Arthur Waley, trans., *The Book of Songs* (New York: Grove, 1960) 287.

and strapped a big wicker cradle across its frame.
They lifted off its hook a boxwood yoke for the mules,
its bulging pommel fitted with rings for guide-reins,
brought out with the yoke its yoke-strap nine arms long
and wedged the yoke down firm on the sanded, tapered pole,
on the front peg, and slipped the yoke-ring onto its pin,
strapped the pommel with three good twists, both sides,
then lashed the assembly round and down the shaft
and under the clamp they made the lashing fast.
(24.313–325)

Coming as it does at a moment of great emotion, as the grieving father, lamenting the death of his favorite son and the now-certain destruction of Troy, faces the dangers of a night visit behind enemy lines, such a technical digression is puzzling, for it impedes the development of the story. The delay, of course, may have heightened the suspense,[39] but it is the nature of the delay that concerns me. One supposes that both Homer and his audience knew a lot about the activity being described—in this case the harnessing of mules to carts—and took pleasure in hearing such details. I know of no comparably detailed Zhou passages about carts or indeed about any aspect of secular activity. The only texts that display such a passion for technical minutiæ are the ritual texts like the *Book of Etiquette and Ceremonial* (see 31) and the third-century *B.C.* legal texts like the coroner's reports from Shuihudi.[40] In

[39]For the dramatic function of Nestor's various hortatory and apologetic digressions, see Norman Austin, "The Function of Digressions in the *Iliad*," *Greek, Roman, and Byzantine Studies* 7 (1966): 301–3.

[40]Derke Bodde, "Forensic Medicine in Pre-Imperial China," *Journal of the American Oriental Society* 102, 1 (January-March 1982): 1–16, translates four such legal texts. The degree of detail is remarkable. Here is an example from the section "Death by Hanging": "C's corpse, facing south, was hanging from the rafter at the northern wall within the bedroom on the east side of the house. The neck was encircled by a hemp rope as thick as one's thumb, which came together [i.e., was knotted] at the nape of the neck.... Upon releasing the rope, the breath issued with a gasp from the mouth and nose. The rope left a compression bruise mark [around the neck], except for an untouched two-inch space at the nape of the neck." This and other cases have also been translated by Katrina C. D. McLeod and Robin D. S. Yates, "Forms of Ch'in Law: An Anno-

both cases the details had their particular religious or administrative, but not artistic, function. The authors of most Zhou texts that have survived were not interested in descriptions of manual labor and artisan skill.

Several conclusions can be drawn from these two examples from Homer. First, I should like to propose as a suggestive generalization that realistic details—such as the sweat from horses and the equipage of a cart—are regarded as uninteresting, even as threatening, by nonheroic (and here I am still using "heroic" in its Western sense) elites. In the Greek world men of action—such as the heroes about whom, and the audiences for whom, the Homeric bards performed—presumably take pleasure in descriptions of things they can do for themselves. In the Chinese world civilian, literati elites who do not get their hands dirty find such accounts of sweat, horses, carts, and fighting uninteresting and, because they cannot or do not do these things for themselves, threatening and delegitimizing. If early Chinese texts and art have been "edited" in the ways that I have been implying in this essay (see 35), one may associate this "editing" with the hierarchical nature of Zhou society. It is precisely what one would expect of authors and transmitters who conceive of a world divided, as *Mencius* puts it, between the rulers (who keep their hands clean) and the ruled (who get their hands dirty): "Hence it said, 'Some labor with their minds and some labor with their muscles. Those who labor with their minds rule others; those who labor with their muscles are ruled by others (*Gu yue: 'huo lao xin, huo lao li. Lao xin zhe zhi ren, lao li zhe zhi yu ren*)" (3.A.4.6).

Second, I would suggest that oral story-telling—as entertainment—encourages realistic detail. The kind of perceptual description that we have encountered above brings tales alive for listeners who know horses, harness, dust, sweat, and carts. It attracts and entertains by enhancing the familiar, making it fresh and wonderful, and giving it structure. The conceptual, expository tradition in the Zhou texts that have been preserved is less one of entertainment, and more one of instruction and exhortation. Their authors or transmitters were interested in stories about protagonists who promoted

---

tated Translation of the *Feng-chen shih*," *Harvard Journal of Asiatic Studies* 41 (1981): 111–63.

concepts of moral and religious order, concepts that they, as authors and transmitters, would like to promote themselves. They were less interested in recapturing the existential detail and perception. The difference is that between drama—which must attract its audience—and sermon—to which the audience has, as it were, already committed itself in advance.

Points of View

The absence of critical and dramatic tension—or, to put it positively, the emphasis on nonadversarial harmony—in early Chinese art and literary expression may also be contrasted with one of the characteristic and non-Chinese features of the *Iliad*, namely, that the audience hears various sides of the story. It is taken within the walls of Troy as well as without, seeing Priam's visit to Achilles from the viewpoints of Zeus, other gods, Achilles, the old man himself, and his sons. Early Greek art, by this pluralism of viewpoint, encourages the audience to sympathize with and to understand the motivations of both victor and vanquished. Achilles and Penthesileia are presented with equal force in the vase paintings. By the classical age, neither Creon in *Antigone*, nor Oedipus in Sophocles' tragedies are presented as unsympathetic or unremittingly evil figures. This ambiguity about what and who is right, about what and who is important, already present in Homer's *Iliad*, lies at the essence of the tragic view of the hero; our sympathies are not, should not be, and cannot be all on one side.[41]

---

[41]"Before Greece and outside the Greco-Western tradition, societies are instituted on a principle of strict closure: our view of the world is the only meaningful one, the 'others' are bizarre, inferior, perverse, evil, or unfaithful. As Hannah Arendt has said, impartiality enters this world with Homer.... Not only can one not find in the Homeric poems a disparagement of the 'enemy,' the Trojans, for example, but the truly central figure in the *Iliad* is Hector, not Achilles, and the most moving characters are Hector and Andromache." See Cornelius Castoriadis, *Philosophy, Politics, Autonomy* (New York: Oxford University Press, 1991) 82, 118; he cites Arendt, "The Concept of History," in her *Between Past and Future* (New York: Viking, 1968) 51.

Greek epics also derive much of their complexity and dramatic tension from the frank recognition that unresolvable conflicts exist in the world. This fundamental assumption is symbolized in the conflict between the values and wills of men and gods. It underlies the recognition that choices are frequently made not between good and evil but between one good and another. Early Chinese writings, by contrast, adopt a less detached, less complex view of the human condition. The vanquished in early China, from the San Miao of the South, who troubled Yao, Shun, and Yu, to Jie of the Xia and Di Xin of the Shang, who led their dynasties to destruction, were categorized as immoral. Their points of view were not presented. From the *Documents* down through *Mencius* and beyond, the last rulers of dynasties were by definition bad, and those who overthrew them, whom the ruled should unquestioningly trust, were by definition good; no "loyal opposition" was conceivable, let alone desirable or human. There are few admirable and vanquished "Trojans" in early Chinese literature; there are generally only admirable and virtuous victors and misguided and defeated villains. This lack of pluralism in politics and artistic representation (and also, as we shall see, in mythology), must have been reinforced by the Chinese cult of ancestor worship (see 42), in which only one viewpoint—that of the fathers and grandfathers—was conceived, both in this life and the next.

Death, Morality, and the Absence of Theodicy

As I have discussed elsewhere, the themes that attracted early Chinese mythologists were social order and social morality; stories of dying and death were not emphasized. The general harmony that pervades the relations of the Chinese to their gods contrasts strongly with the heroic and adversarial universe of early Greece, in which warrior gods and goddesses like Apollo, Artemis, and Pallas Athena involve themselves in the lives of mortals like Achilles or Hector. Early Chinese society was dominated by kinship ties, the royal ancestors representing the most senior members of the kinship unit in heaven. There was little discord between gods and men.[42] Obedience and filiality ruled on earth as they did in Heaven.

There was little expectation, accordingly, that in such a benevolent world, virtue would not be rewarded. Early Chinese thinking, like early Chinese mythology, showed little interest in theodicy; a fundamental optimism seemed to render any explanations for the presence of evil unnecessary.[43] The main function of the Chinese flood myth, for example, however rich its original narrative details might once have been, was to serve as a background for the sage emperor Yu as he laid out the political geography of ancient China.[44] No extant version of the myth addresses the moral significance of the flood.[45] Early Chinese mythology thus does not present malevolent gods who resented human success or conspired to destroy man. The Chinese knew neither a Prometheus nor a Zeus. Reflecting this lack of divine hostility, death in China was not regarded, to the degree that it was in Greece, as an affront to the living; it was, rather, regarded as part of the inevitable and harmonious order, as a subject for ritual rather than tragedy.

Art and Ancestor Worship

The impersonal unselfishness of the early Chinese hero was encouraged and validated by an ancestor worship that stressed the continuity of the lineage and defined the individual in terms of his generational role and status in a highly

---

[42]Keightley, "Early Civilization in China" 34.

[43]On the question of philosophical optimism in early Chinese culture, see Thomas A. Metzger, "Some Ancient Roots of Modern Chinese Thought: This-Worldliness, Epistemological Optimism, Doctrinality, and the Emergence of Reflexivity in the Eastern Chou," *Early China* 11–12 (1985–1987) especially 64, 66–76. Metzger's discussion of the imperfect distribution of sanctions in this world, a concern that was much on the mind of Confucius, provides additional grounds for remarking the unexpected lack of theodicy in early Chinese thought (98–99).

[44]For an introduction to the flood story, see William G. Boltz, "Kung Kung and the Flood: Reverse Euhemerism in the *Yao Tien*," *T'oung Pao* 67, 3–5 (1981): 141–53.

[45]Keightley, "Early Civilization in China" 34.

ritualized system of sacrifice, descent, and unequal distribution of power. The Chinese hero derived his authority from operating within formal boundaries rather than by overstepping them, from emulating previous heroes, who were now ancestors, so that he might be emulated and become an ancestor in his turn.

The early Chinese lack of æsthetic and even philosophical interest in particular detail is entirely congruent with the assumptions underlying ancestor worship. "The ancient Greeks," as Meyer Fortes has noted, "appear to have had elaborate cults concerned with beliefs about ghosts and shades, but no true ancestor cult." He has proposed that ancestor worship be regarded as "a representation or extension of the authority component in the jural relations of successive generations; it is not a duplication, in a supernatural idiom, of the total complex" of kin or other relationships.[46] Ancestor worship, in this view, does not merely involve belief in the dead; it involves beliefs about the dead, who are in turn conceived in a certain way. It does not involve the perceptual commemoration of the total personality of the deceased; it involves an appeal to certain powers that the deceased is conceived as possessing.

The spirit of Achilles, when he appears to Odysseus in Book 11 of the *Odyssey* (see 24), is thus not an ancestor. As when alive, he still has no knowledge of his descendants: "But tell me something of my worthy son:/ Has he, a lord of men, gone off to war,/ become a chieftain?"[47] Above all, Achilles has no power. Whereas our early Chinese texts contain many accounts of ghosts who return to wreak moral vengeance on the living,[48] the powerlessness of the dead in Homer is well

---

[46]Meyer Fortes, "Some Reflections on Ancestor Worship in Africa," in M. Fortes and G. Dieterlen, eds., *African Systems of Thought* (London: Oxford University Press, 1965) 125, 133.

[47]*The Odyssey of Homer* 234.

[48]See, for example, Alvin P. Cohen, "Avenging Ghosts and Moral Judgment in Ancient Chinese Historiography: Three Examples from *Shih-chi*," in Sarah Allan and Alvin P. Cohen, eds., *Legend, Lore, and Religion in China: Essays in Honor of Wolfram Eberhard on His Seventieth Birthday* (San Francisco: Chinese Materials Center, 1979) 97–108.

known.[49] Greek ghosts were powerless precisely because they were shades of their former personalities; their powers had not been abstracted and formalized; they were still truly personalities but they were also truly dead. The Archaic Greeks, one might also observe, were not afraid of ghosts because, in a culture ridden with a sense of tragedy, ghosts could do nothing worse to man than man and the gods had already done to himself.

Three instances of the empowerment and "ritualization" of the dead in the early Chinese evidence will demonstrate the contrast with Greek religious conceptions. First, the Shang practice of conferring temple names on their dead kings and other elites, so that the dynasty founder, who, according to later texts, had been called Cheng Tang, was instead worshiped under the name of Da Yi,[50] indicates the loss of individual personality that was involved in becoming an ancestor. These impersonal temple names were typological and jural; taken from the names of the ten days of the Shang week, they were used primarily for scheduling the ancestral sacrifices on appropriate days. Da Yi, for example, received cult on *yi* days, Wu Ding on *ding* days, and so on.[51] The Shang ritualists used the temple names to place the depersonalized dead in their ritual slots.

Second, the "Pan Geng" chapter (probably written during the Western Zhou) of the *Documents* provides a clear instance of a Shang ruler using his ancestors as authority figures to legitimate his decision, which was evidently unpopular with his

---

[49]See, for example, Erwin Rohde, *Psyche: The Cult of Souls and Belief in Immortality Among the Greeks*, trans. W. B. Hillis (London: Kegan, Paul, 1925) 24; Christiane Sourvinou-Inwood, "To Die and Enter the House of Hades: Homer, Before and After," in Joachim Whaley, ed., *Mirrors of Mortality: Studies in the Social History of Death* (London: Europa, 1981) 22.

[50]Keightley, *Sources of Shang History: The Oracle-Bone Inscriptions of Bronze Age China* (1978; reprint Berkeley: University of California Press, 1985) 204, 207, n. a.

[51]For a detailed analysis of the system of temple names and the way they were awarded after death, see Keightley, "Lucky Days, Temple Names, and the Ritual Calendar in Ancient China: An Alternative Hypothesis" (unpublished manuscript, 1987); for an earlier version (but published later) see Ji Dewei (David Keightley), "Zhongguo gudai de jiri yu miaohao (Lucky Days and Temple Names in Ancient China)," *Yinxu bowuyuan yuankan* (1989): 20–32.

people, to remove the capital to Yin. Not only did Pan Geng appeal to the wise and benevolent government of the former kings when they had been alive, but he spoke of the continuing relationship—entirely jural and impersonal—among the dead ascendants:

> Now when I offer the great sacrifices to my predecessors, your forefathers are present to share in them.
>
> (pt. 1, para. 14)

> Were I to err in my government, and remain long here, my High sovereign (the founder of our House), would send down great punishment for my crime, and say, "Why do you oppress my people?" If you, the myriads of the people, do not attend to the perpetuation of your lives, and cherish one mind with me, the one man, in my plans, my predecessors will send down on you great punishment for your crime, and say, "Why do you not agree with our young grandson, but so go on to forfeit your virtue?" When they punish you from above, you will have no way of escape.... Whereas my royal predecessors made happy your ancestors and fathers, your ancestors and fathers will cut you off and abandon you, and not save you from death.... Your ancestors and fathers urgently represent to my High sovereign, saying, "Execute great punishments on our descendants." So they intimate to my High sovereign that he should send down great calamities.
>
> (pt. 2, paras. 11–14)[52]

Thus was the Shang king thought to have assigned functions to the dead, both royal and nonroyal, legitimating his needs and imposing sanctions on those who would oppose him.[53] Although these dead have power, they have no personality.

Third, the *Zuozhuan* relates the following story for the year 554 *B.C.*:

---

[52]Based on James Legge, trans., *The Chinese Classics: Volume III, The Shoo King or the Book of Historical Documents* (London: Frowde, 1865) 230, 238–40.

[53]For another instance of this use of the dead, see Keightley, *Sources of Shang History*, "Preamble" 1–2.

> Xun Yan [a victorious general from the state of Jin who commanded the army of the center] was now suffering from an ulcer, which grew upon his head; and after crossing the Yellow River [on his way back from campaigning in Lu to return to his state] and getting as far as Zhuyong, he was quite ill, and his eyes protruded. The great officers who had returned [to Jin] before him all came back, and Shi Gai [his deputy commander] begged an interview with him which he did not grant. [Shi Gai] then begged to know who would succeed [Xun Yan as commander], and Yan said, "My son by the daughter of Zheng can do it." In the second month, on the day *jiayin*, he died with his eyes staring, and (his teeth so firmly closed that) nothing [such as a ritual jade] could be put into his mouth. Xuan Zi [= Shi Gai] washed [the corpse's face], and stroked it, saying, "Shall I not serve Wu (Yan's son) as I have served you?" But still (Yan) stared. Luan Huaizi said, "Is it because he did not complete his campaign against Qi?" And he also stroked [Yan's face], saying, "If you are indeed dead, it would have to be something like the Yellow River that would prevent me from carrying on your work [i.e., the campaign] against Qi." The eyes of the corpse then closed, and the [customary jade] was put between his teeth. When Xuan Zi [= Shi Gai] left the room, he said, "As a man of valor how shallow I am [when I compare what I said to what Luan said to the corpse]."[54]

This remarkable story of necrodivination, in which the corpse itself was used, rather like an oracle bone, to determine the wishes of the deceased, dramatizes the first step on the path from corpse to ancestor. Xun Yan is still conceived as having wishes, but they are precisely wishes involving official appointments and succession; just as Pan Geng was using the ancestors to validate his policies, so too were Xun Yan's survivors using his recently dead body to legitimate their own decisions. In accounts such as these, the dead are not grieved; they are put to work.

---

[54]Based on Legge, trans., *The Chinese Classics: Volume V, The Ch'un Ts'ew with the Tso Chuen* (London: Trübner, 1872) 482–83, and Séraphin Couvreur, trans., *La Chronique de la principauté de Lou: Tch'ouen ts'iou et Tso tchouan*, vol. 2 (1914; reprint, Paris: Cathasia, 1951) 345–46.

There is no doubt that the Greeks of the Geometric and Archaic Ages commemorated their dead, and that by the second half of the eighth century various hero cults proliferated, frequently centered on Late Bronze Age or Mycenæan graves. The demonstrable genealogical link, so central to early Chinese ancestor worship, however, appears to have been lacking, as does the systematic articulation and instrumentality of the cult. Furthermore, the Greek hero cult was associated with a decline in the importance of the family and the increasing strength of the polis, so that its role in early Greece increasingly diverged in significant ways from the role of the ancestral progenitors in early China.[55]

Following these lines of thought I would speculate that heroic cultures (such as that represented in Homer's universe) are unlikely—at the time the heroes are conceived as having been active—to produce a strong ancestral cult. We have seen the way in which Achilles was ready to devalue his family ties when his friend Patroclus died (see 29); martial heroes, filled with their own sense of individual glory, are not likely to venerate, and may even be at odds with, their kin group. Ancestor worship, by contrast, is created and nurtured by civilian elites anxious to stabilize the good order and hierarchy that strong lineage units both encourage and replicate.

I would further speculate that an inverse relationship exists between the degree to which an ancestor cult is articulated and the degree of attention paid to the actual circumstances of the soul in the afterlife. In this view, cultures such as early Greece that provide imaginative, perceptual depictions of the afterworld, and also of this one, may not need a well-structured ancestral cult. Indeed, they may well depict postmortem existence in detail precisely because the ancestors are missing. The presence of an impersonalized ancestral cult in early China, by contrast, would help explain the classical texts' general lack of interest in the particulars of death and the afterlife. It would also explain the well-known fact that, although many mythic personages appear very briefly in ancient Chinese texts, they do not participate in a sustained,

---

[55]See Walter Burkert, *Greek Religion*, trans. John Raffan (Cambridge, Mass.: Harvard University Press, 1985) 204; he concludes that "the hero cult, in fact, is not an ancestor cult at all"; Hurwit, *Art and Culture* 121.

anecdotal mythology.[56] In this view, early Chinese elites would have felt less need for the precision of event and personality and for the existential details that are such notable features of the art and mythology of early Greece precisely because they did not conceive their ancestors in these ways. The problems, including that of theodicy, that the Greeks had treated as "mythological issues," had been resolved by the Chinese creation of ancestors, who, following Fortes's definition, were ancestors precisely because they were *not* comprehensive or detailed representations of personality and social role.[57] The concern with unstructured and potentially adversarial personality—in both religion and art—had been displaced by harmonious order and design. Chinese ancestors, like Chinese heroes, were valued for the good order of what they did, as in the "Pan Geng," not for the uncertain individuality of what they were. They were, once again, conceived rather than perceived.

The Chinese Hero

Although I have more than once suggested that early China "lacked" certain features of representation and content present in the culture of early Greece, this does not necessarily imply that such features ought to have been present. I find nothing admirable, for example, in having gods who, like Zeus, assume the form of a swan to rape a woman, or who, like Kronos, devour their own children. I find nothing attractive in what has been called the Greek "lust to annihilate."[58] That the martial heroism of the Greeks has found its emulators in later Western history is as much a cause for concern as for pride. It has indeed been argued that Greek models of war-

---

[56]Derk Bodde, "Myths of Ancient China," in Samuel Noah Kramer, ed., *Mythologies of the Ancient World* (New York: Doubleday Anchor, 1961) 369–370; he notes that "the gods of ancient China ... appear very rarely or not at all in art, and are commonly described so vaguely or briefly in the texts that their personality, and sometimes even their sex, remains uncertain."

[57]Keightley, "Early Civilization in China" 42–43.

[58]Eli Sagan, *The Lust to Annihilate: A Psychoanalytic Study of Violence in Ancient Greek Culture* (New York: Psychohistory Press, 1979).

fare and diplomacy have had a disastrous impact on western history. "The Classics, it is the Classics!" said William Blake, referring to Homer, "that Desolate Europe with wars."[59] For Eric Havelock, the classics helped explain the outbreak and continuation of World War I (and the Vietnam War), most of the statesmen and officers of the early twentieth century having been educated in the Greek classical tradition.[60]

In answer to the question, "Where have all your heroes gone?" the Zhou—or later—Chinese answer might well be, "Who needs them?" And the answer to that, presumably, is that certain kinds of civilizations, like Western civilization, do. All great civilizations have their costs as well as benefits. It would be instructive, accordingly—and I encourage the readers of this essay to make the attempt—to rewrite it from the Chinese point of view, stressing and seeking to explain all the features that early Greek culture "lacked."

Such an essay would begin by defining the hero differently, presumably offering various types: the hero as inventor of culture, as dynasty founder, as sage, as patriarch, as plebeian or recluse raised, on the base of merit, like Yi Yin or Tai Gong Wang, to great status and administrative influence.[61] The Chinese hero would be older, more mature. He would be literate. All Chinese heroes, moreover, would be socially engaged. Rather than employing the alien concept of "hero," the essay would, I suspect, base its categories of comparison upon the radically different Chinese term, *junzi*, originally a lord's son but, by the time of the Eastern Zhou, a moral "noble man."[62] Great stress would be laid on the *junzi's* respectful

---

[59]Cited by Fagles, "Translator's Preface" xiv.

[60]Eric A. Havelock, "War as a Way of Life in Classical Greece" and "War and the Politics of Power," Georges P. Vanier Memorial Lectures, University of Ottawa, 21 and 28 October 1970.

[61]For Yi Yin, see, for example, Chang Kwang-chih, "*T'ien kan:* A Key to the History of the Shang," in *Ancient China: Studies in Early Civilization*, ed. David D. Roy and Tsuen-hsuin Tsien (Hong Kong: Chinese University Press, 1978) 15, 38–40; *Shang Civilization* (New Haven: Yale University Press, 1980) 177, 192. For Tai Gong Wang, see Sarah Allan, "The Identities of Taigong Wang in Zhou and Han Literature," *Monumenta Serica* 20 (1972–1973): 57–99.

[62]On the way this term evolved, see Cho-yun Hsu, *Ancient China in Transition: An Analysis of Social Mobility, 722–222 B.C.* (Stanford: Stanford University Press, 1965) 158–74.

treatment of his parents and on his numerous male progeny. He would primarily be a man of peace not war, an administrator, a harmonizer, a man whose own personal desires were downplayed. There would be little evidence of dramatic conflict, of ironic or tragic incapacities, and there would be little interest in particular detail. The hero's role would be a generalized one.

Using this Chinese definition of "hero," the essay would then note the way in which these traits had been deemphasized in favor of the more particularistic, combative, bloodthirsty, juvenile features of the Greek heroic tradition. Major questions would be asked or implied. Why do the early Greeks and the heroes whom they admire place so little emphasis on kindness, benevolence, a concern for the people, and social harmony? Why does early Greek art lay such unsettling and, in a way, parochial, egotistical, and youthful stress on individual detail and the human form? Why did the Greek city-states, despite, or perhaps because of, their curious conception of heroism, virtually commit suicide?[63] Why, in the Greek case, had something displaced the good sense of order and abstraction with which the Zhou Chinese had come to represent their own society and its leaders and ancestors? An understanding of that "something" would be, and should be, the focus of the discourse. The essay might well conclude with the suggestion that in the perspective of world history, Greece and its heroes and its art were an unusual case. Sima Qian, in any event, would have relegated the Greeks, had he known of them, to a monograph, along with the Xiongnu, Hu, and other barbarian tribes.

Our Western conceptions of man and art, of the individual and the body, of the epic and heroic in both life and literature,

---

[63]For one instructive answer to this question, see W. G. Runciman, "Doomed to Extinction: The *Polis* as an Evolutionary Dead-End," in *The Greek City from Homer to Alexander*, ed. Oswyn Murray and Simon Price (Oxford: Clarendon Press, 1991) 347–67. He argues in part that within the polis there was never "internal consensus on a value-system entitling either the rich or the well-born to deference from their superiors," nor was there ever "any doctrine of legitimate accretion of power at the expense of fellow-Greeks" (354). The contrast with most Eastern Zhou religious, social, and political assumptions is palpable.

and of man's place in the cosmos, still resonate, whether we like it or not, in sympathy with the powerful, imaginative creations of the early Greeks. For their creations have the power to move us still, to be beautiful for us, in ways that defy easy explanation because they are so central to our conception of ourselves. Early Chinese conceptions of man and art have stirred, with equal profundity, the elites of traditional China for a period of some two millennia. If we would understand China and what it means to be Chinese, we must understand its early art and its early protagonists as the Chinese themselves have chosen to see them. And if Westerners would more fully understand themselves, understand the authority of their own past and how its religious conceptions have shaped their views of the individual protagonist and his responsibilities, an understanding of China and its cultural imperatives provides a valuable perspective.

THE AUTHORITY OF THE HINDU EPICS: Genealogy, Authenticity, and Authorship

Barbara Stoler Miller

As the countries of South Asia have struggled to establish their national identities in the postcolonial era, communal factions in the region have frequently appealed to distinct religious authorities in order to authenticate their claims to cultural and political independence. Recent scholarship in different disciplines has amply documented the complicated religious forces at work in the cultural politics of South Asia among groups of Hindus, Muslims, Sikhs, and Buddhists. My inquiry here focuses on Hindu culture in India. I examine alternate conceptions of Hindu authority, emphasizing the way the ancient Hindu epics, the *Mahābhārata* and the *Rāmāyaṇa*, have functioned over time as sources of authority on various levels of Hindu society.

In the dominant Hindu view of the past, origins are crucial, and genealogical authority derives from complicated intersections of divine and human activity. While scholars agree that these epics probably have their roots in events that took place in the period following the entry of the Indo-Aryan-speaking nomadic tribes into northwestern India around 1200 *B.C.*, their historicity is highly controversial. During the centuries of their composition, they became vast repositories of myths, ideals, and concepts that Hindu scholars, priests, rulers, and politicians continue to draw on to legitimate their authority. Since the central narratives of both epics focus on issues of legitimate authority, I analyze the epic vocabulary of "authority" to explore the related realms of textual, moral, ritual, and sexual authority that these narratives display. In this context, it is important to understand how the epic bards constructed their own authors and represented their own authority within the texts, and what significance this has for the transmission of the texts.

Like the multiarmed deities holding various weapons emblematic of Hindu culture, what we call Hinduism is a dynamic complex of rituals and ideologies that have evolved over millennia. Some have their roots in ancient Vedic religion, while others are based on local cults that developed through time in different regions of the subcontinent. The term

"Hindu" as a religious category is not an ancient Indian term; its usage in this sense is traceable to Arab writers of the ninth century, for whom it meant the inhabitants of the subcontinent who worshiped images of various gods. Today, the majority of those who identify themselves as Hindus adhere to cults centered on the gods Viṣṇu, Śiva, and the goddess called Kālī or Devī, all in multiple forms, many of which have regional and caste specificity. Likewise, Hindu practice and values rest on a multiplicity of institutional and textual sources of authority.

In contrast with Islam, Christianity, Judaism, and Buddhism, the heterogeneous traditions of Hinduism claim no single founder, no foundation text, and no fixed canon of texts. While the social hierarchies of caste (*jāti*) and class (*varṇa*) have determined Hindu economic, political, and kinship relations for centuries, even in these spheres, conceptions of legitimate authority have been neither uniform nor static. The custodians of Sanskritic Brahman religion have been remarkably successful in maintaining the timelessness of a Hindu orthodoxy rooted in Vedic ritual, but their constant need to remystify and reauthenticate the Vedic past suggests that their authority did not go unchallenged, even in ancient times.[1] This highly privileged group has proved masterful at inventing mythologies and traditions that retrospectively justify its role in society, even if that role otherwise makes little sense.

In brahmanic terms the Vedic hymns are the ultimate religious authority, considered to be the revelation (*śruti*) that ancient Brahman poets "heard" in ecstasy and orally transmitted with timeless purity to their descendants. In the process of guarding Vedic literature, the Brahmans developed elaborate means for ensuring the authenticity of the hymns and the supremacy of Vedic textual authority over other criteria of religious truth. Twentieth-century historical and anthropological criticism has done much to dispel the brahmanical biases that were incorporated into early Orientalist readings of Hindu culture. Still, contemporary scholars of India remain vulnerable

[1]See Wendy Doniger O'Flaherty, *Dreams, Illusions, and Other Realities* (Chicago: University of Chicago Press, 1984) and A. K. Rāmanujan, "Classics Lost and Found" in *Contemporary Indian Tradition*, ed. Carla Borden (Washington: Smithsonian Institution Press, 1989) 131–46.

to the weight of timeless discourse, articulated in learned texts that give an imposing scholastic authority to brahmanic social theories.[2]

For upper-class Hindus, the authority of Vedic literature still sanctifies brahmanic rites of birth, initiation, marriage, and death, but a broader level of religious authority comes from the body of literature called "memory" or "tradition" (*smṛti*). This includes brahmanical lawbooks, mythic narratives, and heroic epics. Though much of *smṛti* is nonbrahmanical in origin, the category itself is brahmanical and textual evidence shows that Brahman scholars continually influenced the compiling, editing, and transmission of even the epic and mythological traditions they did not totally control.

The paramount works of non-Vedic brahmanical tradition were theoretical textbooks of Hindu customary law (*dharmaśāstra*), the paradigm of the which is *The Laws of Manu.*[3] These books were constructed by Brahmans in their attempt to codify Hindu religious activity in terms of their dominant position atop a hierarchically ordered society defined by ancient brahmanical rites and customs. They called their idealized religious authority *sanātana-dharma*, the eternal religion.[4] The books of *dharmaśāstra* were composed in highly technical Sanskrit and have they been the property of a privileged class of Brahman scholastics throughout their history.[5]

In a series of studies of Sanskritic culture, Sheldon Pollock has argued that the lawbooks were themselves based on a transcendent model of the Veda as an eternal, infallible source of all sacred activity. They defined a genre of Hindu theory whose legitimacy and claim to practical authority involved a "regressive re-appropriation of the past" rather than a dynamic relation between theory and practice, past and pre-

---

[2]Ronald Inden, *Imagining India* (Oxford: Blackwell, 1990).

[3]Georg Bühler, *The Laws of Manu* (Oxford: Oxford University Press, 1886).

[4]Wilhelm Halbfass, *India and Europe: An Essay in Understanding* (Albany: State University of New York Press, 1988) 344–46.

[5]Robert Lingat, *The Classical Law of India*, trans. J. Duncan Derrett (Berkeley: University of California Press, 1973).

sent.[6] This attitude toward the past has dominated Sanskritic India, but it remains questionable how deeply it influenced other layers of Hindu culture until the nineteenth century, when the East India Company became interested in locating an indigenous Hindu legal code to be the basis of a legal system for governing Hindus in India.

Romila Thapar and other historians of India show the extent to which ancient Hindu texts of social observance and customary law were transformed by British lawyers in the employ of the Company.[7] Thapar writes: "The concept of law required that it be defined as a cohesive ideological code. The Manu *Dharmaśāstra*, for example, which was basically part of brahmanical *smṛti* was taken as the laws of the Hindus and presumed to apply universally."

The narrative traditions, though their texts owe much to brahmanical ingenuity and editing, have more popular origins and spheres of influence. They exist in two main genres: mythological narrative, called *purāṇa*, and the heroic epic, called *itihāsa* or *kāvya*. *Purāṇa*, which means "ancient lore," is the name of a class of Sanskrit mythic narratives that were composed according to formulaic rules by anonymous Brahman authors and dedicated to the cults of Viṣṇu or Śiva. In order to extend the religious authority of their myths, rituals, and doctrines to those whom they barred from Vedic ritual, the authors of these *purāṇas* remythologized the Vedic gods and demons in new sectarian genealogies.

The epics, in their extant Sanskrit and regional versions, share some features with the mythological narratives, but their characters are mainly human and their stories explore human social, political, and religious concerns.[8] Though the

---

[6]Sheldon Pollock, "The Theory of Practice and the Practice of Theory in Indian Intellectual History," *Journal of the American Oriental Society* 105 (1984): 499–519.

[7]See Romila Thapar, "Imagined Religious Communities? Ancient History and the Modern Search for a Hindu Identity," *Modern Asian Studies* 23 (1989): 209–31 and David Washbrook, "Law, State, and Agrarian Society in Colonial India," *Modern Asian Studies* 15 (1981): 649–721.

[8]Stuart Blackburn, Peter Claus, Joyce B. Flueckiger, and Susan S. Wadley, eds., *Oral Epics in India* (Berkeley: University of California Press, 1989). See also Alf. Hiltebeitel, *The Ritual of Battle: Krishna in the Mahābhārata* (Ithaca: Cornell University Press, 1976), *The Cult of Draupadī* vol. 1, *Essays on*

Mahābhārata and the *Rāmāyaṇa* do not easily fit within the Western genre of "epic," in view of the works' heroic language, action, characters, and scale, the label "epic" has comparative value. The Sanskrit genre terms used to define them reflect the distinct place that each epic has within Hindu culture. The *Mahābhārata* is called *itihāsa*, which literally means "thus it was said." The *Rāmāyaṇa* is called *kāvya*, which means "poetry;" the term was first used in the *Ṛg Veda* to refer to the inspired hymns of the Vedic poets.

The *Mahābhārata* is a vast archive of cultural genealogy, political struggle, and morality. With its brutality, moral ambiguities, and bloody war, its tone is in marked contrast to the piety of the *Rāmāyaṇa*. The *Rāmāyaṇa* is a shorter poem of family loyalties, adventure, love, loss, and mythic renewal. In its regional versions, especially the Hindi *Rāmcaritmānas*, it is the iconic text of devotional Hinduism.[9]

Within the narrative universe of the epics, temporal and moral dimensions of heroic action are governed by distinctive conceptions of time (*kāla*) and moral order (*dharma*). The narratives unfold in terms of the grand model of time that represents cosmic history as cycles of four degenerating ages, named *kṛtayuga*, *tretāyuga*, *dvāparayuga*, and *kaliyuga*, for different throws of dice used in gaming. According to Hindu reckoning, our present time belongs to Kali Yuga, the dark age, signified by snake eyes on the dice, the losing throw, personified as the destroying spirit of time. In Kali Yuga, the past is not something readily discoverable in a clear regression; it is an elusive minefield of secrets, obscured by disguises, deceptions, and false memories. Whereas the *Rāmāyaṇa* marks the golden age of Tretā Yuga, the Kali Yuga is thought to have begun with the *Mahābhārata* war. The *Mahābhārata* is not a narrative of an idealized past, but an epic drama of the destruction that initiates cosmic dissolution and recreation.

Analogous to this on the level of individual time and history is the idea that all existence is made up of cycles of birth, death, and rebirth (*samsāra*). The history of an individual or a

---

the Mahābhārata, ed. Arvind Sharma (Leiden: E. J. Brill, 1991), and *Mythologies: From Gingee to Kuruksetra* (Chicago: University of Chicago Press, 1988).

[9]Philip Lutgendorf, "Ramayan: The Video," *The Theater Review* 34 (1990): 127–76.

lineage includes not only the events of this life, but actions buried in former lives, which reveal themselves only to those of extraordinary wisdom. In the Hindu conception, succession, whether within a family lineage (*vaṃsa*) or a cultural tradition (*paramparā*), can be determined by events beyond the range of historical time.

Like time, moral authority in the epic universe is effective on different levels. The basic idea of moral authority is contained in the concept of *dharma*. *Dharma*, which literally means "what sustains," generally refers to the order or law that sustains the cosmos, human society, and the individual. On the human scale, it is religiously ordained duty, represented through the actions of the epic heroes.

The hero of the *Rāmāyaṇa*, Rāma, considered an incarnation of the cosmic deity Viṣṇu, is the embodiment of *dharma*. His heroism triumphs through self-sacrifice, devotion to paternal authority, and spiritual victory over evil. Sacred sites throughout India are associated with events in the epic, and Hindu rulers through the centuries have constructed their moral authority with reference to Rāma. Varied examples range from village *rājputs* of North India, whose past is defined in epic terms, to kings of medieval Vijayanagara, who identified themselves with the divine king Rāma and equated their capital with his city of Ayodhya.[10] In Vijayanagara, the capital of the Hindu kingdom that controlled much of South India from the fourteenth to the sixteenth century, the visual representation of Rāma's mythology in the architecture, sculpture, and urban design served to reinforce the legitimacy of the king.[11]

In the twentieth century, ideologies shaped by the colonial experience have led leaders like Gandhi to glorify the moral reign of Rāma as a golden age, while Hindu nationalists have sought archæological evidence of Rāma to confirm their idealized vision of an ancient pre-Islamic Indian glory. Hindu archæological scholarship has attempted to historicize Rāma

[10]Bernard S. Cohn, "The Pasts of an Indian Village," in his *An Anthropologist among the Historians and Other Essays* (New Delhi: Oxford University Press, 1987).

[11]John Fritz and George Michell, with photographs by John Gollings, *City of Victory: Vijayanagara, The Medieval Hindu Capital of Southern India* (New York: Aperture, 1991).

in a line of Ikshvaku kings that ruled the Gangetic kingdom of Kosala from their capital in Ayodhya in the sixth and fifth centuries *B.C.*[12] These claims are echoed in the militant Hindu campaign for restoration of the so-called Rām Temple in Ayodhya, which has been the scene of ongoing communal violence during the past few years.[13]

Though there has also been considerable controversy over the historicity and dating of the *Mahābhārata*, the text has never proved as congenial to orthodox Hindu values as the *Rāmāyaṇa*, nor has it lent itself to a coherent theological agenda.[14] The frame stories and many of the subnarratives seem to suggest that the ideological unwieldiness of the *Mahābhārata* frustrated ancient Brahman redactors, even as they sought to recast it in Vedic terms, calling it the "fifth veda."[15] Likewise it seems to have defeated early Western Indologists like Hermann Oldenberg (1903) and E. Washbrook Hopkins (1901), who called it "the most monstrous chaos" of an epic narrative, "a text that is not a text."[16] In fact, a characteristic of the *Mahābhārata* "text" is its unbounded quality, which has complicated twentieth-century attempts to edit it critically. Even in its critically edited version, the epic defies the notion of a "definitive," timeless text, though the recovery of such a text is at least in part what its editors sought. The editing of Sanskrit texts began in the first half of the nineteenth century. The idea of a critical edition of the *Mahābhārata* began at end of the century, and the work was initiated in Poona in 1919 under the direction of Vishnu S. Sukthankar, a student of the German Indologist Heinrich Luders. Sukthankar considered the *Mahābhārata* to be the

---

[12] H. D. Sankalia, *Rāmāyaṇa: Myth or Reality* (New Delhi: People's Publishing House, 1973).

[13] B. S. Miller, "Contending Narratives: The Political Life of the Indian Epics," *Journal of Asian Studies* 50 (1991): 783–92.

[14] See S. P. Gupta and K. S. Rāmachandran, eds., *Mahābhārata: Myth and Reality* (Delhi: Agam, 1976) and G. C. Agarwala, ed., *Age of the Bharata War* (Delhi: Motilal Banarsidass, 1979).

[15] James L. Fitzgerald, "India's Fifth Veda: The Mahābhārata's Presentation of Itself," in Arvind Sharma, ed., *Essays on the Mahābhārata* 150–70.

[16] See Hermann Oldenberg, *Die Literature Des Alten Indien* (Stuttgart and Berlin, 1903) and E. W. Hopkins, *The Great Epic of India* (1901).

Indian "national epic."[17] In a lecture delivered at the University of Bombay in 1942, he said, "Whether we realize it or not, it remains a fact that we in India still stand under the spell of the *Mahābhārata*. There is many a strand that is woven in the thread of our civilization, reaching back into hoary antiquity."[18]

In the "Prolegomena" to the first book of the Poona Critical Edition, Sukthankar delineated the particularities of editing a Sanskrit text like the *Mahābhārata*, with its widely divergent regional variations, in contrast with the more homogeneous texts of classical Western antiquity.[19] He also included a brief history of the project. After World War I "a band of young and hopeful Sanskritists who had returned to India after completing their philological training abroad, with their heads full of new ideas" took up the idea of a critical edition. The Bhandarkar Oriental Research Institute, founded in 1915, initiated the work on 1 April 1919 when Sir Ramkrishna Gopal Bhandarkar entered the first line of the text on a collation sheet. The main patron was the ruler of Aundha, Bhawanrao Pandit Pratinidhi. With the exception of Franklin Edgerton of Yale, Raghu Vira of Lahore, and S. K. De of Dacca and later Calcutta, the editors were scholars of Poona Brahman families.

Despite layers of accretion that shaped the *Mahābhārata* into a religious text of Hindu Vaishnavism, the reader is frequently aware of theological and moral rationalizations embedded within an episode that is otherwise mainly heroic and at odds with brahmanical values. The way in which the heroic, moral, and theological strands of the text are interwoven gives a peculiar dimension to the text. The narrative core is a martial saga whose sources lie in oral tales of a tribal war that was probably fought in the Punjab early in the first millennium *B.C.* The main story revolves around a feud of royal succession between two sets of cousins distantly descended from the legendary king Bharata: the Pāṇḍavas, five sons of Paṇḍu, and the Kauravas, one hundred sons of Dhṛtarāstra. The feud it-

[17]V. S. Sukthankar, *The Mahābhārata: Critical Edition*, Book 1 (Poona: Bhandarkar Oriental Research Institute, 1933).

[18]V. S. Sukthankar, *On the Meaning of the Mahābhārata* (Bombay: The Asiatic Society, 1957) 32.

[19]Sukthankar, *The Mahābhārata: Critical Edition*, Book 1, i-iv.

self is based on genealogical complications involving a series of mythic antecedents and divine interventions, some of which belong to the original saga, others of which were added by the later redactors in their attempts to mythologize the Bharata lineage within their own religious ideas.

As the saga was taken over by bards and Brahmans, it gradually expanded into a universe of legend, myth, and speculative thought. The whole epic landscape seethes with contradictory values, autochthonous forces, and trials of power, potency, and legitimacy.[20] Its layers of textual history suggest a series of patrons, poets, and scholars who recast its symbols of authority according to their own ideologies.[21] The critically edited text of the *Mahābhārata* consists of over one hundred thousand verses divided into eighteen major books and one hundred interwoven minor books. The purely didactic portions of the text, concentrated in postwar books twelve and thirteen, are brahmanical additions that have much in common with *dharmaśāstra* literature; they are largely ignored by the regional vernacular versions of the epic that proliferated in India and Southeast Asia.[22]

In the title, *Mahābhārata*, *mahā* means "great," and *bhārata* refers to the descendants of a tribal group prominent in early Vedic times whose land was known as *bhāratavarṣa*. The epics heroes trace their ancestry to the mythical prince called Bharata, whose birth is the subject of the famous story of "Sakuntalā" in the opening book. The land of the Bharatas was given new political meaning in the 1920's by V. D. Sarvarkar, the ideologue of the anti-Muslim Hindu Mahasabha. He defined a Hindu to mean a person who regards the land called Bhāratavarṣa as both fatherland and holyland. In modern Indian languages, the Indian nation is officially called, not India, but Bhārat, or Bhārat-Mata, "Mother India."

---

[20]D. D. Kosambi, "The Autochthonous Elements in the Mahābhārata," *Journal of the American Oriental Society* 84 (1964): 31–44.

[21]See R. P. Goldman, *Gods, Priests, and Warriors: The Bhrgus of the Mahābhārata* (New York: Columbia University Press, 1977) and J. A. B. Van Buitenen, *The Mahābhārata*, Books 1–5 (Chicago: University of Chicago Press, 1973–1978). See also Sukthankar, *The Mahābhārata: Critical Edition*, Book 1.

[22]Barend Van Nooten, *The Mahābhārata* (New York: Twayne, 1971) 81–108.

Though the genealogy of the Hindu nation is traced to the *Mahābhārata*, it has no eponymous hero like Rāma as its authoritative moral figure. Its multiple heroes are constellations of authority who represent not a single truth, but the paradoxical multiplicity of truth. The god Kṛṣṇa guides the *Mahābhārata*, but his power is ambiguous and dependent upon other characters in the drama. He is a cousin and teacher to the heroes, as well as a god whom they worship. He is an enigma whose seemingly capricious actions work to overturn all preconceptions about truth and falsehood, good and evil.[23]

To some extent, the paradoxes that Kṛṣṇa embodies are represented in the two authoritative figures of the grandfather generation, Vyāsa and Bhīṣma. Both are born of extraordinary parentage outside legitimate marriage. Their relationships to the heroes dramatize the ironies of genealogy that govern the *Mahābhārata*. A Brahman, Vyāsa is the natural grandfather of the warrior heroes of the Bhārata lineage and also the author of the epic. Bhīṣma is the great-uncle, also called "grandfather" (*mahāpitā*), who is revered for his spiritual power, symbolized by a terrible vow of celibacy. Several scholars have analyzed the overdetermined correspondence between Vyāsa and Bhīṣma.[24] One is the offspring of a wandering sage and a low-caste fisherman's adoptive daughter; the other is the offspring of a king and the sacred river Gangā. Vyāsa and Bhīṣma are the collaborators whose actions and advice define and animate the narrative universe they inhabit.

In its own terms, the *Mahābhārata* is a repository of *dharma*, not the clear moral order of a golden age, but the subtle (*sukṣma*) order that is played out on the field of moral combat (*dharmakṣetra*) in the Kali Yuga. Despite the ultimate value of *dharma* in the world of the *Mahābhārata*, order is inextricably bound up with its obverse, *adharma*. Values are ambiguous and the epic's heroes continually act outside their *dharma*—Arjuna, the great warrior, loses his nerve and Yudhiṣṭhira, the truth-teller, lies. Like the order of the cos-

---

[23]Bimal K. Matilal, "Kṛṣṇa: In Defence of a Devious Divinity," in Arvinda Sharma, ed., *Essays on the Mahābhārata* 401–18.

[24]See Van Buitenen, *The Mahābhārata* and Bruce Sullivan, *Kṛṣṇa Dvaipāyana Vyāsa and the Mahābhārata: A New Interpretation* (Leiden: E. J. Brill, 1990).

mos, the order of narrative time and space is baffling to conventional thought. The epic idea of the world's complexity resonates with what modern mathematicians call "chaos," unpredictable behavior that defies our conventional linear notions of order. They say that nature is in a state of flux and any change in even the smallest component of the system changes the dynamics of the whole system.[25] In a parallel way, we might see the world of the *Mahābhārata* as one of ordered randomness—past and present turning into one another, twisting into intricate patterns that seem elusive to our conventional thought. In such a world, linear explanations of events in the past do not suffice. Even a seemingly simple event may involve an endless web of past lives or forgotten moments in another age of this cycle of existence.

How did such a text originate? This is difficult problem to solve if one agrees with scholars like Van Buitenen that the critical edition of the *Mahābhārata* takes us back to a text no older than the sixth century *A.D.* Though the actual origin of the epic remains opaque, we can begin to trace the changing concerns of the epic redactors from this period. They had an ideological stake in representing their version of the origin and orderly transmission of the text. To this end, a history of the epic's origin and transmission was woven into the genealogy of the Bhārata lineage. Given the absence of an historical author, the presence of the legendary figure Vyāsa at the head of a transmission process that begins within the text itself gives the text a peculiar reflexive legitimacy. Vyāsa, whose name means "compiler," literally exists as a character within the text attributed to him, making explicit the author implied by the work.[26] He has a particular status within the text, coexistent with it and intimately involved with its characters.

The legendary author of the *Rāmāyaṇa* also exists within the text, but a comparison between the frame episodes of the *Rāmāyaṇa* and the *Mahābhārata* is illustrative of how differently the two texts were shaped. The text of the *Rāmāyaṇa* begins with a mythic dialogue between the sage Vālmīki and the divine messenger Nārada, who is a repository of Vedic wisdom.

---

[25]Heinz Pagels, *The Dreams of Reason* (New York: Simon and Schuster, 1988) chap. 3.

[26]Michel Foucault, "What is an Author?" in Donald Bouchard, ed., *Language, Counter-Memory, and Practice* (Ithaca: Cornell University Press, 1977).

In answer to Vālmīki's question about who in the world is the perfect man, Nārada outlines the story of Rāma, who was exiled by his father and whose wife, Sītā, was abducted by the demon king, Rāvaṇa. Obsessed by the story, Vālmīki walks along the bank of the Tamasa river, where Rāma, his brother Lakṣmaṇa and his wife Sītā had crossed on their way into exile. There the sight of a female crane lamenting the death of her mate arouses in him a sympathy for the long separation of Rāma and Sītā. Through divine inspiration, he transforms the ancient legend he learned from Nārada into lyric narrative, and then the god Brahmā appears to sanctify the poem. Two rhapsodists (*kuśilavas*), who are literally the sons of Rāma and Sītā, named Kuśa and Lava, learn the poem from Vālmīki in his hermitage in the forest and sing it before Rāma. Thus, Rāma, whose story Vālmīki heard from the gods, comes to hear about himself from his own two sons through Vālmīki.

The episode of Vālmīki's inspiration is cited by Sanskrit poets and literary critics when they refer to him as the "original poet" (*ādikavi*). In designating the *Vālmīki-Rāmāyaṇa* as the "original poem" (*ādikāvya*) the critics were not talking about the Rāma story, but about the inspired epic poem to which later religious poets looked as a source of their art.[27]

By contrast, Vyāsa is not represented primarily as a poet, but as a sage elder of his family. He is said to have composed what he witnessed with his own eyes. Vyāsa's presence at the events of the narrative and his relation to the characters in his story gives him authority over the poem, validating the authenticity of his account. Vyāsa not only precedes the heroes, but he lives long into the succeeding generations to tell their story in all its secret turnings. So powerful is Vyāsa's figure in the *Mahabharata* that it suggests correspondences with the mythic Brahmā. Just as brahmanic traditions attribute the creation of the Veda to Brahmā, they attribute the division of the Veda into four parts and the composition of the *Mahābhārata* as a fifth Veda to Vyāsa. From this, he bears the epithet "Vedayāsa."[28] While Vyāsa's Vedic associations are undeniable, his activity in epic time seems as crucial to his character as his mythic aspect.

---

[27]B. S. Miller, "The Original Poem: Vālmīki and Indian Literary Values," *Literature East and West* 17 (1973): 163–73.

[28] See Sullivan, *Kṛṣṇa Dvaipāyana Vyāsa and the Mahābhārata*.

Within the *Mahābhārata* text there are multiple frames that recount its transmission. The entire work is cast in the form of a dialogue between a young prince named Janamejaya and a student of Vyāsa named Vaisampāyana. Janamejaya is the great grandson of the hero Arjuna. The occasion for the narration is a sacrifice being held at Janamejaya's court in honor of his father Parikṣit, the grandson of the Pāndava hero Arjuna and the only survivor of the war. The sacrifice is rationalized within the text by an intricate series of explanatory tales.[29]

Though this is the basic narrative framework, it is not the outermost frame of the multilayered work. There are two further frames. One, which appears in only one version of the *Mahābhārata* and is thus deemed of questionable authenticity by the editors of the critical edition, portrays Vyāsa's presentation of his poem to the god Brahmā, to whom he appeals for help in transmitting it to his students. Brahmā advises him to invoke the auspicious elephant-headed god Gaṇeśa as his scribe. Gaṇeśa's role must have been introduced to give the enterprise of committing the epic to writing divine sanctity.[30]

The next frame involves a wandering bard, a *sūta* named Ugraśravas, who proposes to recite an auspicious story for some Brahman sages gathered in a royal ritual assembly. It is a story he had heard some years before from Vaisampāyana, as he was telling Janamejaya the story of his ancestors. In this frame, which seems to represent the passage of the epic from the bardic tradition to the Brahmans, Ugraśravas identifies his material as "auspicious stories connected with ancient lore (*purāṇa*) and moral order (*dharma*), which tell of the exploits of kings and great-spirited sages."[31]

After introducing Vyāsa into the narrative, and quoting him directly, Ugraśravas begins the account again, giving another version of the genealogy of the gods, the heroes, and the epic. The epic author is represented as recording and transmitting what he had witnessed and gathered from the past

[29]Van Buitenen, *The Mahābhārata* 2–4, 44–123.

[30]James L. Fitzgerald, "India's Fifth Veda: The Mahābhārata's Presentation of Itself," in Arvind Sharma, ed., *Essays on the Mahābhārata* 150 ff.

[31]*Mahābhārata* 1.1.14; Sukthankar, *The Mahābhārata: Critical Edition*, Books 1, 6.

through his special powers. We learn that Vyāsa first taught it to his son Śuka and later to other disciples, who recited it to the gods, the ancestors, and other superhuman beings. The disciple who recited for the gods was Nārada, the same divine messenger who told the story of Rāma to Vālmīki. The disciple who narrated the story for humans was Vaisampāyana, who told it to Janamejaya. Embedded within Vaisampāyana's narrative are various interrelated and subordinate narratives, many with their own narrators and audience. This subnarration is crucial to the compositional style of the epic.

The most famous subsection of the epic is the *Bhagavadgītā*, a dialogue between the god Kṛṣṇa and the warrior Arjuna which is contained in the sixth book of the *Mahābhārata*,[32] but which has an independent existence as a Vaishnava philosophical text that has attracted a variety of theological commentaries and modern interpretations. In its highly eclectic philosophy of action, the *Gītā* absorbs Buddhist and Saivite ideas into the cult of Kṛṣṇa. The setting of the *Gītā* is the battlefield of Kuruksetra, as the war is about to begin. When the assembled troops are arrayed on the field awaiting battle, Vyāsa appears to the blind Dhṛtarāṣṭra and grants him a boon. He will be able to hear an account of the battle from his charioteer Sañjaya, whom Vyāsa has endowed with immediate vision of all things past, present, and future. Sañjaya narrates not only the *Bhagavadgītā*, but all of the six war books. He reveals Kṛṣṇa's mystical teaching to the epic audience to temper the horrors of war.

Within the narrative mode of the *Mahābhārata*, the story of Vyāsa's own ancestry offers clues as to how the ancient Indians conceived the *Mahābhārata* text. Vyāsa's father Parāsara, whose name means "destroyer," was raised by his grandfather Vasistha to be a mighty sage. His most significant epic act is the seduction of Satyavatī, the daughter of a king and a nymph who is raised by a fisherman—a story that is repeated in different versions in the opening of the epic. It first appears in response to a Janamejaya's request to hear the *whole* epic text.

The narrator begins by telling of King Vasu, through whose city a river flowed. A mountain fell in love with the

[32] B. S. Miller, *The Bhagavad Gita: Krishna's Counsel in Time of War* (New York: Bantam Books, 1986).

river, waylaid her, and begot twins on her. The king freed her by kicking the mountain with his foot. In gratitude, when her children were born she gave them to the king. He made the boy chief of his army and married the girl, whose beauty was so great that thought of her made him spill his seed, which eventually fell into the river Yamunā, where it impregnated a nymph who had been cursed by Brahmā to become a fish. When the fish was in her tenth month she was caught by fishermen who pulled human twins from her belly and presented the marvelous pair to their king. He raised the boy as his son, but the girl, who smelled like a fish, he gave to a fisherman. She plied a ferry on the river Yamunā, and the Parāsara came to see her when he was traveling on a pilgrimage. The "bull among hermits" was instantly smitten by her and began taking his pleasure with her. She protested that there were holy men standing on both sides of the river watching. Then he created a fog that "seemed to cover the entire region in darkness." Again she protested, pleading her virginity and filial piety. The great sage was pleased by her virtue and promised that his love would not ruin her virginity; then he granted her a boon. She chose as her boon that her body would always smell delicious. On the same day that she lay with Parāsara, she gave birth to a dusky son on an island in the river Yamunā, so he was called at birth Kṛṣṇa Dvaipāyana, later Vyāsa. He stood before his mother and set his mind on asceticism. "When you think of me, I shall appear to you if any task needs to be done."[33]

The epic poet's origin and descent, like the origin and history of the epic heroes is a story of seduction, restored virginity, and substitute fathers (human and divine). Vyāsa, like several other key epic figures, is born outside the legitimate bonds of marriage. Also, the representations of the main female figures in the epic—Kuntī, Gandharī, and Draupadī—all contain elements of this story. Just as Kuntī, the mother of the Pāṇḍava heroes is the hub of a multivalent set of relations that constitute the epic story, so is Satyavatī the hub of a set of relations that constitute the formal prologue of the poem, her mating with Parāsara is an epic play-within-a-play that reveals the obscure origins, ambiguities of legitimacy, and shadowy kinship relations that govern the entire epic text.

---

[33]Van Buitenen, *The Mahābhārata* 130–34.

Parāsara is not Satyavatī's only mate, nor is Vyāsa her only son. The sweet smell that Parāsara gives her attracts the affection of King Santanu, father of the other Bhārata grandfather, Bhīṣma. When he proposes marriage to Satyavatī, her fisherman stepfather demands a promise that her sons and their descendants will inherit the Bhārata kingdom, Bhīṣma renounces his rights and makes a vow of chastity to assure that no progeny of his will ever claim the kingdom. So terrible is the vow that thereafter he is known as Bhīṣma, which means "terrible"—until then he had been named Gāngeya, "the son of Gangā," or Gangadatta, "the gift of Gangā," in recognition of his divine maternity. Satyavatī's royal sons die childless and Bhīṣma refuses to break his vow to beget children on her daughters-in-law, so she calls on Vyāsa to sire them. Thus the women whom Bhīṣma abducts for the family are impregnated by Vyāsa to perpetuate the lineage, but again with complications, attributable at least in part to Vyāsa's foul smell and fearsome ugliness.

The vow that Bhīṣma makes is itself the main source of his authority as a teacher of *dharma*, yet the vow is one of the critical events that ironically seeds the internecine war. The social force of the vow and the reverence with which Bhīṣma is held within the epic world is in part explained by the role of the ascetic in India. Romila Thapar observes, "One of the paradoxes of the Indian tradition is that the renouncer is a symbol of authority within society."[34] Certainly, Mahatma Gandhi's vow of celibacy (*brahmacārya*) was a crucial part of his religious-political authority.

Bhīṣma, in exchange for his vow, receives a boon that he can choose the moment of his own death. Later he abducts three brides for his stepbrothers, thereby incurring the curse of one named Ambā, who in her turn vows to kill him and proceeds to perfect her vow with such fierce austerities that she is reborn as an androgynous female named Śikhaṇḍī/Śikhaṇḍinī who has the singular power to make Bhīṣma lay down his life. Bhīṣma is also instrumental in acquiring wives for his nephews, Vyāsa's sons Paṇḍu and Dhrtarāṣṭra.

Paṇḍu becomes king because his elder brother Dhrtarāṣṭra is congenitally blind and is thus ineligible for direct

[34]Thapar, *Ancient Indian Social History* (New Delhi: Orient Longmans, 1978) 62.

succession to the throne. But Paṇḍu, born with the pallor of an albino, is also flawed as a king. Later, he is cursed to die the day he makes love to either of his wives—once carried away by the bloodlust of hunting, Paṇḍu killed a pair of mating sages disguised as deer and the buck hurled the curse in the throes of death. Again the Bhārata lineage is threatened. Paṇḍu is barred from begetting sons. He renounces the kingdom, appoints his blind brother regent, and retires to the forest with his two wives. One of his wives is Kuntī, a princess whose intelligence and virtue endow her with a magic power, a *mantra*—the power to call down a god at will and to have a child by him. Having experimented with the *mantra* as a girl, she called on the sun and bore him a child, whom she abandoned in her fear of social approbation, despite the usual assurance that her virginity was intact. The magic still terrifies her, but in a desperate attempt to save Paṇḍu's life, she reveals it to him and invokes three gods to father her sons; she then lends her power to her cowife Mādrī (a beauty Bhīṣma purchased for Paṇḍu) and so the five Pāṇḍavas, the so-called sons of Paṇḍu, are born. Each is endowed with an aspect of the god Kuntī invoked. Yudhiṣṭhira, the eldest, son of Dharma, the god of justice and order, embodies moral perfection. Bhīma, son of Vāyu, the god of wind, embodies the raw force of nature. Arjuna, son of Indra, the chief of the gods, is the conquering warrior. The twins, Nakula and Sahadeva, sons of the twin gods of dawn, the Aśvins, are as splendid and skillful as the sun's charioteers.

The Pāṇḍavas' rivals, their cousins, the Kauravas, are also the sons of a weak man and a powerful woman. Gandharī, their mother, is tricked by Bhīṣma into marrying the blind king Dhrtarāṣṭra. When she learns that her husband is blind, she ties a band on her eyes and vows to share his darkness forever—but her deep woman's rage is manifest in the ball of hard flesh, like a dense ball of clotted blood, which she aborts from her womb after a two-year-long pregnancy. In her revulsion, she rejects it, but Vyāsa appears before her and instructs her to douse it with water and it falls into a hundred pieces, which are placed in a hundred pots, from one of which the first-born, Duryodhana, emerges howling like a wild jackal that feeds on carrion, foretelling his own lust for destruction. Though she realizes her blind love for her power-mad son, Gandharī is powerless to resist it.

Youthful rivalry between the Pāṇḍavas and their cousins explodes into adult rivalry for control of the kingdom. Although Yudhiṣṭhira, Paṇḍu's eldest son, has the legitimate right to be king, Duryodhana covets the throne, and in various episodes, he attempts to assassinate his cousins or otherwise frustrate their rights. A plot is hatched to kill the Pāṇḍavas and their mother in a fire—they escape and live disguised as poor scholar-priests who beg for food and alms. Vyāsa sends them to the bridegroom-choice ceremony of the princess Draupadī. Arjuna is drawn to participate and wins her by performing a trial of archery. The bride, not alms, is brought that day to Kuntī, who without looking up, tells them as usual to share whatever they have. When she is told that they have brought a woman, Kuntī refuses to retract her command, claiming her vow to keep her word. So Draupadī, a princess born out of a sacrificial fire, becomes the wife of all five brothers. Dark and fiery by nature, she is the force that binds them into to their heroic purpose.

Attempts to rationalize the polyandry of Draupadī in terms of ancient social customs are inconclusive.[35] Within the *Mahābhārata*, it seems reasonable to see Draupadī as the wife of its composite epic hero, whose role it is to keep order in the world and protect the earth. Draupadī embodies the Indian goddess in her two aspects. As Lakṣmī, the goddess of beauty and fortune, she is the female power of earth that is essential for sovereignty. As Kālī, the dark goddess of destruction, her sexual power invites violence and her beauty threatens to produce chaos. In her double nature, Draupadī is the guardian of her husband's lineage. Despite the fact that her sons are all eventually killed in the war, the earth and the Bhārata line are preserved. She integrates their disparate characters and provides the energy (*śakti*) they need to win the battle of order over chaos in the dark age of the Kali Yuga. Within the epic, the stories told to explain her polyandry reflect different layers of mythic and religious authority in the epic. Both stories involve the god Śiva, who on the theological level of interpretation is the symbolic agent of discord and destruction in an epic world ultimately governed by Kṛṣṇa. One story links

[35]A. N. Jani, "The Socio-Moral Implications of Draupadi's Marriage to Five Husbands," in Bimal K. Matilal, ed., *Moral Dilemmas in the Mahābhārata* (Delhi: Motilal Banarsidass, 1989) 69–76.

Śiva with one of the cataclysmic events of the main story, the dice game between the Pāṇḍavas and Kauravas.[36]

The Kauravas invite Yudhiṣṭhira to participate in a ritual dice game that he can't refuse. Though he realizes the game is crooked, he plays until everything he possesses is lost, including his brothers and himself; finally in despair he wagers their wife Draupadī. Although the participants in the dice game are often warned about the danger of their course, once they begin the end it inevitable. They become trapped in a degenerating world over which they have no control, replaying through their actions the degenerating cosmic cycles that measure time and the waning of *dharma*. The destructive dice game in effect dissolves the royal authority of Draupadī's husbands and forces them into exile.

Draupadī is dragged by her hair into the dicing hall, stained with her own menstrual blood to be the slave of her husbands' cousins. Before the entire court she questions Yudhiṣṭhira's right to pledge her since he did so after he had lost himself and so dissolved their relationship. The court judges against her, refusing her claim of independence from her defeated husband. Duryodhana orders her disrobed and bares his thigh to her in a lewd gesture. Though the logic of her argument is rejected, its truth is represented by the endless garment that wraps itself around her nakedness. (In some versions she prays to Kṛṣṇa, who supplies the magical garment in response to her devotion.) Still, her curse takes it course. Her husband Bhīma, seething with rage, vows to kill the man who disgraced her and to drink his blood. She for her part vows to leave her hair unbound until his death and to wash her hair in his blood. Her anger provides the energy that goads her husbands to the war that reestablishes order, symbolized by her act of binding her hair, soaked in the dead warrior's blood. Draupadī, like Kālī in her ferocity, demands her sacrifice before peace can be restored. The *Mahābhārata* war ends with the annihilation of both armies, in Hindu terms marking the final destruction of chaos before a new age can begin.

What authority does this epic of cultural genealogy have for contemporary Hindus? If Rāma is the focus of ongoing attempts to construct a Hindu community in India, the

---

[36]See Alf. Hiltebeitel, *The Ritual of Battle: Krishna in the Mahābhārata*.

Mahābhārata heroes and heroines seem rather to function in an imaginative universe of relations and actions that various groups in Hindu society draw on for inspiration in separate ways. Many aspects of the epic seem to have their origins in folk traditions, which in turn develop with reference to the epic. Were there no *Mahābhārata*, the resources of Hindu culture would be much more limited. Modern Indian writers continue to recast characters and issues in the *Mahābhārata* in new ways.

One of the most startling examples is the story entitled "Draupadi" by Bengali writer Mahasweta Devi.[37] The story is set in the forest region of Naxalbari district of West Bengal during a peasant rebellion. The heroine of the story is a tribal woman, named Dopadi, a tribal form of Draupadī, which she is named in the official records. After her husband and co-conspirator is killed, she operates alone in secrecy, but is betrayed and tracked in the jungle by army men, under the command of a brutally methodical officer of Special Forces named Senanayak, "an elderly Bengali specialist in combat and extreme-Left politics." After she is captured, she is brought to camp and gang-raped before being brought before Senanayak for interrogation. The nobility of her actions as a tribal woman, a fugitive and a prisoner relate ironically to the epic Draupadī's questioning of authority and raise multiple moral and political issues that reflect back onto the epic text. While the epic Draupadī confirms her status by inciting her husbands to act, Mahasweta Devi's Dopadi acts on her own to defeat her adversary, Senanayak, through her refusal to accept the authority of her captors and her personal power to contravene what is expected of her in terms of gender and social status. The story ends with Dopadi refusing to cover her bloody body with the cloth that had been torn from her and she stands before her tormentor, naked, smeared with her own dried blood:

> Draupadi's black body comes even closer. Draupadi shakes with an indomitable laughter that Senanayak simply cannot understand. Her ravaged lips bleed as she begins laughing. Draupadi wipes the blood on her palm and says in

[37]Mahasweta Devi, "Draupadi," trans. Gayatri C. Spivak, in her *In Other Worlds* (London: Routledge, 1988) 179–96.

> a voice that is as terrifying, sky splitting, and sharp as her ululation, What's the use of clothes? You can strip me, but how can you clothe me again? Are you a man?
>
> She looks around and chooses the front of Senanayak's white bush shirt to spit a bloody gob at and says, There isn't a man here that I should be ashamed of. I will not let you put my cloth on me. What more can you do? Come on, *counter* me—come on, *counter* me—?
>
> Draupadi pushes Senanayak with her two mangled breasts, and for the first time Senanayak is afraid to stand before an unarmed *target*, terribly afraid.

Episodes from the epic are regularly performed in folk dramas throughout India; the traditions in Kerala and Tamilnadu are particularly active. A few years ago, I spent the night of New Year's eve in a coconut grove outside a village near Udipi on the southwest coast of India. I arrived there at dusk to watch an all-night performance of a ritual dance drama known as Yakṣagaṇa, based on the final episodes of the war in a local Kannada version of the *Mahābhārata*. The Yakṣagaṇa dance drama took form through the fusion of regional cults like the goddess cult and Bhuta spirit worship[38] with Kṛṣṇa devotional worship, of which Udipi has been a center for centuries.[39]

The night's drama, known as *Karnārunja Kālaga*, shifted between scenes of Draupadī's sexual revenge as the fierce goddess and scenes of the death of Karṇa, Kuntī's abandoned son, who is sworn to kill his own brother, Arjuna. In his youth Karṇa unknowingly becomes the ally of his brother's enemies. Only as the war begins does he learn from Kuntī about his true origins, but he remains loyal to Duryodhana and fights Arjuna to his death. The first episode in the drama showed Karṇa's appointment as general of the Kaurava army. In the next sequence, Draupadī portrayed her unavenged honor and then Karṇa defeated Yudhiṣṭhira in battle.

I looked at my watch; it was past midnight. The villagers here were not celebrating the new year, but the approach of

---

[38]U. P Upadhyaya and S. P. Upadhyay, *Bhuta Worship: Aspects of Ritual Theater* (Udipi: Regional Resources Centre for Folk Performing Arts, 1984).

[39]Martha Ashton and Bruce Christie, *Yaksagana: A Dance Drakma of India* (New Delhi: Abhinay, 1977).

the rice harvest, marked by the lunar calendar. Bhīma had just killed Duḥsāsana, and Draupadī, like one possessed, was washing her hair in bloody vengeance, performing a sacrificial act to restore the honor of her husband's lineage and purify the earth for the new cycle to begin. The drama culminated in a tumultuous duel between Karṇa and Arjuna, in which Kṛṣṇa forced Arjuna to kill his elder brother, even while his chariot wheel was caught in the mire of the battlefield.

Despite the raw horror of Draupadī's bloody bath and Karṇa's death at his own brother's hand, the performance had a sacrificial solemnity. In South Indian ritual drama, all participants (poet, performers, audience) receive blessings from such a performance, which celebrates Kṛṣṇa's triumph and the reestablishment of *dharma* in the Kali Yuga. Here, as in other folk traditions of ritual drama associated with the *Mahābhārata* throughout the subcontinent, the triumph of Kṛṣṇa is linked with that of Draupadī as the fierce goddess Kālī. The local representation of Draupadī as the goddess, related to the ancient and widespread worship of the goddess in South India, gains Hindu authority in the context of epic stories performed as devotional pieces revealing Kṛṣṇa's divinity. It seems clear that the authority of the epic tradition maintains its vitality, not through the critical edition, but through periodic ritual reenactment in these local contexts, which continue to change over time.[40]

Folk forms like Yakṣagaṇa persist alongside film and television versions of the epics. Beginning in 1987, Indian National Television broadcast a synthetic, serialized *Rāmāyaṇa*, which had a strong religious appeal for the mass of Hindu viewers throughout the country. It was based mainly on a Hindi version of the *Rāmayaṇa*, with elements freely drawn from Tamil, Bengali, and other regional versions, as well as from the Sanskrit *Rāmāyaṇa*. The popularity of the series led to its inflation into about eighty episodes, which finally ended in the fall of 1988. It was not uncommon for television sets in towns and villages to be freshly garlanded as a sign of worship before each Sunday broadcast. Many scholars saw the series as an exploitation of religion for both political and financial

[40]See Blackwell, et al., *Oral Epics in India*; Cohn, "The Pasts of an Indian Village"; Hiltebeitel, *The Cult of Draupadī*, especially *Mythologies: From Gingee to Kuruksetra*, vol. 1 and *On Hindu Ritual and the Goddess*, vol. 2.

profit in the midst of a crisis in Hindu-Muslim communal relations, centered around control of a sacred site in the town of Ayodhya in North India, which Hindu militants claimed to be the birthplace of Rāma.[41]

When Doordarshan began to broadcast the Hindi *Mahābhārata*, directed by B. R. Chopra, with a screenplay by Rahi Masum Raza, a Muslim, the drama and the response were very different. Chopra's emphasis was not on the religious dimensions of epic, but on the relevance of the *Mahābhārata*'s fratricidal conflicts to contemporary Indian political ethics, which lessened its appeal for rural audiences. The series appealed more to urban audiences, many of whom avowed learning their "national epic" for the first time. Sanskrit scholars like R. N. Dandekar of the Bhandarkar Oriental Research Institute in Poona, home of the critical edition, decried the liberties taken by and inauthenticities of the production (for example, *Hindusthan Times Magazine*, 15 October 1989), but for many educated Hindus, it was a chance to encounter and debate ancient Hindu values. An unbounded text like the *Mahābhārata* by its nature lacks absolute religious authority, but its powerful characters and the moral dilemmas of their world sustain an ongoing dialogue between the Hindu present and its complex past.

---

[41]See Lutgendorf, "Ramayan: The Video"; Miller, "Contending Negatives"; and Thapar, "Imagined Religious Communities?"

*IMAGINING IDOLATRY: Missionaries, Indians, and Jews**

Judith Laikin Elkin

> Listen like Christians, and believe, for this is no fable such as you had before under the Incas, but the truth, and no one will be saved who does not believe it.... Christ did not just give his life for his friends, but for his enemies. And who were his enemies? The principal persons among the Jews and all idolators. *Sermon delivered during Easter Week by Francisco de Avila, priest of the City of Huanuco, and published in Cuzco in 1648.*

Anti-Jewish invective was a feature of sermons preached by parish priests in Peru and New Spain (Mexico) in the mid-seventeenth century to congregations of recently converted native Americans and *mestizos*, scarcely any of whom could ever have had contact with a Jew.[1] In addition to the traditional charge of deicide and other lesser charges such as avarice, sadism, and subversion, the priests accused Jews of idolatry.

Two aspects of these sermons grip the attention most forcibly. The first is the question why the Jews should have been a subject of sermons at all. There were scarcely any in the Indies (Jews being prohibited from settling there) and none at all in the Andean village of Huanuco. The second concerns the charge of Jewish idolatry. Living among native peoples who appeared to be practicing idolatry, it might seem more rational for the missionaries to anchor themselves in the monotheistic Judaic tradition from which their own beliefs de-

---

*This paper is based on research carried out in 1989 while on a fellowship from the National Endowment for the Humanities and in the summer of 1990 while the author was the Touro National Heritage Trust Fellow and a Visiting Scholar in Judaic Studies at Brown University. A condensed version was presented at the Forty-Seventh Congress of Americanists at Tulane University in July 1991. It has benefited from readings by Ruth Behar, Walter Mignolo, Richard H. Popkin, and Tobin Siebers.

[1] At this date, *mestizos* were almost entirely the offspring of Spanish fathers and Indian mothers.

rived. What purpose was served by casting the Jews as idolaters?

Explaining this paradox requires us to look at the lives of clergy assigned to the Indies. Clearly, they had a heavy teaching burden. The church had undertaken to bring the Amerindians into the mainstream of Western, Christian civilization, a task best described in Ricard's pungent phrase as the spiritual conquest of the New World. In order to teach Christian doctrine, the clergy had first to educate themselves in the various indigenous languages and what we would now call ethnology. The church's "civilizing mission" required a complete reordering of native family life, the conversion of "savage" dress and foodstuffs to European taste, instruction in European agricultural methods and crops to a demoralized and dispossessed peasantry, and coping with predatory *encomenderos* who were concerned more with the regular supply of Indian manual labor than with the condition of Indian souls; all this, while living in stressful, utterly novel, physical surroundings.[2] Why, then, were they concerned with Jews? Why Jews-as-idolaters?

The clergy were for the most part educated and had read the Bible. Some sermons show familiarity with the central tenet of Jewish belief: "Hear, O Israel, the Lord our God, the Lord is One." The stark simplicity of this formula throws into relief the problem the priests faced in teaching their charges to distinguish between the Catholic images they should venerate from the discredited images that the Indians had formerly worshiped and that were now forbidden to them as the work of Satan. The authorized *Christian Doctrine and Catechism for Instruction of the Indians*, published in Lima in 1584 in Spanish, Quechua, and Aymara, instructs the clergy how to handle this problem:

> Q. Why do Christians adore images of wood and metal, if it is wrong to adore idols?
> A. Christians do not adore these images for themselves, as idolators do, nor do we think they have virtue in themselves.

---

[2]Early in the conquest period, in a system known as *encomienda*, Indians were parceled out to Spanish settlers (*encomenderos*) who were allowed to make use of their labor in exchange for exposing them to Christian teachings. *Encomienda* soon deteriorated into a form of serfdom.

> We revere these images for what they represent—Jesus, Maria and the saints, who are in heaven.[3]

This is the response of the sixteenth-century church to the question of idolatry among Catholics. By the mid-seventeenth century, however, a different response has taken over. Idolatry is now the crime of Jews and Muslims (moros), who are the enemies of Christ. How and why did idolatry come to be perceived, in the *judenrein* Spanish Indies, as a Jewish crime? Why, amid apparently idolatrous Indian practices, did evangelizing clerics single out "Jews" as the idolaters? How did this charge fit into their teaching agenda? The answers illustrate the ways in which the authority of the past can be used and abused in the service of ideology.

Does the possibility exist that these charges represent a provincial aberration, some localized delusion that found its public expression at this particular time and place? This explanation is not tenable. The unity of Catholic doctrine and the requirement of conformity in its expression are well established and well known. In the Spanish Indies as in Europe, control over intellectual and cultural expression was exercised by both church and state. A priori censorship for spoken and published utterances was established by the Catholic Kings in 1502 and renewed periodically through the seventeenth century. In its effort to extirpate doctrinal error, the Tridentine Council (1545–1563) mandated its own system of censorship.[4] The priests and friars who preached to the Indians had been trained in Catholic seminaries in Europe or in American extensions of these institutions. Priests were assigned to various parts of the empire at different times in their careers, and the message they delivered was the identical authorized message. The printed versions consulted for the present research typically carry the license and approbation of the preaching order to which the priest belonged, the opinion (*parecer*) of a priest from another order, approval by a church censor, the viceroy's

---

[3]Catholic Church. *Doctrina christiana y catecismo para instruccion de los indios* (Lima, 1584).

[4]For an overview of censorship laws, see Miguel Mathes, "El libro europeo en Nueva España," in Alicia Gojman de Backal, coordinadora, *El Impacto del Encuentro de dos mundos* (Asociación Mexicana de Amigos de la Universidad de Tel Aviv, 1989).

license to publish, and the license of the vicar general of the archbishopric.[5] In some instances, the permits, licenses, and opinions are more extensive than the text that called them forth. The system was designed to enforce conformity to authorized doctrine at every level, not to encourage inspired but idiosyncratic interpretation.

That the sermons against the Jews are a prominent feature of Franciscan and Dominican teachings in the Spanish Indies is all the more puzzling because there were no acknowledged Jews in the Indies at this date. It is well known that the Jews were expelled from Spain in 1492; less well known is the fact that Jews and conversos were excluded by law and license from migrating to the Spanish Indies.[6] The number of conversos in the world increased considerably after 1497 when the Portuguese crown forcibly converted all Jews within its borders.[7] Portuguese policy with respect to conversos was not as consistent as that of the Spanish; but despite the wider latitude allowed conversos in emigrating to Brazil, the practice of Judaism remained illegal in the Portuguese as in the Spanish colonies.

While being a Jew had not been illegal prior to 1492, Christian converts in Spain (and shortly thereafter, in Portugal) came under the scrutiny of the Inquisition, which was empowered to look into their religious practice in order to determine whether they were "Judaizing." Pursuing the "dead law of Moses" came to be defined as the crime of heresy, for which the ultimate penalty was death. In both Iberian nations, conversos very soon became the target of laws of *limpieza de sangre* ("purity of blood") which excluded anyone with a Jewish ancestor from holding public office, practicing a profession, or performing other honorable work. Over the course of

---

[5]See list of primary works consulted for this essay.

[6]Conversos (also known as New Christians) were Jews or the descendants of Jews who had been converted to Christianity either forcibly or voluntarily. At some points in this essay, they will be referred to as Judeo-conversos in order to distinguish them from Indian converts, who were also called New Christians.

[7]Portuguese Jewry included the Spanish Jews who had accepted exile from Spain in order to keep their religious faith. These forced converts are known to Jewish history as *anusim*; in the Spanish Indies, they came to be called, simply, Portuguese.

time, laws of *limpieza* converted what had originally been a religious distinction into a racial one.[8]

Conversos as well as Jews were excluded from the Spanish Indies in a series of laws that began in 1501 and continued to 1802. But some New Christians, like their Old Christian countrymen, were eager to take part in the great adventure of the age, with its promise of gold and glory. Others must have hoped that by removing to the perimeter of empire, they could escape the notice of the Inquisition. Conversos entered the Indies through loopholes in the law or by grace of a license bought from the Crown itself, which, increasingly corrupt and constantly in need of funds, sold emigration rights to people it officially excluded. Thus the laws of *limpieza* were not an impassable barrier for those clever enough to outwit them.

Though individual New Christians might be tolerated to varying degrees, Judaism was not. Crypto-Jews (sometimes called Marranos), who had come in the hope that they could remain faithful to the God of their fathers at the desolate far reaches of the known world, paid a heavy price if caught practicing their ancestral religion. Jews who had never been baptized were beyond the jurisdiction of the Inquisition, but they could be prosecuted for residing in the Indies illegally. However they entered, and for whatever motive, the one certain datum concerning conversos, including those who continued to regard themselves covertly as Jews, is that none practiced Judaism openly. To have done so would have drawn immediate retribution from both church and state.

This had indeed happened in the past. The Catholic Kings, in their order expelling the Jews from Spain, gave as their reason that they posed a threat to the faith of the New Christians. The pretext had some validity in that forcibly baptized Judeo-conversos might well have wanted to return to their Jewish families. But in the Americas, Spanish missionar-

---

[8]On laws of *limpieza de sangre*, see Albert Sicroff, *Les controverses des statuts de "pureté de sang" en Espagne du XVe au XVIIe siècles* (Paris: Didier, 1960). For linkage of these laws to contemporary manifestations of racism, see Ronald Sanders, *Lost Tribes and Promised Lands: The Origins of American Racism* (Boston: Little, Brown, 1978) and Yosef Haim Yerushalmi, "Jewish History and Jewish Memory," *Leo Baeck Memorial Lecture* 26 (New York: Leo Baeck Institute, 1982).

ies confronted an entirely different situation. Recently baptized Indians, far from feeling an atavistic tie to the Jewish people, would not have known about the existence of Jews had not the priests excoriated them in their sermons. The gulf between the two historical situations could not have been greater, but Catholic orthodoxy regarded both Indians and Judeo-conversos as New Christians. In lumping together monotheists and pagans, Catholicism differed from Islam, which traditionally acknowledged its debt to the Jewish and Christian traditions that preceded and nurtured it.

This confusion between different populations of New Christians also had negative consequences for the Indians, the full extent of which lies beyond the scope of this essay. Evidence comes from the rules for admission to the Franciscan order. Like other religious orders, the Franciscans had prohibited the admission of Judeo-conversos since 1488, a time when Jews still lived in Spain. Admission of Indians or *mestizos* to the order was prohibited after 1539 in language derived from the ancient statutes of *limpieza de sangre.* Gradually, these prohibited classes merged, until Indians and *mestizos* came to be included in language that originated in the exclusion of Judeo-conversos. The sixteenth-century historian Jerónimo de Mendieta closed the circle when he commented that "just as those converted from Judaism were new Christians and thus prevented from joining religious orders, so also should Indians be barred because they too were 'nuevos en la Fe.'" The modern historian of the Franciscan order comments that "it is not difficult to surmise that the Indian and the *mestizo* had taken the place occupied by the Jews in Spain."[9]

The merger of Indian New Christians with the class of New Christians who had formerly been Jewish signals confusion between Indians and Jews. Clues to this confusion are scattered in documents of the period. In manuscript, and even in print, *Iudio* easily becomes *indio* and vice versa. In the text of that same sermon by Father Francisco Dávila that is cited at the beginning of this essay, Jesus is guarded by soldiers and some princes of "*los Indias.*" (The masculine definite arti-

---

[9]Francisco Morales, O.F.M., *Ethnic and Social Background of the Franciscan Friars in Seventeenth Century Mexico* (Washington: Academy of American Franciscan History, 1973) 14–18.

cle provides a clue that the noun it modifies was originally masculine). The Quechua translation correctly shows "*Iudios*." Book 7 title 5 Law 29 of the *Recopilación de la leyes de las indias* states that all children of judíos are to be expelled from the Indies. The original, 1681 edition is quite unequivocal about this. However, in the 1756 edition, it is all the children of indios who are to be expelled, a far more difficult order to carry out.[10]

Such orthographic slips mirrored actual confusion in European minds between Indians and Jews. The fever of messianic speculation that gripped Europe in the seventeenth century focused on the supposed descent of the Amerindians from the ten lost tribes of Israel. A considerable literature was generated by partisans of all aspects of the debate.[11] Some authors found remarkable similarities between the two populations: that mothers suckled their own children, for example, or that some Indians appeared to be circumcised. Reading these sermons, one finds characteristics attributed to Jews—cannibalism, for example—that were being attributed to Indians at the same time.[12]

---

[10]The first compilation of the laws of the Indies was edited by Antonio Leon Pinelo, the son of a *converso*, grandson of Jews who had been burned at the stake. A conforming Catholic, Leon Pinelo was harassed all his life because of the "blot" on his escutcheon; he was most unlikely to confuse judío and indio.

The "Freudian slip," however, persists into the twentieth century. Some years ago, I found the famous Argentine novel, *Los gauchos judíos*, listed on the Harvard Library shelf list as *Los gauchos indios*.

[11]The basic reading list on this subject begins with Thomas Thorowgood, *Iewes in America, or Probabilities that the Americans are of that Race* (London, 1650); Menasseh ben Israel, *La esperanza de Israel* (Amsterdam, 1650); and Hamon L'Estrange, *Americans no Jewes or the improbabilities that the Americans are of that race* (London: Henry Seile, 1652). The history of this polemic will be found in Richard H. Popkin, "The Rise and Fall of the Jewish Indian Theory," in Yosef Kaplan, Henry Méchoulan, Richard H. Popkin, eds, *Menasseh ben Israel and his world* (Leiden: E. J. Brill, 1989). The author states, "The history of the theory provides an insight into the changing ways Europeans and European Americans saw their place in the world, and the changing ways they perceived the world" (63). See also n. 16.

[12]Possibly erroneously. For a deconstructed view of the perception of cannibalism among Native Americans, see Peter Hulme, *Colonial Encounters:*

Rolena Adorno notes this anomaly and speculates that "The search for similarities and the elaboration of comparisons, on the one hand, between the Amerindian and the Jew and on the other between the Amerind and the Moor or Morisco, reveal the process of fixing 'otherness' by grasping onto similarities."[13] In trying to understand the otherness of the Indians, Europeans tried to fit these new peoples into categories they thought they understood better. The conflation of Judaism with savage religion was a hallmark of European clerical mentality, and European-educated missionaries transmitted it to the Americas as conscientiously as they did other articles of their faith.

This phenomenon emerges in the life of Diego Durán, sixteenth-century missionary to the Aztecs. This Dominican friar believed the Aztecs to be descended from the ten lost tribes of Israel because of their cowardice. Furthermore, he "could not help but be persuaded" by the similarity of their customs: "the sacrifice of children, the eating of human flesh, the killing of prisoners of war, all of these being Jewish ceremonies." Durán, born in Spain forty-five years after the Jews had been expelled from that country, was brought to Mexico at the age of eight. There, he lived in an Indian village until entering a monastery at age nineteen. What he "knew" of Jews came to him only through the teachings of his church.[14]

We are presented with a tantalizing puzzle. In seventeenth-century Peru and Mexico, the charge of idolatry is leveled at a suppressed population of monotheists who are doing everything possible to keep their beliefs to themselves; hatred of Jews is being taught to congregations of newly converted Indians and *mestizos* who will never meet a Jew. Jewish evan-

---

Europe and the Native Caribbean, 1492–1797 (London and New York: Methuen, 1989).

[13]Rolena Adorno, "El sujeto colonial y la construcción cultural de la alteridad," in *Revista de Critica Literaria Latinoamericana* Año xiv, no. 28, Lima, 2do. semestre de 1988, 63. The contemporary reinterpretation of the encounter between Europe and America begins with Edmundo O'Gorman *The Invention of America* (Bloomington: Indiana University Press, 1961) and continues with Tzvetan Todorov, *La Conquête de l'Amérique* (Paris: Seuil, 1982).

[14]Diego Durán, *Historia de las indias de Nueva España y islas de Tierra Firme* (Mexico, D. F.: Editora Nacional, S.A., 1951) 1–8.

gelism is out of the question: the crypto-Jews who survived in Mexico had no prayer books, rabbis, schools, or synagogues to transmit knowledge of their banned religion. Their heritage had been reduced to half-remembered household routines, scraps of Christianized Hebrew blessings, and rumors of hugger-mugger candle lightings: hardly the stuff of evangelical outreach. But the harassment of Judeo-conversos and the burning of alleged Judaizers continued.

The total number of Jews and Judeo-conversos arrested, tried, and condemned by the Inquisition in the New World, is probably undiscoverable. Seymour Liebman, who examined Inquisition trials for New Spain, New Granada, Peru, and Rio de la Plata, concluded that the first-named tribunal was the most active. In the records for New Spain, he identified 1,744 individuals of both sexes tried between 1522 and 1709 on a variety of charges ranging from blasphemy through seduction in the confessional, of whom 378 or 21.7 percent were convicted of Judaizing.[15] The most frequent punishments for this "crime"—in addition to the expropriation of property exacted from all prisoners—included public lashing (up to four hundred blows), the wearing of a penitential garment that provoked public contumely, life imprisonment, labor in the galleys, death by garroting followed by burning, and death by burning. Beyond the penalty exacted from prisoners, all these punishments brought instant impoverishment to their families and ineradicable shame to their descendants.

Historians have not been negligent in researching the Inquisition in the New World, with respect not only to its operation against accused Judaizers, but also to its proceedings against accused witches, bigamists, concupiscent priests, and others who violated official norms of behavior.[16] Multiple rea-

[15] Seymour Liebman, *The Inquisition and the Jews in the New World: Summaries of Procesos, 1500–1810, and Bibliographic Guide* (Coral Gables, Fla.: University of Miami Press, 1974) 33.

[16] The bibliography for this subject is extensive, and includes José Toribio Medina's five volumes on the various Inquisition tribunals and Henry C. Lea's four-volume *History of the Inquisition in Spain*. Among twentieth-century scholars whose work should be consulted for the Inquisition generally are Richard Greenleaf, Julio Caro Baroja, C.R. Boxer, Antonio Domínguez Ortiz, Julio Jiménez Rueda, Henry Kamen, and Lucia Garcia de Proodian. With specific reference to Jews, see Martin A. Cohen, *The Martyr: The Story of a Secret Jew and*

sons have been adduced for the Inquisition's pursuit of Judeo-conversos to the New World; these may be aggregated into five basic causes.

1. Christian triumphalism, engendered by military victories over, first the Muslims, then the Amerindians, had persuaded Spaniards of their divine mission to bring the entire world to Christ. This spirit was encapsulated by the sixteenth-century Spanish historian, Gerónimo de Mendieta, in the first chapter of his monumental history of the conquest of the Indies:

> Chap. 1. How it would seem that, with the conquest of New Spain by Don Fernando Cortés, God had sent another Moses to liberate the natives from the slavery of Egypt.
>
> One must ponder greatly, how without any doubt God singled out and took for his instrument this valiant captain don Fernando Cortés, as his means for opening the door and making way for the preachers of his gospel in this new world, where the conversion of many souls would restore and compensate the Catholic church for the great damage and harm being done to our ancient Christianity at exactly the same time by the cursed Luther. Fortunately, what was lost in one quarter, was regained in another. Thus, it is not without mystery that in the same year that Luther was born in Eisle-

---

the Mexican Inquisition in the Sixteenth Century (Philadelphia: Jewish Publication Society, 1973); Boleslao Lewin, *Mártires y conquistadores judíos en la América hispana* (Buenos Aires, Asociación pro-cultura judía, 1954) and *La inquisición en Hispanoamérica (judíos, protestantes y patriotas)*, (Buenos Aires: Editorial Proyección, 1962); Seymour B. Liebman's numerous works, including *The Jews in New Spain: Faith, Flame, and the Inquisition* (Coral Gables, Fla.: University of Miami Press, 1970), *The Inquisitors and the Jews in the New World* and *New World Jewry, 1493–1825: Requiem for the Forgotten* (New York: Ktav Publishing House, 1982); and Stanley M. Hordes, "The Crypto-Jewish Community of New Spain, 1620–1649: A Collective Biography" (Ph.D. dissertation, Tulane University, 1980). For Brazil, see Nelson Omegna, *Diabolização dos Judeus* (Rio de Janeiro: Distribuidora Record, 1969); José Gonçalves Salvador, *Cristãos-novos, jesuítas e Inquisição* (São Paulo: Livraria Pioneira Editôra, 1969); and Anita Novinsky, *Cristãos novos en Bahia* (São Paulo: Editôra Perspectiva, 1972).

> ben, a town in Saxony, Hernando Cortés was born in Medellín, a town in Spain; the one to upset the world and to draw under the Devil's banner many of the faithful who from fathers' and grandfathers' time had been Catholic; the other to bring into union with the church an infinite multitude of peoples who for years without number had been under the power of Satan, enveloped in vice and blinded by idolatries.[17]

In this grand triumphal vision, Jews were an obstacle to the preordained triumph of the Catholic faith, an anachronism, and a standing reproach to the efficacy of Christian evangelists.[18] Laws of *limpieza de sangre*, which converted Judaism from a religion to a disease of the blood, extended this vision into the genetic makeup of Spanish and Portuguese New Christians, making it impossible for Old Christians to accept conversions as genuine, though some historians believe that as many faithful Catholics as faithful Jews died at the stake as Judaizers. Laws of *limpieza* institutionalized the prejudice that not just every Jew, but every converso bore the indelible mark of Cain. Father Domingo de Soussa, preaching at the auto-da-fé "celebrated" in Mexico in 1699, taught that Abel was the semblance of the first Christian while Cain was the first Jew and the first heretic.[19]

---

[17]Fray Gerónimo de Mendieta, of the Franciscan Order, *The Ecclesiastical History of the Indies*, (Mexico: Antigua Librería, 1770). Translation mine.

[18]The persistence of this view of Judaism surfaced in recent years with the statement by Dr. John Strugnell of Harvard University's Divinity School, at the time chief editor of the Dead Sea Scrolls, to the effect that what annoyed him about Judaism was "the fact that it has survived when it should have disappeared." Quoted in the *New York Times*, 12 December 1990, 1.

[19]"Bearing the weight of the divine curse with its everlasting opprobrium (which David predicted), fleeing from men who fear that he may kill them, marked like Cain so that they may not kill them, hiding themselves in synagogues, without God, without priests, without church, and without law, remaining obstinate in the perfidy of the first Jew Cain, living shadow of the enrooted hardheartedness of innate perfidy, and congenital blindness, which we see in all Jews, as though their conversion were negated, from their first outline in the beginnings of the world, reserved, at its limits for divine judgment; all the blame because the eternal damnation of Cain was, according to Saint Ambrosio, not for having killed his brother, but for having deprived of life Abel, Abel, Abel was the brother he killed. Consider the significance of the name, in

2. Since expropriation of property was the first action taken by the Inquisitors upon arrest of an individual, it is easy to accuse the institution of being motivated by greed. The historical record provides considerable support for this view, even among historians such as Richard Greenleaf who believe that the Inquisition held itself generally to higher standards of morality than prevailed elsewhere in Europe at the same time. The *visita* (general accounting) of the Mexican Holy Office in the years 1645–1649 determined that massive peculation by the Inquisitors had accompanied the prosecution of Judaizers. The proceeds of the auto-da-fé of 1649 alone came to at least three million pesos, and Greenleaf concludes that "the confiscation of Judaizante wealth laid a firm foundation for the Holy Office's budget in the second half of the seventeenth century."[20] The more than one hundred Portuguese New Christians arrested by the Inquisition in Lima in 1635 included some of the greatest merchants of the Atlantic trade. Several historians have carried out a detailed accounting of the goods expropriated from them, and one concludes,

---

order to understand the saint. Abel means "wail" [Sp., *llanto*], which is the most effective penitential remorse.... For if Cain killed not only Abel, but also his wail, his penitence, to what extent is the death of sorrow the cause of his sentence? If the wail of penitence had remained alive in Cain, if he were not obstinate, he would not be eternally dead; his obstinacy caused his death, and this follows the diabolical malice of Cain...." *Sermon en el auto publico de Fee.* Que el Tribunal de el Santo Officio de Nueva Espana celebró el día catorze de unio de 1699. Mexico, 1699. En el real convento de NPS Domingo de México. Dixolo el M. Father Domingo de Soussa, Qualificador del Santo Oficio, Theólogo, y Examinador Sinodal de la Nunciatura de España, Prior Provincial de la Provincia de Santiago.

Soussa concludes by urging the prisoners who are about to be burned alive not to be obstinate like Cain, but to revive the *llanto* within them. In addition to his other transgressions, Soussa misunderstood his Hebrew. "Wail" in Hebrew is *evel* but Abel's name was *Hevel.* For the uses of anti-Semitism in establishing a Christian identity, see Rosemary Ruether, *Faith and Fratricide. The Theological Roots of Antisemitism* (New York: Seabury Press, 1979).

[20]Richard E. Greenleaf, "The Great Visitas of the Mexican Holy Office 1645–1669." *The Americas* 44, 4 (April 1988): 399–420. The visita was the official accountability review carried out for every Crown official at the expiration of his term of office.

> There is a positive correlation between the New Christian persecutions and the financial consolidation of the Inquisition as an effective and relatively autonomous institution.... A period of major disorder in the Inquisition's sources of income coincided with the main persecution of Portuguese [New Christian] merchants which began in 1635.... After the expropriations of 1635–1641 the Inquisition's budget again acquired its balance.[21]

3. Commercial competition is a traditional stimulus to prejudice against Jews, one that reasserts itself periodically in all ages. The way in which religious prejudice could be placed at the service of commercial competition can be illustrated by an incident in 1529, when a Spanish merchant petitioned the monarch to prohibit the giving of Indians in *encomienda* to the son or grandson of any person burned or reconciled by the Inquisition "because of the danger to our holy faith." The petitioner went on to denounce a competitor, "of whom it is said that his father had been a Jew."[22] Quiroz writes of the Old Christian merchants that they "not only complained constantly about the Portuguese trade, but also were involved directly in the repression of the Portuguese New Christian merchants in the period 1635–39 while performing honorary official tasks for the Inquisition."[23]

4. The mid-seventeenth century was a time when millennial expectations among both Christians and Jews had reached ecstatic proportions. 1648 was the date interpreted by kabbalists to be the year of redemption, for which all Europe had strong need following thirty years of harrowing religious

---

[21]Alfonso W. Quiroz, "The Expropriation of Portuguese New Christians in Spanish America, 1635–1649." *Ibero-Amerikanisches Archiv* N.F. Jg 11 H.4 1985: 407–65, especially 410 and 423–24. See also José Toribio Medina, *Historia del Tribunal del Santo Oficio de la Inquisición de Lima (1569–1820)* (Santiago, Imprenta Elzeviriana, 1887); Boleslao Lewin, *El Santo Oficio en América y el más grande proceso inquisitorial en el Perú* (Buenos Aires, Sociedad Hebraica Argentina, 1950); Rene Millar Corbacho, "Las confiscaciones de la Inquisición de Lima a los comerciantes de origen judio-portugues de "la gran complicidad' de 1635," *Revista de Indias* (Madrid) 43 (1983): 27–58.

[22]José Toribio Medina, *La primitiva inquisición Americana, 1493–1569* (Santiago de Chile, Imprenta Elzeviriana, 1914) 32.

[23]Quiroz, "Expropriation of Portuguese New Christians" 418.

warfare. Among Jews, the Chmielnicki pogroms in Poland and renewed pressure by the Inquisition in territory under Spanish rule (which now included most of the Western hemisphere), increased the traditional yearning for the coming of the Messiah. In 1650, Rabbi Menasseh ben Israel published his apocalyptic book, *Esperanza de Israel*, based on the sworn testimony of a converso traveler who claimed to have made contact with Jews living hidden away in the Andes Mountains.[24] Here was evidence that the dispersion of the Jews was nearly complete. If Oliver Cromwell would only readmit the Jews to England, the way would be clear for advent of the Messiah. Sabbatai Zevi declared his messiahship in Smyrna in 1665, setting off a wave of religious exaltation among Jews and Christians alike. Christian millenarians had set 1660 as the date of the Second Coming of Christ, at which time they expected that all surviving Jews would be converted overnight. With chiliastic sects proliferating in the ruins of central Europe, apocryphal writings were studied for clues as to when the Messiah would appear, an occurrence that seemed increasingly likely. In that eventuality, from the point of view of those in power, it would be better if it were not another Jewish messiah.

5. By mid-seventeenth century, the outposts of the Spanish empire were under attack by Portuguese and Dutch corsairs. In an atmosphere of tension generated by the presence of ships of foreign rivals trespassing in waters claimed by Spain—with papal backing—by divine right, the search for subversives and traitors began. Prosecutions of alleged Judaizers increased during periods when attacks by hostile foreign powers on Spanish territories were expected.

The pattern of suspicion was set by events surrounding the capture of Bahia by the Dutch in 1624. The defeat of the Portuguese on the important sugar exporting coast of Brazil

---

[24]The best edited text of this work is Henry Méchoulan and Gérard Nahon, eds., *Menasseh ben Israel, The Hope of Israel. The English Translation by Moses Wall, 1652*, trans. Richenda George (London: Oxford University Press, 1987). For informed commentary on Menasseh in the context of his times, see Kaplan, Méchoulan, and Popkin, eds., *Menasseh ben Israel and his World*. A compact discussion of millenarianism is to be found in David S. Katz, *Philo-Semitism and the Readmission of the Jews to England, 1603–1655*. (Oxford: Clarendon Press, 1982).

was charged to the account of New Christians who had lived there for generations, and who were alleged to have assisted the invaders because of a desire to benefit from Dutch religious toleration, which would permit them to return to Judaism. A Brazilian historian has shown convincingly that New Christians in Bahia, far removed from their Jewish origins, reacted to invasion in the same ways as their Old Christian neighbors: some supported the Portuguese, some the Dutch. An inquest held by Bishop Dom Pedro da Silva following the reconquest of the city by the Portuguese heard denunciations of eighty persons for cooperation with the Dutch. Among those denounced were forty-eight Old Christians, twenty-four New Christians, and eight priests.[25]

The canard of Jewish treachery was employed to spook the citizens of Lima in 1635 when the entire converso community was arrested overnight in an operation that went down in history as *la gran complicidad.* Interestingly, in the interrogations carried out in Inquisition cells, there are references to some merchants' association with the Dutch West Indies Company, but no evidence of involvement in a "conspiracy." Nor did the priests who delivered the self-congratulatory sermons that accompanied the auto-da-fé take credit for nipping a conspiracy in the bud. Father Fernando Montesinos, speaking at the auto-da-fé performed in Lima on 23 of January 1639, at which ten persons were burned at the stake and various other punishments meted out to those who had not already died in their cells, describes the prisoners as comprising a "gran complicidad." The only proof he brings forward is that the prisoners attempted to communicate between cells by tapping out words alphabetically.[26] No prisoner was in fact

---

[25]See Anita Novinsky, *Cristãos Novos na Bahia.* For the invasion and the inquests that followed, see Novinsky, "A Historical Bias: The New Christian Collaboration with the Dutch Invaders of Brazil." *Fifth World Congress of Jewish Studies* 22 (1972): 141–54; Novinsky, "Uma Devassa do Bispo D. Pedro da Silva," in *Anais do Museu Paulista* (São Paulo: Universidade de São Paolo, 1968); and Stuart Schwartz, "The Voyage of the Vassals: Royal Power, Noble Obligations, and Merchant Capital before the Portuguese Restoration of Independence, 1624–1640," *Hispanic American Historical Review* 96, 3 (1991): 735–62.

[26]Presbitero Fernando Montesinos, *El auto de la fe celebrado en Lima La 23 de enero de 1639.* (Madrid, 1640). Nor is a "conspiracy" mentioned by Father

charged, convicted, or executed for conspiracy during this "gran complicidad," raising the question of who, in fact, conspired against whom.

The major period of repression of accused Judaizers in New Spain occurred in the years 1642–1649, triggered by the revolt of the Portuguese Duque de Bragança against Spanish rule, and the corresponding fear that Portuguese living in the Americas would collaborate in attacks on the colonies. The ensuing xenophobia created the conditions for a crackdown on a specific class of Portuguese, the conversos. Two hundred and twelve conversos were arrested during this period, appearing at a series of autos-da-fé to receive their punishment. The charge brought against the prisoners was not treason, but the criminal heresy of Judaizing; nevertheless, a lasting perception was created of New Christians as traitors and subversives. Their confiscated property never was remitted to the Spanish Suprema, as regulations required, but remained in the pockets of members of the local tribunal.[27]

The conjunction of these five elements: Christian triumphalism, greed, commercial rivalry, millenarianism, and fear of a foreign enemy, all came together to create a congenial atmosphere for what in later centuries would be called a pogrom. In this context, "great conspiracies" were discovered in Peru, Brazil, and New Spain, and the Inquisition stepped up its prosecution of supposed Jews and New Christian Judaizers.

One question, however, remains unanswered: what is the meaning of the charge of idolatry that starts to figure in priestly rhetoric in the mid-seventeenth century? In Inquisition records of "sinagogas" claimed to have been discovered in Lima and Mexico, no mention is made of idols having been found. The inquisitors who interrogated Portuguese New Christians accused of Judaizing did not ask whether they were worshiping idols, but whether they were following "the dead law of Moses," in the cant phrase of the time. In the absence of any evidence of Jewish idolatry, we must ask, what

---

Joseph de Zisneros, who delivered the sermon on this occasion. Medina, who examined the trial records (procesos), found in them no mention of conspiracy.

[27]Hordes, "The Crypto-Jewish Community," chap. 4, and Greenleaf, "The Great Visitas."

was on the church's agenda when it leveled this charge? The answer provides us with a new perspective on a complex and self-contradictory age; it removes the supposed relationship between Indians and Jews out of the realm of humor and into the inferno of religious bigotry.

The herculean efforts of frontier missionary friars, backed by the force of invading armies, led within a generation of the conquest to the apparent conversion to Catholicism of the remnant of Native American peoples that survived the encounter. But the friars of the various teaching orders and the secular priests who followed in their footsteps came to realize over the course of time that, beneath the newly acquired veneer of Catholicism, many Indians continued to cling to their old beliefs.[28] The discovery of images hidden in caves or behind false walls in village churches, the existence of priests of the old faith who taught that abandoning ancestral beliefs would lead to disaster (as indeed it had), or who at best suggested that this new god, Jesus Christ, could be comfortably accommodated among the other gods, all under the guise of Catholic ritual, caused severe anguish to the clergy, who had imagined the task of evangelization complete and who now feared that their authority over the Indians would be eroded.[29] Outraged by the discovery that their congregants, apparently so obedient, could spurn the promise of salvation in favor of familiar pagan rituals, the Catholic priests fought back with the harsh measures deemed necessary for the task of routing the forces of Satan: the destruction of anything that could be related in any way to the old religion; and imprisonment, torture, confis-

[28]Priests who spent long years in close contact with the Indians recognized that at celebrations such as Corpus Christi, something else, something distinctly non-Christian, was going on. Louise Burkhart argues in a recent book against the traditional view that a religious syncretism harmonized Christianity with Nahua religious belief. "Syncretism implies a resolution of contradictions, but that did not occur." Rather, Nahua structures and functions imposed themselves on Christian content, while the logical structure of the universe remained Nahua. Christianity was "patched in where it fit." *The Slippery Earth: Nahua-Christian Moral Dialogue in Sixteenth Century Mexico* (Tucson: University of Arizona Press, 1989) 187ff.

[29]Burkhart comments in passing that "Catholicism's emphasis on images permitted an easy transition for idolators," but nothing in the record supports that view.

cation of goods, and burning at the stake for those accused of practicing it.

In 1539 in Mexico, Franciscan bishop Juan de Zumárraga prosecuted the Indian cacique Chichimecatecotl, known by his baptismal name of don Carlos de Mendoza, for heretical dogmatizing against the faith and for idolatry. No witness was presented who claimed to have seen him serve or worship an idol in any way. But enough witnesses testified to don Carlos's subversive speech to cause his conviction as a heretic.[30] At the auto-da-fé where he was to be punished, don Carlos requested permission to speak to his people in their own language. Permission granted, he confessed his faith as a Christian and urged his people likewise to be good Christians. In these circumstances, the prisoner should have been admitted to reconciliation. He was not, but in clear contravention of the Inquisition's rules of due process, was apparently burned to death on the spot.

Don Carlos had been accused of idolatry by his nephew. One aspect of the matter that the bishops failed to investigate was whether there might have been an ulterior motive for the denunciation. In fact, the nephew was a rival claimant to the estate of his late father, don Carlos's brother. With the execution of don Carlos, the suit was settled: the Church expropriated the disputed land for itself. The resemblance to Inquisitorial practice with respect to Judeo-conversos is unmistakable. A charge of religious deviation is leveled against a New Christian who is perceived to hold subversive political ideas, and who owns property that will be free for the taking once the deviant has been convicted. This resemblance has never been remarked upon by historians of the "spiritual conquest" of the Indies.

---

[30]At secret meetings with other caciques, don Carlos had spoken in ways calculated to rouse rebellion against the Spanish. Richard Greenleaf provides a transcription of one of his speeches in *Zumarraga and the Mexican Inquisition*, 70: "Who are those that undo us and disturb us and live on us and we have them on our backs and they subjugate us? Well here I am, and there is the Lord of Mexico, Yoanize, and there is my nephew Tezapille, Lord of Tacuba, and there is Tlacahuepantli, Lord of Tula, that we are all equal and in agreement and no one shall equal us, that this is our land, and our treasure and our jewel, and our possession, and the dominion is ours and belongs to us."

The case of don Carlos shows the church proceeding against New Christians who were Native Americans in the same manner, and with the same mixed motives, as against New Christians who were descended from Jews. But the cacique's trial and execution led to an entirely different outcome than the trials and executions of suspected Judaizers. The absence of approved legal procedures during don Carlos's trial sparked an investigation and removal of the inquisitorial power from the bishops. This was not a situation that could be tolerated by the Spanish Crown, which from the start had taken the Indians under its protection.[31] Partly as a result of the atrocious mismanagement of don Carlos's case, the Crown never placed Indians under the jurisdiction of the Inquisition; as newcomers to the faith, they were not to be charged with heresy.

In this manner, the church lost an important weapon for enforcing doctrinal conformity among the Indians. This loss must have been particularly galling as successive generations of priests became aware that Indian life continued to be based on pre-Columbian values. The longer the Spanish friars stayed in the Indies, the more aware they became that the Indians were following Catholic form while living the substance of their native tradition. Frustrated in their effort to remake the Indians in the mold of the European peasantry, the priests came to form the opinion that the Indians' "brutish nature" could only be dealt with by the enforcement of strict discipline.[32] They faced a frustrating situation: practices that they perceived as idolatrous were going on all about them, but they were helpless to punish the perpetrators in what they re-

[31]The philosophical basis for Spanish policy toward the Indians is set forth in Lewis Hanke, *Aristotle and the American Indians. A Study in Race Prejudice in the Modern World* (Bloomington: Indiana University Press, 1975).

[32]The execution of don Carlos did not end the prosecution of Native Americans for heresy. In 1562, Bishop Diego de Landa carried out a reign of terror among the Maya of Yucatan. Although complaints concerning the violence of his methods led to his recall to Spain for questioning, he was exonerated and returned to his post. "Lesser" penalties than burning—such as two hundred lashes, seven years in the galleys, and so on—continued to be imposed throughout New Spain in the sixteenth century. However, the Indians were never formally placed under the jurisdiction of the Holy Office of the Inquisition.

garded as just measure for their sin. Fortunately, there was someone else whom it was not only legal, but meritorious, to burn: those other New Christians, the Judeo-conversos.

Although no record exists of Jews found worshiping idols, perhaps we should not be surprised that the friars' rhetoric failed to match the evidence of their senses. In the mid-seventeenth century, the authority of the past was still for them the final arbiter. Reading the sermons, we learn that the "evidence" of Jewish idolatry came not from contemporary testimony but from the teaching of St. John Chrysostom, one of the church fathers who preached in Antioch in the fourth century of the Christian era. John Goldenmouth is the most frequently quoted patristic author in this group of sermons from the seventeenth-century Spanish Indies, and he delivered eight homilies against the Jews, which we find quoted at autos-da-fé thirteen centuries later. John's purpose at the time was to break Christians newly converted from paganism of their habit of going to the source by frequenting synagogues, which he referred to as "lairs of demons, no different from pagan temples."[33] His twentieth-century biographer

---

[33]Robert L. Wilken, *John Chrysostom and the Jews: Rhetoric and Reality in the Late 4th Century* (Berkeley: University of California Press, 1983). The importance of John's teachings on the Jews is underscored in the epilogue to this book, which is generally sympathetic to Chrysostom as a creature of his time. Wilken writes:

> Many religious works from antiquity have double lives, a life in the time in which they were first composed and a second life as they were read, studied, and used by later generations. Because of John's popularity as a preacher, the purity of his Greek style, and his exemplary life and martyrdom, his writings have exerted a powerful influence on later Christians. In the generation immediately after his death, some of his works began to circulate through the Church.... Today hundreds of manuscripts of his writing are to be found in the libraries of Western Europe, the Soviet Union, Greece, the Middle East, and the United States.... Given the popularity of these homilies among the writings of John Chrysostom, *it is apparent that the sermons on the Jews have been a factor in forming Christian attitudes in times and places far removed from ancient Antioch.*
>
> (161–62; emphasis added)

states that it is most unlikely that anyone hearing John preach took his rhetorical charges literally, but goes on to say that this would not be the first text to be wrenched out of its temporal context by later generations.[34] Indeed, Chrysostom himself made a habit of doing precisely this in his sermons. In this saint, the Spanish friars found an authority who spoke directly to their need.

At an auto-da-fé in New Spain on 14 June, 1699, Domingo de Soussa addressed an audience of Old Christian Spaniards, their *mestizo* offspring, and the newly christianized Indians. Quoting John Chrysostom, he added that, in worshiping the golden calf, "the Hebrew people opposed themselves to their zealous inquisitor, Moses." He followed up this piece of biblical hermeneutics with this cry to the prisoners at the stake: "Go, then, in your arrogance, to the all-embracing voracity of the flames of hell. And you, distinguished members of the Tribunal, enjoy the triumph you have won."[35] This was one of the last autos-da-fé to take place in the New World, in part because of a change of regime in Spain, in part because there were no identifiable Judeo-conversos left to prosecute. The great autos-da-fé of Lima and Mexico City erased the last vestiges of Judaism. Descendants of conversos who succeeded in hiding their Jewish ancestry had been totally absorbed into the general population by the end of the seventeenth century.[36]

In addition, it is fascinating to learn that John's homilies against the Jews were in fact aimed, not at them, but at the Aryans. An early example of vituperative surrogacy.

[34]The Real Academia Española continues the tradition in the twentieth edition of its *Diccionario de la Lengua Española* (1984), by defining *sinagoga* figuratively as "a meeting for illicit ends."

[35]Domingo de Soussa, *Sermon en el auto público de Fee que el Tribunal de el Santo Officio de Nueva España celebró el día catorze de junio de 1699 en el convento de NPS Domingo de Mexico* (Mexico, 1699).

[36]The effectiveness of measures to repress Judaism can still be observed among descendants of conversos in the American Southwest who continue to follow ambiguous religious practices and refuse to identify themselves publicly. Presentations by Stanley E. Hordes, Tomas Atencio, and Frances Hernandez at the International Conference on the Inquisition in the Americas and the Hidden Jews of the Southwest, University of Arizona, 27–28 January 1991.

In the waning years of their existence, the marginalized class of Portuguese New Christians, cut off from the living body of Judaism but still vulnerable to the charge of Judaizing, came to be used as surrogates for that other class of New Christians—Native Americans—whom the Crown had placed beyond the reach of the Inquisition. The theme of Jews-as-idolaters was a teaching device, a visual aid for nonliterate, idolatrous—and untouchable—neophytes. In short, Jews were charged with idolatry not because they worshiped idols, but because the missionaries believed that the Indians did.

The need for surrogates is stated quite plainly in sermons being delivered to the Indians at that time. During the years of the "great conspiracy" in Peru, Father Francisco Davila, wrestling with the devil in Huanuco, wrote a number of essays that were published posthumously, at a time when the author presumably was enjoying the correction he had prescribed for others whom he considered to be false Christians. Two of the essays report the discovery of entire villages of Indians who, he believed, continue to worship idols. The third is a sermon delivered to the Indians of Huanuco:

> For God's sake, I beg you to listen with attention. Because what I have to say to you must be believed; it is an article of Faith. Look ye, how we pray the Credo.... It is imperative to believe ... *and he who does not believe is a heretic and deserves to be burned to death. Have you understood?*
>
> (emphasis added)[37]

---

[37]Francisco de Avila (Davila), *Tratado de los evangelios que nuestra madre la iglesia propone en todo el año* (Cuzco 1648) 431. This and other sermons were published within a year of their oral delivery and widely disseminated throughout Peru and New Spain.

Davila himself presents a rewarding subject for psychohistorians. Born in Cuzco in 1592, he attended the University of Lima, where he studied canon law. He wrote and published a book of sermons for the entire year in Quechua. The document naming him canon states that he is "*hombre de moderadas letras, buena opinión en sus costumbres, criollo deste reino, y aunque hay opinión que son conocidos sus padres, el se cuenta por expuesto, y en cualquiera destos dos caminos es mestizo, segun se tiene por mas cierto* (He is moderately well learned, of good habits, a criollo of this kingdom, and although opinion holds that his parents are known, he holds himself to be a foundling; and by what-

Ultimately, most Native Americans living under Spanish rule "understood" what was required of them, at least in part because they were required to attend the periodic burnings of those other New Christians, those who descended from Jews. The sight of presumed idolaters being burned alive must have concentrated their minds wonderfully.

To the five reasons already given for prosecuting Judeo-conversos in the Indies, a sixth must now be added. The missionaries, faced by the challenge of extirpating idolatry among Native Americans recently converted from paganism, were powerless to punish them as they thought they should be punished. But when the political climate was right, it became possible to reach the Indians through a favorite teaching method of the church. The auto-da-fé was the ultimate parable.

---

ever way he came to it, he is certainly *mestizo*)" (Medina, *La imprenta en Lima*, item #45). Recalling that *mestizos* were prevented from entering holy orders, we find this man denying his own mother in order to become a priest, and going on to a successful career extirpating idolatry by, among other things, denying the mother of Christ.

PRIMARY WORKS CONSULTED FOR THIS ESSAY

Sermons and Ecclesiastical Documents

Avila, Francisco de [Davila]. Presbitero, cura y beneficiado de la Ciudad de Huanuco. *Tratado de los Evangelios que Nuestra Madre la Iglesia Propose en Todo el Año.* Cuzco, *1648.*

Catholic Church. *Doctrina christiana y catecismo para instruccion de los indios.* Spanish, Quechua, Aymara. Lima, 1584.

Copilacion de los instrucciones del Officio de la Sancta Inquisicion. Granada 1537.

Dias de Antequera, Fray Diego. *Sermon que en la solemne procession de la madre Maria Magdalena de la Soledad predicó Fray Diego Dias de Antequera.* Mexico, 1694.

Escaray, Fray Antonio de. *Deseos de Asertar.* Sermon Gratulatorio. Mexico, 1683.

Escoto, Antonio de. Familiar, calificador proprietario de el Santo Officio, Guardian del Convento de Tlalmanalco. *Sermon de las Tres Horas que Christo Estuvo en la Cruz.* Predicado en la Iglesia Parrochial de San Luis de Tlalmanalco, 12 April 1715. Mexico, 1715.

Estrada y Escovedo, Pedro de. *Relacion Sumaria del Auto Particular de Fee,* que el tribunal del S. O. de la Inquisicion de los reynos y provincias de la Nueva España celebró en la muy noble y muy leal Ciudad de Mexico, 16 abril 1646. Dr. don Pedro de Estrada y Escovedo, racionero de la S. O. Mexico, abogado de presos y del real fisco del mismo tribunal. Mexico, 1646.

Farias, Manuel Ignacio. Soberano maestro de orthographia. *Christo senor nuestro crucificado, venerado en su milagrosa imagen de Tziritziquaro.* Provincia Michoacan (Mexico), 10 enero 1745.

Llana, Joseph de la. *Impresion mysteriosa de las llagas de nuestro Redemptor.* Mexico, 1686.

Montesinos, Fernando. *El Auto de la Fe Celebrado en Lima a 23 de Enero de 1639.* Dedicado a el Tribunal de la Inquisición de los Reynos del Peru, Chile, Paraguay, y Tucuman. Madrid, 1640.

Nos los Inquisidores contra la heretica pravedad y apostisia in Mexico [formula for determining purity of blood]

Soussa, Domingo de. *Sermon en el auto publico de Fee.* Que el Tribunal de el Santo Officio de Nueva España celebró el día catorze de junio de 1699 en el real convento de NPS Domingo de Mexico. Dixolo El M. Father Domingo de Soussa Qualificador del Santo Oficio, Theologo, y Examinador Sinodal de la Nunciatura de España, Prior Provincial de la Prov. de Santiago. Mexico, 1699.

Torres Cano, Juan. *Sermon a la Publicación del Edicto de la Fee del Sancto Tribunal de la Inquisición.* Cura Actual, vicario juez eclesiastico, etc. de la Santa Cruzad Tehuacan. Mexico, 1695.

Zisneros, Joseph de. Calificador en la Suprema y General Inquisidor ... del Peru. *Discurso que en el Insigne Auto de la Fe Celebrado en Esta Real Ciudad de Lima.* Lima, 1639.

Laws, Regulations, Ordinances

Constituciones y Ordenanças de la Universidad, y Studio General de la Ciudad de los Reyes del Piru. Lima, 1602.

Ley Sobre a gente de naçam. Lisbon, 27 January 1587.

Manzano Manzano, Juan. *Historia de las Recopilaciones de Indias.* Vol 1 Siglo XVI. Madrid, 1950.

Recopilacion de Algunas Bulas. Valladolid, 1504.

Recopilacion de las leyes de los reynos de las Indias, mandadas imprimir y publicar por la majestad del Rey Don Carlos II. 4 vols. Madrid, 1681. Also 2nd ed. Madrid, 1756.

Reglas y Constituciones que han de guardar los senores inquisidores ... del Santo Oficio de la Inquisicion en Mexico. 1659 en la imprenta del secreto del Santo Oficio, por la viuda de Bernardo Calderon, en la calle de San Agustin, 1659.

Royal Instructions to Fray Nicolás de Ovando, Comendador of Lares, of the Order of Alcántara, from Ferdinand and Isabela, done in Granada on 16 September 1501. Colección de document de Indias, 31: 13-25.

*EMPIRE TO COMMONWEALTH: Consequences of Monotheism in Late Antiquity**

Garth Fowden

The angle from which most historians approach late antiquity can be summed up in a single phrase: the formation of Christendom. Even in the most sensitive hands, this approach tends to exclude the Islamic empire and impose a Christian and Eurocentric perspective. An important part of the story is left uninvestigated. But the very idea of "Christendom" is also problematical. It is not just that we begin already in late antiquity to detect the continental drift that eventually produced the Greek East and the Latin West. There is an ambiguity implicit in the term "Christendom" itself. What is Christendom? We think, instinctively, of the knights of Christendom, the Crusaders, going into battle against the infidel. Underlying the image is a strong link between political authority and religious ideal. But we also use the term Christendom to describe the values and traditions shared across the cultural zone of Christian Europe, regardless of political affiliation or of whether these values were being projected aggressively against Europe's non-Christian neighbors. The purpose of this paper, then, is first to ask how these two senses of the term Christendom, the imperial and the cultural, emerged from the Roman emperor Constantine's decision to become a Christian; and second to conduct this investigation with exclusive reference to the lands that eventually became Muslim, in order to integrate Islam into our story and abandon the identification of Christendom with Europe alone. Late antiquity cannot be understood unless we follow its own dynamic toward its fullest expression in the Islamic empire during the period, from 750 onward, when it was ruled by the Abbasid dynasty.

The emperor Constantine inherited a throne to which, it was claimed, the whole world was subject;[1] and he chose a re-

---

*For fuller documentation of the arguments advanced in this article, see my book of the same title (Princeton, N.J.: Princeton University Press, 1993).

[1]Attilio Mastino, "*Orbis*, κόσμος οἰκουμένη: aspetti spaziali dell'idea di impero universale da Augusto a Teodosio," in *Popoli e spazio romano tra diritto e profezia. Atti del III seminario internazionale di studi storici "Da Roma alla Terza Roma"* (Naples, 1986) 63–162.

ligion whose founder had bidden his disciples "go, make disciples of all nations."[2] During the thirty-one years during which he ruled either parts or, from 324 *A.D.* until his death in 337, the whole of the Roman Empire, Constantine strove to fuse a revived empire's imperial impetus with the Church's missionary monotheism. His biographer, Bishop Eusebius of Cæsarea, spoke of him as God's "friend" and vicegerent on earth.[3] It is well known how this worked in practice: we have only to think of Constantine summoning the bishops to the Church's first ecumenical council at Nicæa in 325, or Constantine being buried in Constantinople in a tomb surrounded by cenotaphs of the twelve apostles. But the full implications of the first Christian emperor's position are best brought out by the assault he planned on late antiquity's other superpower, Sasanian Iran. Because Constantine died just as he was setting out on this campaign, scholars have given it very little attention.

Since its revival by the Sasanian dynasty in the 220s, Iran had proclaimed its intention to reconquer all the lands that once belonged to the Achæmenid Empire.[4] According to Shapur II, who ruled Iran at the same time as Constantine ruled Rome, that meant all territories as far as the river Strymon in Macedonia.[5] Thanks to its founder Cyrus the Great and his successors Cambyses and Darius I, the Achæmenid Empire had achieved the basic precondition of world empire, namely simultaneous control of the Iranian plateau and of the eastern Mediterranean, and by obvious consequence of the Fertile Crescent that lies in between. Despite its importance in the history of civilization, the Fertile Crescent cannot on its own support autonomous empires for any length of time, because it is exposed on all sides to enemies whose power bases

---

[2]*Matt.* 28:19–20.

[3]Eusebius, *Vita Constantini* I:3.4, I:6, I:52; Eusebius, *De laudibus Constantini* II.

[4]In interpreting the controversial evidence for this policy I follow (e.g.) Engelbert Winter, *Die sāsānidisch-römischen Friedensverträge des 3. Jahrhunderts n. Chr.—ein Beitrag zum Verständnis der aussenpolitischen Beziehungen zwischen den beiden Grossmächten* (Frankfurt am Main: P. Lang, 1988) 26–44, 51–52, 75–77, 122–23, against sceptics such as Benjamin Isaac, *The Limits of Empire. The Roman Army in the East* (Oxford: Clarendon Press, 1990) 21–22.

[5]Ammianus Marcellinus XVII:5.5–6.

are much more homogeneous and easily defended—Iran to the east, Anatolia to the north and northwest, the Mediterranean to the west, Egypt to the southwest and Arabia to the south. But whoever controls, as the Achæmenids did, both Iran and the eastern Mediterranean can more or less assure the security of the Fertile Crescent too. In terms of the known ancient world, which stretched from the Atlantic to the Ganges and from southern Russia to Ethiopia, such an empire could not seriously be threatened by any other power, and deserved to be called a world empire. The last ruler of the Achæmenid world empire was the Macedonian usurper Alexander, who insisted that he had lawfully acceded to the Iranian throne;[6] and in the wake of this disastrous episode the Achæmenid Empire dissolved into several less stable successor-states. Despite many attempts to imitate Alexander's conquests, nobody else has ever succeeded in equaling the Achæmenid achievement, with the sole exception of Muḥammad and his heirs. But the Islamic empire did have an important antecedent in Christian Rome.

The difference between the Achæmenid empire, the Hellenistic empires and polytheist Rome on the one hand, and Constantine's Christian Rome on the other hand, is that these empires of the ancient world lacked the cultural and above all the religious motive-force that is inherent in missionary monotheism. They were tolerant, culturally pluralist states in which a more or less homogeneous elite ruled but did not strive to convert a wide range of subject races. Hellenism, for example, lacked the focus a single god and a revealed scripture afford. Gods, of course, it offered in abundance, along with a language and Homer. Thanks not least to Alexander, Hellenism spread almost unimaginably far beyond its Ægean home; and thanks to the durable *pax Romana* it sank dccp roots in the lands around the eastern Mediterranean. Even so, Hellenism lacked Christianity's and Islam's sense of mission and power of penetration. Its most characteristic benefits were

---

[6]Pierre Briant, "Conquête territoriale et stratégie idéologique: Alexandre le Grand et l'idéologie monarchique achéménide," in *Actes du colloque international sur l'idéologie monarchique dans l'antiquité, Cracovie-Mogilany du 23 au 26 octobre 1977* (Warsaw, 1980) 37–83.

accessible only to the literate, and "nothing like mass literacy ever came into being in antiquity."[7]

Constantine's fusion of imperial impetus with missionary monotheism obviously created a much more favorable climate for dreams of world empire; and world empire presupposed the suppression of the Sasanid state and its Zoroastrian religion, and the annexation of the eastern Fertile Crescent and the Iranian plateau to the western Fertile Crescent and the Mediterranean that Rome already controlled. As his biographer Eusebius points out, Constantine was very much the sort of person who planned ahead.[8] A project as grand as the Iranian campaign, the fruit of the emperor's mature years, was clearly intended as the culmination of his whole career, as the logical next step after the Christianization of Rome.[9] Constantine died just as he was setting out. Had he lived, the campaign would probably still have failed, for the same practical reasons that assaults on Iran usually failed. But even if the enterprise had succeeded, the flaws in the ideas that inspired it would soon have undermined the victory. Only by grasping what these flaws were can we appreciate the dynamic by which, in late antiquity, monotheist empires evolved into commonwealths.

Constantine saw himself as "God's friend." As the single ruler of a single empire, his regime reflected the heavenly monarchy and replaced the polyarchy of polytheist Rome. Rome's first Christian ruler perceived monotheism as an especially appropriate creed for an autocrat who aspired to rule the whole world. His philosophy can be summed up as "one god—one empire—one emperor." But monotheism is a less effective friend of monarchy than may at first appear.

The particular monotheism Constantine espoused was as careless about the unicity of God, whom it defined as a trinity, as Constantine himself was about that of his empire when he divided it among his three sons and his half-nephew Dalmatius. Eusebius must have been aware of the connection between these two problems when he formulated the idea that

[7]William V. Harris, *Ancient literacy* (Cambridge, Mass.: Harvard University Press, 1989) 327.

[8]Eusebius, *Vita Constantini* III:29.

[9]On the Iranian campaign see Timothy D. Barnes, *Constantine and Eusebius* (Cambridge, Mass.: Harvard University Press, 1981) 258–59.

Constantine's three sons and actual heirs (Dalmatius having been eliminated) were little more than reflectors of their deceased father's heavenly glory.[10] It was in any case inevitable that, eventually, somebody would invoke Trinitarianism to justify division of the empire between two or more rulers, or even the existence of several Christian states. The former argument—that Trinitarianism requires three emperors—is not unattested[11] (though it can hardly be said to have changed the course of Byzantine political thought). And the growing controversies about the nature of Christ, particularly about the relationship between his divine and human aspects, certainly reflected Christianity's ambiguous position on the unicity of God. The political consequences of these controversies are not so easily dismissed. Not only did they destroy the Church's aspiration to be one and undivided. Some feared that they might even undermine the very security of the empire in the face of the barbarian threat.[12]

But the root of the Christian empire's problems was not Trinitarian or Christological. Islam too, after all, was to be afflicted by heresies. And Islam too was a monotheism, albeit more austere than Christianity. We should consider the possibility that monotheism itself may, under certain circumstances, have divisive effects. For where polytheism diffuses divinity and defuses the consequences if not necessarily the intensity of debate about its nature by providing a range of options, monotheism tends to focus divinity and ignite debate by forcing all the faithful, with their potentially infinite varieties of religious thought and behavior, into the same mold, which sooner or later must break. Monotheism often (though not necessarily) follows its own internal logic and addresses itself to the whole world, proclaiming universally the One God who is, by definition, potentially knowable to all mankind. That makes it seem like a suitable ideology for universal empire and/or autocracy. But the progress of its missions cannot be wholly uncoupled from that of intolerance and heresy. Even before the Roman Empire acquired a Christian ruler, Origen had foreseen that, desirable though it might be for all men to

---

[10]Eusebius, *Vita Constantini* I:1.

[11]Theophanes, 352 de Boor (under Constantine IV: 668–85).

[12]Ambrose, *De fide* II:16.139.

follow the same doctrine, they were more likely to do so in the next world than in this.[13]

This then is the background against which we need to examine the relationship between Christianity and Rome in the fourth to seventh centuries, from Constantine to Muḥammad. Constantine's attempt to graft Christianity onto Rome had mixed results. Christianity's evolution into an imperial Church may be judged a success or failure, depending on one's point of view. But even if we call it a success, we have to accept that Christianity failed to impart to its imperial partner the energy to keep up with the missions that were already in Constantine's and Constantius's day spreading beyond the frontiers. And the success of Christianity beyond the frontiers was often inversely proportionate to the degree of its association with Rome. It is striking how often the ecclesiastical historians represent captives, especially captive women, as responsible for the Christianization of peripheral regions such as Georgia or Ethiopia—and not only before but during and after Constantine's reign too.[14] This is a topos the degree of whose historical accuracy or romantic inventiveness is less interesting than the proof it offers that the missionary process could be seen in a humble and evangelical as well as an aggressive and imperial context.

As for the Church in Iran, the only way it could survive at all in the aftermath of Constantine's declaration of Christian war was by gradually distancing itself from Rome and eventually adopting a version of Christianity, Nestorianism, that was persecuted as a heresy within the Roman Empire. The Nestorians' famous Asiatic missions took them as far as China, where they are first attested in 635, at the same time as the Islamic armies were pouring into Romc's eastern provinces. In terms of geographical extent, Nestorianism was Christian Rome's might-have-been. Yet in the long term it failed to maintain its position, and the western and central Asiatic world came to be dominated by Islam and Buddhism. Rome may have been a dangerous ally, but Nestorianism never found an alternative political patron, despite the favor it was often shown at the Sasanian court, and its initial influence on

---

[13]Origen, *Contra Celsum* VIII:72.

[14]For example, Rufinus, *Historia ecclesiastica* X:9–11; Sozomen, *Historia ecclesiastica* II:6.2.

the Mongol elite. Though religions may be forced to make painful concessions when they ally themselves with empires, they cannot do without political patronage if they aspire to become world religions.

Between these two extremes of identification with the Roman state represented by the imperial Church, and divorce from it represented by the Nestorians, there lay an enormously ambiguous zone, the Monophysite world. The Monophysite world emerged very slowly in the aftermath of the Council of Chalcedon's definition of the nature of Christ in a way that was or became unacceptable to most of Rome's Eastern subjects (451). In geographical terms it was identical with the southwest Asian Mountain Arena—in other words the Fertile Crescent and the Syro-Arabian desert together with the mountainous rim that encloses them, a vast oval whose circumference touches on and interacts with but does not include the Black Sea in the North, the Iranian plateau in the East, the Arabian Sea and the Gulf of Aden in the South and the Egyptian desert (beyond the Nile valley) and the Mediterranean in the West. The almost continuous mountain rim is itself in places of such great extent that it constitutes subregions that independently interact with as well as defining the edges of the great expanse of plain and desert that lies at the region's heart.

In late antiquity this vast area was divided into Roman and Iranian spheres of influence, though these became very fluid and often quite tenuous in the Mountain Arena's southern segment. There, it was the coastal regions along the Red Sea and Persian Gulf trade routes that mainly mattered. But even in the North there were wide variations in the level of dependence on Rome or Iran. Politically, Antioch was as Roman as could be and Ctesiphon as Iranian. But the Armenians in their mountains astride the frontier, or the Arabs in their desert between frontiers, were another matter. Even so, until a cultural, more specifically religious, motive could be found, beyond dim memories of the Assyrian or Babylonian Empires, potentially independent identities were bound to remain potential.

Christianity spread early in this region—it was born here after all, and there were Parthians, Medes, Elamites, people from Mesopotamia, and Arabs all present at Pentecost. But from that point onward the *Acts of the Apostles* gradually distracts our eye westward. Christianity had to become a Greek religion before it could acquire distinctive Eastern versions too. The various branches of Monophysite Christianity, as well as Nestorianism, all began as translation cultures. The ideas that underlay the emergent identities of Armenians, Syrians, Copts, and Ethiopians were Greek ideas, the heresies of Alexandria and Antioch. What we see in the endless Christological disputes of the fifth to seventh centuries is the indigenization of these ideas and the establishment, from the 520s onward, of an institutional framework for them, a parallel and independent clerical hierarchy, so that in Alexandria, for example, there was always a "Coptic" Monophysite patriarch alongside the Chalcedonian patriarch, the emperor's man. There were also Monophysites beyond the Byzantine frontier, subjects of the Iranian "King of Kings" or even of independent Monophysite princes—the rulers of the Ghassanid Arabs, for example, or of Nubia or Aksum (Ethiopia). But the Monophysites within the empire were not secessionists inspired by nationalistic ideas. They might dream of a Monophysite emperor, but they accepted the alliance of throne and altar as readily as any other Byzantine. After all, it was the Monophysites who preached one-nature Christology, which meshed much better than Chalcedon's apparent dualism with the one god—one empire—one emperor ideology.

The Monophysite world's political and/or cultural dependence on Constantinople was, in short, profound and enduring. Recent excavations at Nubian sites such as Faras and Qasr Ibrim have shown how thoroughly Byzantine the Nubian church and court remained even after centuries of isolation from the Mediterranean caused by the Muslim conquest of Egypt. This Monophysite world of the Mountain Arena, as flourishing beyond as within the Byzantine frontier, is the First Byzantine Commonwealth, in parts less politically independent but theologically much more distinct from Constantinople than the Second Byzantine Commonwealth in eastern Europe, for our understanding of which we are indebted to Sir Dimitri Obolensky.[15] The First Byzantine Commonwealth is well described by the sixth-century Monophysite bishop John of Ephesus as "the commonwealth of the party of the believ-

[15]Dimitri Obolensky, *The Byzantine Commonwealth: Eastern Europe, 500–1453* (London: Weidenfeld and Nicolson, 1971).

ers."[16] Its primary touchstone of identity was its faith. But its secular identity adds up to more than just the geographical contiguity of its parts within the Mountain Arena. We can see this most clearly in the Ethiopian kingdom of Aksum, and in the campaign successfully mounted by its ruler Kaleb to protect the Monophysite Christians of Najran in southern Arabia, who in 523 were violently persecuted by the Jewish ruler of Himyar, what we know as Yemen. Not only was this "an unprecedented confrontation between Judaism and Christianity as two state religions, a confrontation unique in the history of the Near East," as Irfan Shahîd has pointed out;[17] it was also a campaign explicitly encouraged by the Byzantine emperor Justin (518–527). Justin had no sympathy for Monophysites, but was eager to protect Byzantine interests in the Red Sea from intervention by Iran. And Justin recognized that the only Christian state capable of acting effectively in this area was Monophysite Ethiopia.

This important recognition of Ethiopia's role by Constantinople is reflected in the Ethiopian national epic, the *Kebra Nagast*, whose original version may go back to this very period.[18] The *Kebra Nagast* depicts Kaleb as a righteous Christian king, a Crusader against the Jews, who travels to Jerusalem to meet the Emperor Justin and agrees with him to partition the *oikoumene* between Ethiopia and Byzantium. But Ethiopia is superior to Byzantium—the Negus is descended from Solomon's firstborn, while the Byzantine emperor can claim only a younger son as ancestor. And Byzantium, having deviated from (Monophysite) orthodoxy, will be destroyed by Iran, while Ethiopia will endure for ever. That this prophecy is placed in the mouth of St. Gregory the Illuminator, the apostle of Armenia, is remarkable testimony to the sense of cultural cohesion and shared tradition that, thanks in large part to the mediating role of Syria, might unite even the remotest extremities of the Byzantine commonwealth. The implication both of St. Gregory's appearance and of the division of the

---

[16]John of Ephesus, *Lives of the Eastern Saints* XLIX, 490 Brooks.

[17]Irfan Shahīd, *Byzantium and the Semitic Orient before the Rise of Islam* (London: Variorum Reprints, 1988) X:148.

[18]Shahīd, *Byzantium and the Semitic Orient*, X. The *Kebra Nagast* was edited and translated into German by C. Bezold (Munich: Königliche Bayerische Akademie der Wissenschaften, 1905).

world between Byzantium and Ethiopia is that Ethiopia is the protector of the Monophysite world, the First Byzantine Commonwealth.

The *Kebra Nagast* is of course an expression of an ideal, not a description of reality. And its point of view is firmly Ethiopian. Elsewhere in the First Byzantine Commonwealth there were other identities and other aspirations. The commonwealth's common theological denominator, Monophysitism, suffered from severe internal divisions, which often congealed around differences in local outlook, as for example between Syrians and Egyptians. So too the commonwealth's political aspect was diverse and fluctuating. This was unavoidable in a region that was sandwiched between two superpowers and whose peoples had to take advantage, as and when they could, of the ebb and flow of relations between Rome and Iran. This was what lay behind the loyalty of the Church in Iranian Armenia to the non-Christian Sasanians, but also the omission of the rulers of the Lakhmid Arabs, allies of Iran, to follow their people and become Christian, until the end of the sixth century. The greater the number of apparent contradictions one introduced into one's position, the wider the choice of exits from the tight corners in which one was bound to find oneself. One of the themes of the Byzantine commonwealth's history is precisely this interplay, in which smaller nations have been caught at all periods of history, between the search for cultural identity and the longing for political allies or protectors. It is striking, for example, how Armenian writers loved to draw parallels between their people's struggles and those of the Jews, especially the Maccabees. Monophysite Christianity and the Byzantine Commonwealth compensated up to a point for this sense of isolation, giving the Armenians a context, a reassuring sense of not being alone in the world, that the Jews lacked.

The early seventh century saw further developments in the political attitudes of many of Byzantium's Eastern subjects. The inhabitants of the eastern provinces began to acquire a clearer sense of the limits of Byzantine power, but also a greater sensitivity to its encroachments and abuses. The campaigns of Khusrau II and Heraclius reopened in spectacular fashion the whole question of frontiers and allegiances. For a time the Sasanians absorbed most of the Byzantine East. A generation grew up that had known only their rule. Then Heraclius struck back, right into the Sasanian heartlands. The old lines of political demarcation could already be seen to be crumbling, before the Arab armies appeared. It was only natural that the Byzantine commonwealth *intra fines* should at such a juncture come into clearer focus as a political as well as cultural entity, especially when Constantinople began to repress the newly reconquered populations. "The hostility of the people to the Emperor Heraclius, because of the persecution wherewith he had visited all the land of Egypt in regard to the orthodox faith,"[19] made the Muslim conqueror seem, at least to some, a tolerable alternative.

And so it fell to the Muslim conqueror to realize fully the Byzantine commonwealth's political potential (though not of course as a Byzantine commonwealth). From Georgia and Armenia to southern Arabia and Ethiopia, Monophysitism had become a fertile common spiritual ground and a community. Within that community one is struck by the growing importance of southerly regions such as Arabia and Ethiopia. When on top of this Khusrau II demonstrated that the political reunification of the eastern Mediterranean and Iranian spheres was once more a practical option, it began to become clear to what an extent, politically as well as culturally, Islam and its empire was already implicit in late antiquity.

With the formation of the Islamic empire on the ruins of the Sasanian Empire and of much of the Byzantine empire too, we come to late antiquity's second and this time successful attempt to fuse an imperial impetus with a monotheism that was, at least potentially, a missionary monotheism. Some hold that "the advent of Islam in the Mediterranean sealed the end of Late Antiquity";[20] but the Muslims themselves took the view that they had consummated all that was most essential in the late antique world. Their clearest statement of this attitude was the Dome of the Rock in Jerusalem, built on the site of the Jewish Temple and near to the Church of the Resurrection. And the fact that the Islamic empire too eventually evolved into a commonwealth confirms the validity of what has already emerged from the experience of Christian Rome as

---

[19] John of Nikiu, *Chronicle* CXV:9, trans. R. H. Charles; see also LXXI:2.

[20] J. Herrin, *The Formation of Christendom* (1987; reprint, Princeton, N.J.: Princeton University Press, 1989) 134.

regards the difficulty of using monotheism as an ideology of world empire. The Islamic empire's achievements and problems grow out of late antiquity, and before the Abbasid dynasty enters in the ninth century on its long period of political decline we cannot say that the dynamic of late antique history has fully worked itself out.

For the first time since the demise of the Achæmenid-Macedonian state, Muḥammad and his successors reunited under a single authority the Iranian plateau and the eastern Mediterranean basin. They set in motion a sequence of conquests that resulted in world empire. And besides a new secular order Muḥammad also proclaimed a fresh revelation from the One God, and in doing so created (whether or not this was fully understood at the time) a new religion as well as giving impetus to the emergence of a new culture. Muḥammad shared Constantine's ability to perceive the historical moment; but he was both more radical and luckier. And he did not merely choose one religion rather than another (as Constantine had) and then rewrite history accordingly (as the ecclesiastical historians did). Instead he gave history new impetus by proclaiming a new revelation and a new religion, while cleverly drawing on the momentum built up by earlier monotheist prophets. Muḥammad's career was the product of a conjunction of opportunities, but also of his personal ability to recognize that conjuncture and communicate it to others. Within a decade of the Prophet's death in 632 his followers had invented a brand-new system of numbering years, counting from his flight from Mecca to Medina—this at a time when the Christian world had still after six centuries not become used to numbering years from the birth of Christ. As for the problem of dissent, it took Christ's followers three centuries to come to see heresy as an object of attention for political authority, for the simple reason that previously they had little access to political power. For Muslims, heresy was a problem almost from the beginning; but that was because Islam was from the beginning in a position of dominance, not subjection. What was the secret of the Islamic empire's success?

Among the many possible answers to this question, the one that concerns us here has to do with the mutually reinforcing but at the same time flexible relationship between the religion of Islam and the empire within which it existed and spread. This is an enormous and complex subject that cannot be properly dealt with here. But in the context of our interest in the evolution of empire into commonwealth, one aspect of the relationship between religion and authority within Islam stands out as especially relevant, namely the question of conversion.

Whereas acceptance of the caliph's secular authority was the attribute of all his subjects, Islam for long remained the faith of the relatively few, and primarily of the Arabs. This does not mean that Islam was an Arab religion, or in any way less universal than its rival Christianity. But Islam took an attitude to conversion that helped to counteract monotheism's tendency, which we have already seen at work in the Byzantine world, to impose an unrealistic and dangerous level of uniformity and so to generate heresy. Islam banned polytheism absolutely, but the "peoples of the book," notably the Jews and Christians, it was prepared to tolerate, for they too were monotheists, whose doctrines had been revealed by God himself. In other words, the Islamic empire's policy was to enforce universal monotheism. Islam itself, a monotheism so pure that it did not allow itself to say of God, as the Christians did, that he is "three,"[21] was open to all who chose it, and was the only sure passport to the heavenly city. But it was first enjoyed by the Arabs; and although the Arabs knew well that they were but messengers to the rest of mankind, they always cherished a special relationship with the faith proclaimed in the Qur'ān. What made the Islamic empire into a successful world empire was the combination of imperial impetus with a universalist monotheism that was inflexible as regards doctrinal essentials and full of missionary zeal toward polytheists but flexible, or at least prepared to exercise economy, in its dealings with other monotheisms. The Islamic empire was actually and aggressively universal, Islam only potentially—and the empire consented to tolerate a degree of cultural-religious pluralism. Had the Islamic empire been prepared to tolerate only Islam, it would have had to impose the inhuman uniformity for whose sake Constantinople had vainly struggled through more than three centuries of Christological debate. It would have dissipated its energies in internal strife, and "might well have shrunk back to the wastes of Arabia

[21] *Qur'ān* V:74.

from which it had sprung."[22] Alternatively, Islam would have become the very diverse religion it eventually became anyway, but without the memory of the golden age of Abbasid Baghdad—one god, one empire, one emperor—to sustain it. If we look for the origins of that diversity, we will at the same time understand how and why the Islamic world empire eventually evolved into the Islamic commonwealth.

When the Abbasid dynasty overthrew the Umayyads in 750, relatively few of the empire's non-Arab subjects had accepted Islam. But a recent estimate places the Muslim population of early ninth-century Iran at about 40 percent, growing to over 90 per cent by the mid-tenth century. Iraq, Syria, Egypt, and North Africa lagged behind this very rapid conversion rate from the mid-eighth to the late-tenth century, but the end result was the same—an almost entirely Muslim population by the eleventh century.[23] An increasing diversity of people, living further and further from the Arab heartlands, came to feel they had a stake in the fortunes of what was now a decidedly Muslim rather than Arab empire, a politico-culturally universalist empire in which conversion, though not imposed by mission, had nonetheless come to seem expedient.

Richard Bulliet has argued that once the growing rate of conversion made the Islamic religion's hold seem no longer in peril, it became legitimate to reassert local identities long submerged. Anything that might have looked like revolution against Islam had been inconceivable; but revolution within Islam became less and less objectionable as the strong center came to be seen as an exploitative obstacle to provincial development, which could be handled much better by local dynasties. This interpretation is quite speculative and certainly not above criticism.[24] There continues to be dispute about the speed and chronology of conversion. And it was certainly also

---

[22]Roy P. Mottahedeh, *Loyalty and Leadership in an Early Islamic Society* (Princeton, N.J.: Princeton University Press, 1980) 20.

[23]Richard W. Bulliet, *Conversion to Islam in the Medieval Period. An Essay in Quantitative History* (Cambridge, Mass.: Harvard University Press, 1979), especially the graphs on 82, 97, 109, and the summary, 128–38.

[24]Michael G. Morony, "The Age of Conversions: a reassessment," in M. Gervers and R.J. Bikhazi, eds., *Conversion and Continuity. Indigenous Christian Communities in Islamic Lands, Eighth to Eighteenth Centuries* (Toronto: Pontifical Institute of Mediæval Studies, 1990) 135–50.

true that Islam's political hold on the empire's provinces was an essential factor in encouraging further conversion and giving the process critical impetus. Nor should we assume that the only way Islam could become impregnable was by absorbing a "democratic" majority of the population. Some converts were more influential than others. But it remains likely that the conversion process, along with other developments such as the growth of agricultural wealth thanks to diversification of crops and improvement of farming techniques,[25] did create an atmosphere in which the political disintegration of the Abbasid Empire seemed less unthinkable.

The probability that there was such a connection appears most clearly when we consider the relationship between the upswing in conversions and the multiplication of heresy—or perhaps it would be better to say the subdivision of "orthodoxy," since Islam's doctrinal center was to begin with relatively ill-defined, a considerable variety of teachings being allowed to pass for orthodox. Here the causative role of conversion is less in dispute. Admittedly it takes only two to make an argument—the possibility of doctrinal discord was present in Islam as in all other religions from the moment the Founder acquired his first follower. And the chronological priority of orthodoxy over heresy or vice versa is a notorious conundrum, in Islam as in Christianity. But here, as in our discussion of the First Byzantine Commonwealth, we are concerned with heresy's acquisition of stable, nonclandestine structures and hence of political potential or actual power; and that can hardly come about until heresy has at least some mass together with unmistakable momentum, while orthodoxy has lost full control of the situation, even within the wide parameters Islam permitted. Despite the considerable disruption caused by such early dissenting movements as Kharidjism, this did not happen until the Abbasid period. Bulliet has argued that the different schools of law and theology came into being at different points on the "conversion curve" and reflected needs and attitudes characteristic of those who were converting at that time.[26] Although Islam had no clergy, it did

---

[25]Andrew M. Watson, *Agricultural Innovation in the Early Islamic World: The Diffusion of Crops and Farming Techniques, 700–1100* (Cambridge: Cambridge University Press, 1983).

[26]Bulliet, *Conversion to Islam* 59–63.

have its local learned elites—the *ulama*. The cohesiveness of the *ulama* as a group is easily overestimated—it was closer to that of modern "intellectuals" than to that of the medieval European Church.[27] Even so, particularist feelings slowly congealed around them, somewhat as local loyalties had focused on late antique bishops. Once teachings became movements and acquired regional roots they could hardly be ignored; and official attention, especially if heavy-handed, naturally led them—and of course the center as well—to sharpen their ideological profile.

This was certainly the case with the Sunnī-Shī'ī divide, which had started as a difference over the role of Ali in Muḥammad's succession but came to acquire extremely specific associations with the various parties contending for power amidst the ruins of the Abbasid state. By the tenth century Sunnīs and Shī'īs were generating not only religious but also social milieux, often in separate quarters of the self-same city, but of very different emotional texture: the Shī'īs peripheral (in the universal if not always in the local perspective), speculative and esoteric, the Sunnīs insistent on the codification and preservation of tradition and precedent (*sunna*), especially the gathering and interpretation of Muḥammad's "sayings" (*ḥadīth*). For the rewriting of history did not leave even the Prophet unscathed—his sayings became a battleground for rival aspirants to legitimacy. This was scarcely a problem under the Umayyads; but toward the end of their period there are signs that the *ulama* were developing a *sunna* supposedly derived directly from the Prophet and his *ḥadīth*, without caliphal intermediaries and indeed often conceived in opposition to caliphal claims. This was the beginning of the process that was complete by the mid-ninth century, whereby the caliphate was reinterpreted as a largely political institution without substantial religious authority and obliged therefore to follow those who did have religious authority, the *ulama*.[28] The consequences of this reinterpretation are still with us, not least in the difference between on the one hand the Sunnīs' willingness to make do with the Prophet's example

---

27Mottahedeh, *Loyalty and Leadership* 136–38.

28Patricia Crone and Martin Hinds, *God's Caliph. Religious Authority in the First Centuries of Islam* (Cambridge: Cambridge University Press, 1986) 58–99.

and the scholarly tradition, and on the other hand the Shī'ī assumption that, at least in an ideal world, religious and secular authority are united in the person of the Imam. The caliphate was still further undermined, and such symbolic unity as the *umma* had retained was shattered, when in the course of the tenth century rival dynasts—the Umayyads in Spain, and the Ismaili Shī'ī dynasty that ruled Egypt, the Fatimids—adopted the title of "caliph" for themselves.

Ultimately, then, and to some it may seem paradoxically, the quickening pace of conversion in the ninth to tenth centuries—the reduction, in other words, of the distance and flexibility that had once existed between the empire that was for all and the religion of the Arab few—helped to bring about the fragmentation of the Islamic world empire, whose birth and growth had owed so much to the power of religion. Gradually the Islamic empire ceased to be the dominant player on the stage of world affairs. What remained was the Islamic commonwealth or the Muslim world, at first alongside a decaying remnant of world empire, then just nourishing a memory of a golden age associated particularly with Baghdad.

But the Islamic commonwealth was not exactly like either the First or the Second Byzantine Commonwealth. Although important parts of the First Byzantine Commonwealth lay outside the Byzantine empire, much of it occupied soil universally acknowledged to be under Byzantium's rule. The Second Byzantine Commonwealth, the Slavic world of eastern Europe, consisted entirely of autonomous states; but unlike most of the First Byzantine Commonwealth, these states were orthodox in Constantinople's eyes, so that tensions between center and periphery were mainly political rather than ideological—therefore reasonably soluble. In other words, both Byzantine commonwealths enjoyed a dynamic relationship with a living and vigorous parent—one could even say, in the case of the earlier of the two commonwealths, that the relationship was more like that between an elder and a younger sibling. The Second Byzantine Commonwealth did in fact outlive its parent, and Moscow succeeded Constantinople as the "third Rome" when the latter fell to the Turks; but by that time the commonwealth seemed as mature as the empire itself.

The Islamic commonwealth was different. Whereas Christianity had far outstripped Rome's imperial impetus, the Islamic empire had never left the religion of Islam to fend for itself. The sword had everywhere been at the service of the Qur'ān, even if it had more often been wielded to defend than to impose the new faith. But perhaps in the process of expansion the empire had exhausted itself; certainly dissolution rather than consolidation was its response to the mounting curve of conversion to Islam. Far from being built in a mission-field that the imperial armies and bureaucracy were still striving to reach, the Islamic commonwealth arose on the ruins of the empire that had generated it. When the first political cracks appeared in the Abbasid edifice, the caliphs of Baghdad still on the whole continued to recognize the rulers of the successor-states, whom they called "kings." In this way, the Islamic empire's notional unity was maintained. But when, after the fall of Baghdad to the Turks in 1055, the power of the Abbasids dwindled to insignificance, the Islamic commonwealth was left with no single point of political reference, no secular equivalent of Mecca where the *hajj* remains to this day a spectacular statement of the ultimate oneness of Islam, Sunnī and Shī'ī. The caliph's title continued to bestow a certain political legitimacy on the power that possessed it; but both the legitimacy and the power were as likely to be shadow as substance. The commonwealth, whose common denominator was cultural and religious much more than political, related better to its senescent or dead parent, Baghdad, than to more vigorous siblings such as Fatimid or Mamluk Cairo or Ottoman Istanbul, except in so far as the commonwealth was identical with the possessions of Cairo or Istanbul. Inevitably, the Islamic commonwealth was even less coherent than either of the Byzantine commonwealths.

Nonetheless, the Islamic commonwealth's emergence was far from being the negative experience described by those historians who concentrate on the central political structures of the Abbasid state. Despite its political and to some extent doctrinal multipolarity, the commonwealth was founded on a faith confessed by peoples more numerous and in lands more extensive than could be claimed by any other religion. And at least to begin with—which is all that seriously concerns us here—it was founded on the Arabic language and a shared bureaucratic culture that allowed top administrators to move from one Muslim court to another; on recognition that only the caliph could confer political legitimacy; and on freedom of travel and trade between the commonwealth's constituent parts. Not a few of the commonwealth's parts were at times prosperous and well-governed—a condition for which strong central government is far from being a sine qua non.[29] And the availability of a number of competing patronage-centers encouraged a remarkable cultural efflorescence in the tenth century, which itself in turn strengthened the Islamic commonwealth and confirms its importance for us. It was above all this cultural strength of the Islamic commonwealth that allowed it to absorb and convert the Turkish invaders who arrived in such force during the eleventh century, and captured Baghdad in 1055. That the energy of the Turks was turned to Islam's account was one of the decisive events in history. It ensured that the Byzantine empire would eventually be eliminated and that the Umayyads' goal of taking Constantinople for Islam would one day be achieved—but not before Eastern Christianity had been deeply influenced by eight centuries of interaction with Islam, first Arab and then Turkish.

Islam's role in the evolution of Western Christendom was no less fundamental, molding it by forcing it to recoil, then retaliate, and once more, under Ottoman leadership, threatening its integrity as recently as the seventeenth century. Today the Islamic commonwealth continues to provide a powerful bond between Asia and Africa and, in the opinion of many of its intellectual and political leaders, a potential base for less fragmented and unstable political structures than those in place at the moment. At the same time the religion of the Qur'ān goes on expanding beyond its own territories. Islam today affords, along with but often more self-confidently than Christianity, clear proof that late antiquity's difficult marriage of political and religious universalism, the emperor Constantine's greatest vision and legacy, still endures.

---

[29]Note Hugh Kennedy's intelligent remarks in this connection, *The Prophet and the Age of the Caliphates. The Islamic Near East from the Sixth to the Eleventh century* (London: Longman, 1986) 249, 266; and in general his chapter on "The Structure of Politics in the Muslim Commonwealth," especially 201, 204–5.

CURRENT ARAB PARADIGMS FOR AN ISLAMIC FUTURE

Yvonne Yazbeck Haddad

The authority of the past has a time-honored place in Islamic intellectual thought and theology, preserving what is received of revelation and prophetic teaching from deviance, innovation, and error; at the same time, it has played a unique role in justifying change. The current attachment to this authority, however, in a very important way is intricately bound up with the violent encounter of Muslim societies with a dominant "West" during the last two centuries that has insisted that the only universal truths and values worth adhering to in the modern world are those developed in the West as a consequence of the Renaissance, the scientific and industrial revolutions, and the challenge of liberal and Marxist thought.

Visitors to various Muslim countries today encounter a dynamic Islamization project engaged in by various sectors of society.[1] The cherished dream of a small group of committed Muslim revivalists for over half a century, Islamization increasingly has become the dominant preoccupation of a growing number of Muslims, a community-wide endeavor to liberate Muslim countries from allegiance to the intrusive values of Western society and to recreate a vibrant Islamic society. It is seen by its advocates as a necessary corrective to Westernization "run amok" and an effort to ground modernization in an

---

[1]For a comprehensive bibliography on Islamization worldwide, see Yvonne Yazbeck Haddad, John Obert Voll, and John L. Esposito with Kathleen Moore and David Sawan, *The Contemporary Islamic Revival: A Critical Survey and Bibliography* (Westport, Conn.: Greenwood Press, 1991); For regional studies, see Haddad, "Islamic 'Awakening' in Egypt," *Arab Studies Quarterly* 9, 3 (1987): 234–59; Imran Muhammad, "Muslim Liberation Movements in Africa," *Islamic Literature* 17 (May 1971): 35–58; Henry Munson, "Islamic Revivalism in Morocco and Tunisia," *Muslim World* 76 (1986): 203–18; Javid Iqbal, "Islamization in Pakistan," *Journal of South Asian and Middle Eastern Studies* 8 (1985): 38–52; Fred R. Von Der Mehden, "The Political and Social Challenge of the Islamic Revival in Malaysia and Indonesia," *Muslim World* 76 (1986): 219–33; Shahrough Akhavi, *Religion and Politics in Contemporary Iran: Clergy-State Relations in the Pahlevi Period* (Albany: State University of New York, 1980).

authentic Muslim environment, governed by the values and mores of the faith.[2]

In the last two decades, there has been a notable growth in the number of publications addressing the utility and validity of the Islamic heritage, discussing in great detail what is worth saving, negotiating, highlighting, or discarding. A lively debate about the merit of the recovery of the past has ensued in which its authority for the future and its utility as a means of engendering authenticity are examined as Muslim societies chart their course in the modern world. Some of this literature appears to be driven by an internal incentive for change in an attempt to determine what is truly relevant for Muslim society.[3] At the same time it seems charged by a feeling of profound urgency, formulated in a desperate effort for survival in the face of mounting losses in wars of resistance against colonial encroachment. It also appears to be driven by a frantic fear of what is perceived as a militant cultural invasion or intellectual onslaught by the West.[4]

Some of the ideas advocated have been formulated as attempts to counter what are perceived as religiously motivated attacks designed to denigrate Islam. That European colonialism in the last century was accompanied by a concerted missionary movement that sought to convert Muslims away from their faith has had a profound impact on the response. Islamist literature is painfully aware that basic to the mission-

---

[2]See for example Muḥammad 'Amāra, *Taḥaddiyāt lahā Tārīkh* (Beirut, 1980); 'Abd al-Shāfi Ghānim 'Abd al-Qādir, *Qaḍāyā Islāmiyya Mu'āsira* (Cairo, 1980).

[3]For Islamic reflections on concern for the future, see Fu'ād Muḥammad Fakhr al-Dīn, *Mustaqbal al-Muslimīn* (Cairo, 1976); 'Abd al-'Azīz Kāmil, *Al-Islām wa al-Mustaqbal* (Cairo, 1975).

[4]See for example 'Abd al-Ḥalīm 'Uways, *Al-Muslimūn fī Ma'rakat al-Baqā'* (Cairo, 1979); Ḥassan Muḥammad Ḥassan, *Wasā'il Muqāwamat al-Ghazū al-Fikrī li-al-'Ālam al-Islāmī*, (Mecca [1981]); 'Abd al-Ḥalīm Maḥmūd, *al-Ghazū al-Fikrī wa-Atharuhu fī al-Mujtama' al-Islāmī al-Mu'aṣir* (Kuwait, 1979); Muḥammad Muḥammad Ḥusayn, *Ḥuṣūnunā Muhadada min Dākhilihā* (Beirut, n.d.); 'Alī Muḥammad Jarīsha and Muḥammad Sharīf al-Zaybaq, *Asālīb al-Ghazū al-Fikrī li-al-'Ālam al-Islāmī* (Cairo [1977]); Muṣṭafā al-Rafi'ī, *al-Islām wa-Mushkilat al-'Aṣr* (Beirut, 1972); Muḥammad al-Ghazālī, *Kifāḥ Dīn* (Cairo, n.d.) Muḥammad Faraj, *al-Islām fī Mu'tarak al-Sirā' al-Fikrī al-Ḥadīth* (Cairo, 1962); Muḥammad Jalāl Kishk, *al-Ghazū al-Fikrī* (Cairo, 1975).

ary message is the conviction that the only way Muslims can "catch up" with the West is by abandoning Islam.[5] In an effort to alert the current generation to the impending danger, they have rummaged through the missionary literature and translated passages that essentially target Islam for eradication[6] and defame the prophet Muḥammad as a possible agent of the devil.[7] The apologetic nature of their discourse is inspired by the effort to respond directly to what is seen as Christian contempt for Islam and its institutions, an attitude used and reinforced by the colonial governments so they can undermine the areas they governed in an effort to divide, disempower, and dispossess Muslims of their natural resources.[8]

---

[5]Anwar al-Jundī, *Āfāq Jadīda li al-Da'wa al-Islāmiyya fī 'Ālam al-Gharb* Beirut, 1984) especially 19–27; Anwar al-Jundī, *Al-Islām wa al-Isti'mār* (Cairo, 1948); 'Umar Farrūkh, *Al-Tabshīr wa al-Isti'mār* (Beirut, 1957).

[6]The Christian missionary's dependence on and cooperation with colonial powers in Muslim countries is highlighted in a 1911 quotation from W. M. Wherry and Samuel M. Zwemer: "It is a fact not to be ignored or lightly regarded that almost the only really open doors to reach Islam are in countries where Moslems are under Christian or non-Moslem rule. The Turkish Empire, Western Arabia, Persia, Turkestan, Afghanistan, Tripoli, and Morocco, under Moslem rule, are virtually sealed against liberty of conscience and belief. On the other hand, in India, the East Indies, North West China, Egypt, Tunis and Algiers, the door may be regarded as open, so that about 140,000,000 are in a measure accessible to the Christian missionary." Wherry and Zwemer, *Islam and Mission* (New York: Fleming H. Revell Co., 1911) 22; see also Ibrāhīm Khalīl Aḥmad, *Al-Istishrāq wa-al-Tabshīr wa-Ṣilatuhumā bi-al-Imberialiyya al-'Ālamiyya* (Cairo, 1974); 'Abd al-Raḥmān Ḥabnakat al-Mīdānī, *Ajniḥat al-Makr al-Thalātha wa-Khawāfīhā: al-Tabshīr-al-Istishrāq-al-Isti'mār* (Damascus, 1395H); Muṣṭafā Khālidi wa 'Umar Farrūkh, *al-Tabshīr wa-al-Isti'mār fī al-Bilād al-'Arabiyya* (Beirut, 1973).

[7]Missionary literature published by Fleming H. Revell Company in New York included such works as: *The Mohammedan World of Today*, James L. Barton, S. M. Zwemer and E. M. Wherry, eds.; *Islam and Christianity: The Irresponsible Conflict* by E.M. Wherry; Annie van Sommer and S. M. Zwemer, eds., *Our Moslem Sisters: A Cry of Need from Lands of Darkness Interpreted by Those Who Heard It* (1907). See also Dr. and Mrs. Samuel M. Zwemer, *Moslem Women* (West Medford, Mass: The Central Committee on the United Study of Foreign Missions, 1926).

[8]Muḥammad al-Ghazālī, *Kifāh Dīn* (Cairo, n.d.); Muḥammad al-Ghazālī, *Ma'rakat al-Muṣḥaf fī al-'Ālam al-Islāmī* (Cairo, 1964).

More recent Islamist literature on the heritage of Islam is aimed at correcting what is perceived as politically motivated orientalist and Zionist literature in such fields as history, sociology, and anthropology that Muslims see as geared specifically to undermine the various Islamic communities. They believe that the goal of this material is not knowledge for its own sake, but knowledge to be put to use in the "national interest" of the colonial countries that produce it. This material cannot be trusted, they believe, because its goal is to learn how to manipulate and subjugate the Muslim people, rather than to empower them and celebrate the glories of Islam.[9]

The Islamization project, on another level, is the latest answer in the continuing intellectual quest for the empowerment and reconstitution of Muslim society, perceived by its advocates as the key component that could trigger the industrialization of the Muslim world; a growing number of intellectuals since the 1970s have begun to see it as the way to mobilize the masses for this development.[10] Others believe that such a goal is not attainable unless Muslim societies are purged of alien Western institutions and laws that have transformed Muslim nations during the colonial and postcolonial period.[11]

---

[9]For a selection of papers presented to the Conference on Islamic Jurisprudence at the Islamic University of Imam Muhammad Ibn Sa'ud in 1976, see *The Intellectual Invasion and Anti-Islamic Attitudes* (Riyad: Imam University Press, 1984); Najīb al-'Aqīqī, *al-Mustashriqūn* (Beirut, 1937); al-Jundī, *Āfāq* 20–22; al-Bahnasāwī, *al-Ghazū* 111–47; Anwar al-Jundī, *al-'Ālam al-Islāmī wa-al-Isti'mār al-Siyāsī wa-al-Ijtimā'ī wa-al-Thaqāfī* (Cairo, 1970); 'Abd al-Mun'im Nimr, *al-Islām wa-al-Gharb Wajhan li-Wajh* (Beirut, 1982).

[10]See for example Galāl Amīn, *Al-Iqtiṣād wa-al-Siyāsa wa-al-Mujtama'* (Cairo, 1984); 'Ādel Ḥusayn, *Al-Iqtiṣād al-Miṣrī min al-Istiqlāl ilā al-Taba'iyya* 2 vols. (Cairo, 1982).

[11]'Abd al-Ghanī 'Abbūd has written extensively about the inadequacy of the values of the Western systems. In *Al-Yawm al-Ākhar wa-al-Ḥayāt al-Mu'āṣira* (Cairo, 1978), he argues that although Muslims have been told that this is the age of the human being, in reality "it is the age of international slavery where the strong oppress the weak and life is for the powerful." He goes on to say that the then-third world experienced oppression under communism in the name of the preservation of human dignity. At the same time, democratic countries allowed the individual to destroy this dignity by himself in the name of freedom. Only the idea of accountability on the day of judgment that Islam

Some of the literature that focuses on the Islamic heritage consists of government-commissioned studies that have varied according to the needs of those in power. They range from texts glorifying the past, whether to instill a commitment to Arab nationalism, Arab socialism, or Islamic modernism. Some are initiated in response to the demands of opposition Islamic groups, while others are efforts to co-opt and manipulate those groups' agendas and provide more moderate interpretations. Other studies have come into existence as a result of outside pressures, or in response to international forums such as those dealing with the definition of human rights in various cultures or the United Nations-sponsored conferences on women.[12]

Intellectual efforts have also been directed toward this project by Islamic funds made available for such research.[13] Graduates of foreign universities who felt alienated by what they perceived as amoral or immoral Western societies turned

---

teaches can restore human dignity to the individual (143–44). See also 'Abd al-Ḥamīd Mutawallī, *Azmat al-Fikr al-Siyāsī al-Islāmī fī al-'Aṣr al-Ḥadīth* (Alexandretta, 1975).

[12]See for example S.M. Sayeed, "Human Rights in Islam," *Hamdard Islamicus* 9, 3 (1986): 67–75; Sayed Ḥassan Amīn, *Islamic Law in the Contemporary World* (Glasgow: Royston, 1985); David Little, Abdulaziz Sachedina and John Kelsay, *Human Rights and the Conflicts of Culture: Western and Islamic Perspectives on Religious Liberty* (Columbia: University of South Carolina Press, 1988). The Year of the Woman (1975) and the Decade of the Woman (1985–1995) sponsored by the United Nations produced a variety of self-studies in preparation for the conferences. See, for example, the two books published by the Women's Cultural and Social Society of Kuwait on women in Kuwait. *Dirāsāt 'an Awḍā' al-Mar'a fī al-Kuwait wa-al-Khalīj al-'Arabī* ([Kuwait], [1975]); *Al-Mar'a wa-al-Tanmiya fī al-Thamānīnāt* (Kuwait, 1982). See also the volume on women in Islam published by al-Azhar in Egypt as a counter to government studies on the subject in preparation for the Year of the Woman, *Makānat al-Mar'a fī al-Usra al-Islāmiyya* (Cairo, 1975).

[13]Funds have also been allocated by international Islamic organizations such as the Muslim World League and the Organization of Islamic Conference. The latter is operating three international Islamic universities charged with instructing students from an Islamic perspective.

to a study of the Islamic past in search of viable alternatives.[14] Scholars at various universities who sought lucrative salaries at Gulf universities began to write on Islamic topics in order to obtain employment, such scholarship in turn serving to affirm that they were not atheists, socialists, or other undesirables who might corrupt the youth in the Gulf countries.[15]

Thus the context of the new reflection on the role of the past is global in perspective and not limited to internal considerations. It proceeds from a feeling of weakness and defeat that has enveloped the Muslim world and a perception that it is virtually encircled by hostile powers bent on the destruction of the community's strength by keeping it underdeveloped and dependent.[16]

The Encounter with the Modern World

Modernity—and its challenge to the prevailing political, economic, social, and cultural order—arrived in the Arab world having evolved in a different environment in response to a different set of issues. Advocates of the modernization of Muslim countries during the nineteenth and early part of the twentieth century perceived the European models as prefabricated systems, transferable and ready for borrowing and implementation simply because they had proven to be efficacious in Western society. Those who advocated and initiated change in the Muslim world included two sets of agents with conflicting agendas: 1) those internal to the Muslim countries them-

---

[14]See for example the works of Sayyid Qutb, especially *Ma'ālim fi-al-Ṭarīq* ([Cairo], 1968) and *Naḥwa Mujtama' Islāmī* (Cairo, 1975). See also Haddad, "Sayyid Qutb Ideologue of Islamic Revival," in *Voices of Resurgent Islam*, ed. John L. Esposito (New York: Oxford University Press, 1983); Haddad, "The Qu'ranic Justification for an Islamic Revolution: The Views of Sayyid Qutb," *Middle East Journal* 37, 1 (Winter 1983): 14–29.

[15]'Abd al-Ghanī 'Abbūd, *Al-'Aqīda al-Islāmiyya wa-al-Idyulojiyyāt al-Mu'āṣira* (Cairo, 1967); 'Abd al-Ghanī 'Abbūd, *Allāh wa-al-Insān al-Mu'aṣir* (Cairo, 1977); Zaidān 'Abd al-Bāqī, *'Ilm al-Ijtimā' al-Islāmī* (Cairo, 1984).

[16]See for example Muḥammad al-Ḥasanī, *Al-Islām al-Mumtaḥan* (Cairo, n.d.); see also Muḥammad al-Bahī, *Al-Fikr al-Islāmī al-Ḥadīth wa-Ṣilatuhu bi-al-Isti'mār al-Gharbī* (Cairo, n.d.).

selves, concerned with the condition of the Muslim nation, and 2) external agents attempting to control these nations and effectively undermine them.

The first group included government officials in Istanbul, Cairo, and Tehran as well as other centers of waning Muslim power worried about the quality of their armed forces and their inability to withstand European encroachments, as well as the few intellectuals they enlisted in their attempt to break out of the "noose of backwardness" of their societies vis-à-vis Europe.[17] The external forces included colonial agents and bureaucrats who sought to subjugate the political and economic systems of Muslim countries in order to facilitate their integration into the expanding European industrial and capitalist system, to control their economy so as to provide raw materials needed by European markets, and to create a local demand for manufactured consumer goods. These external forces also included Western Christian missionaries who were eager to subvert Islam and undermine its spiritual and intellectual hegemony over its people.

Interest in the West, its philosophy and culture, was strong in the Muslim world during the nineteenth century and the early part of the twentieth. Muslim intellectuals who traveled to Europe were dazzled by its modernity and progress, its freedom and discipline, and its promise of a revitalized society, and they became enthusiastic advocates of its emulation. Some went as far as to adopt the French revolutionary slogan of liberty, equality, and fraternity, interpreting those qualities as intrinsically Islamic values. They saw such a philosophy as shedding the shackles of traditionalism, destroying prevailing medieval conditions, and opening new vistas for progress. They thus initiated a modernist interpretation of the world, producing thereby what has been called the "Arab liberal age."[18]

---

[17]For a discussion of Muḥammad Abduh's interpretation of the sources of Islamic backwardness at the end of the nineteenth century, see 'Abd al-'Ātī Muḥammad Aḥmad, *Al-Fikr al-Siyāsī li-al-Imām Muḥammad 'Abduh* (Cairo:, 1978) 98–115. For the corpus of 'Abduh's works on political and social issues, see Muḥammad 'Amārah, *Al-A'māl al-Kamīla li-al-Imām Muḥammad 'Abduh*, vol. 3 (Beirut, 1972).

[18]Albert Hourani, *Arabic Thought in the Liberal Age, 1798–1939* (New York: Cambridge University Press, 1983).

The image of a progressive and modern West in the nineteenth and early twentieth century precipitated a rupture in the traditional Islamic belief in its own superiority.[19] Increasingly many came to believe that anything Western was implicitly valuable and that any assessment of the Islamic world was to be made only in comparison to the West. Islamic writers and thinkers saw serious challenges confronting their community. How were they to recognize the Islamic world's underdevelopment and decadence in comparison with the West? Why were they "backward" vis-à-vis Western civilization? How could they catch up and what might have to be sacrificed in the process?[20] Perhaps most importantly, what must *not* be sacrificed in the process, what was indispensable for the Islamic community's survival? The answers were varied and conflicting, reflecting the class, intellectual, and political backgrounds of those who posed the questions. Reaction to the West, of course, was not uniform. Some intellectuals devoted themselves to the revival of the classical heritage, such as Muṣṭafā Sadiq al-Rafi'i, Zakī Mubārak, and 'Abd al-'Azīz Jāwīsh. Others, such as Salāma Mūsā (a Copt), Maḥmūd 'Azmī, and Ḥussein Fawzī sought total westernization and rejected the Arab Muslim past. Still others tried to integrate the two, including Rif'at Rāfi' Ṭahṭāwī, Muḥammad 'Abduh and Ṭāhā Ḥussein. (These early twentieth-century writings grappling with Muslim "backwardness" in relation to the West continue to be influential today.[21])

Nationalism, an import from Europe, attempted to tap into a rich preserve of memories, both real and mythic, that could help endow the community with a sense of patriotism based both on a shared past and on mutual trust and commitment to refashioning the future. The wars of liberation in such places as Egypt and Algeria against the common enemy

---

[19]One Qu'ranic verse has during this century been interpreted to teach that Muslims have been elected by God to provide leadership for the world. "You are the best community brought forth to humanity commanding what is good and forbidding what is evil and believing in God (Sūra 3:10).

[20]Shakīb Arslān, *Li-Mādhā Ta'akhkhara al-Muslimūn wa li-Mādhā Taqaddama Ghayruhum* (Beirut, 1965); Abū al-Ḥasan al-Nadawī, *Mādhā Khaṣira al-'Ālam bi-Inḥiṭāṭ al-Muslimīn* (Al-Doha, Qatar, 1974).

[21]Muḥammad Arkūn, *Al-Fikr al-Dīnī: Naqd wa-Ijtihād*, trans. Hashem Saleh (London: Ta Ha Publishers Ltd., 1983) 269.

of Islam, colonialism, provided common ground and common experiences as well as a new set of common memories and the will to perpetuate them. Muslims grieved over defeats in those wars and rejoiced in victories. Nationalism was accompanied by free public education, which led to a rise in literacy. A whole new genre of literature came into being, haunting poetry and music that sang of sacrifice and struggle in the single cause of a unified future, words and music to bind together a people and a nation.

In the 1920s and 1930s the secular nationalist trend was gradually replaced by a reformist Islamic trend whose roots are to be found in the writings of Muḥammad 'Abduh and Jamāl al-Dīn al-Afghānī. The reaction to secularization as instituted by Atatürk and the elimination of the office of caliph in 1924 gave rise to such Islamic revivalist groups as the Muslim Brotherhood in Egypt and the *ulema* in Algeria in the 1930s. This was accompanied by attempts to recover the glorious past of Islam. By the mid-1930s Muḥammad al-'Aqqād was writing about the genius of the prophet Muḥammad and the caliphs 'Umar and Abu Bakr, and Ṭāhā Ḥussein and Aḥmad Amīn lauded the Islamic contribution to civilization.[22]

This trend toward Islamization with its strong *salafi* element of reviving the model of the original and ideal Islamic community challenged the liberals who sought to imitate the West. It was driven by two powerful realities: 1) perception of the disparity between European philosophies and values as preached, and colonial policies and treatment of the indigenous peoples as practiced—increasingly seen as "Western hypocrisy"—and 2) the intense need for the preservation of the dignity and self-worth of the Arab people. The initial response to colonial domination and European military campaigns brought a dramatic reappraisal of the prevailing worldview. While admitting to the superiority of Western technology and military prowess, there was an increased reluctance to allow what amounted to a Westernizing and Christianizing of Islamic thought and tradition. Many rejected outright the Christian missionary affirmation that such leadership was a consequence of a superior faith. The legacy of Western violence and intolerance, however, far from effecting the downfall of Islam,

---

22. 'Abbās Muḥammad al-'Aqqād, *'Abqariyyat Muḥammad* (Cairo, 1942); *'Abqariyyat 'Umar* (Cairo, 1943); *'Abqariyyat al-Ṣiddīq* (Cairo, 1943).

sent the Muslim thinkers back to their own heritage for reassessment and reintegration.

Tensions between those who looked to emulate the West and those who rejected all Western values came to a head with the end of World War II and the creation of the state of Israel. This was followed by Nasser's rise to power in Egypt in 1952 and the Algerian war of 1954, both of which tried to elevate nationalism as a counterforce to imperialism and Zionism,[23] leading to the disparagement of liberal intellectuals as "bourgeois lackeys" of the West.[24]

There is a vast difference, then, between the openness Muslim thinkers showed to Western ideas in the nineteenth century and the reaction to the violent confrontation with the West that unfolded in the twentieth. While earlier some were willing to accept European civilization as representing a model for all, a "universal" civilization, firsthand experience of colonial oppression precipitated a questioning of the values underpinning Western civilization, values that, many argue, make it a culture built on violence.[25] The liberal trend of earlier years was halted in its tracks by events that overwhelmed the local cultures in the last four or five decades. By the 1970s the West, with its bid for universal hegemony, was increasingly being rejected.

The Encounter with the West

The affirmation of the authority of the past and the scavenging of the heritage of Islamic contributions to world civilization that is currently taking place is part and parcel of the

---

[23]Arkūn, *Al-Fikr* 48.

[24]Arkūn, *Al-Fikr* 15.

[25]"The world has neither in the past nor in the present renounced force. The great nations perpetrate a variety of means of violence and oppression in Asia, Africa, and Latin America. The military camps dispersed throughout the [world] ... are nothing but a frank declaration that force is a legitimate weapon in international affairs, and the use of force to defend the luxury and comfort of western man, or the greed of the great nations, is a legitimate endeavor, a given, in the logic of western nations." See Fahmī Huwaidī, *Muwaṭinūn, lā Dhumiyyūn* (Beirut, 1985) 224.

continuing and essential process of decolonization. It is a response to several centuries of European hegemony over Muslim lands, assumed after World War II by the United States. Muslims are painfully aware of Western intervention in the area, the consequences of which have been the fragmenting of formerly unified regions and a legacy of displaced peoples. When European nations started encroaching on Muslim lands in the sixteenth century there were three Islamic empires: the Moghul, the Safavid, and the Ottoman. By the end of World War I, Western nations, including the Soviet Union, had managed to carve up these Muslim empires, dividing them into what are now forty-eight nation states, forty-five of which were occupied by European nations until the second world war. In 1969, forty-two nations formed the Organization of the Islamic Conference. (With the breakdown of the Soviet Union, six additional states with primarily Muslim populations became independent.[26]) These territorial divisions left an estimated 30 percent of the Muslim population of the world with minority status under the hegemony of other religious groups.[27] More tragic, in the Muslim perception, is the fact that an estimated 70 percent of the twelve million refugees in the world are Muslim. The current state of affairs is perceived as the devastating consequence of Western policies of divide and conquer, what Islamists now call efforts to "Lebanonize" the various countries to keep them from becoming integrated, independent, and self-sufficient. The perception that dominates the rhetoric is that Muslim people continue to be decimated by anti-Muslims.

Islamists increasingly have expressed the belief that it is naive to think that the Crusader mentality that characterizes European history has disappeared as a consequence of capitalist progress or development or of the rise of Marxist or socialist parties, or that the racist history of the European white man who enslaved Africa and massacred the Indians in the Americas has been eradicated, or his imperialistic tendencies in any way mitigated by the development of technology and

---

[26]Azerbaijan, Kazakhstan, Kirgizia, Tajikistan, Turkmenistan, and Uzbekistan.

[27]M. Ali Kettani, *Muslim Minorities in the World Today* (London: Mansell Publishing Ltd., 1986) 18–20.

industrialization.[28] This realization, along with the vagaries of American foreign policy in the Middle East—increasingly perceived as driven by innate Jewish and Christian hatred of Islam—have led to a growing feeling of victimization on the part of Muslims. Historical events such as the Crusades, the Spanish Inquisition (which gave Muslims a choice: forced conversion to Christianity, expulsion from Spain, or death at the stake), the colonial heritage, and what is perceived as American-supported Israeli violence against Palestinians are cited as proof of this heritage.[29]

The Arab experience of the West has generated complex feelings of inspiration and subjugation, almost always embedded in conflict. For many, the West continues to be the source of creative political and technological progress, a symbol of positive values that the Arabs have emulated and continue to imitate in styles of dress, modes of thinking, scientific research, and social organization. The other side of this relationship is the West's use of its power and superiority to dominate the Arab world, what Burhān Ghalyūm refers to as the legacy of colonialism, which includes "eradication, killing, and direct control over people and their resources." In the case of North Africa, Ghaylūm cites as the specific products of Western intervention the destruction of the local intellectual center, the ban on the teaching of Arabic, distortion of the religion and culture, and discord among Arab nations and sectarian strife among different groups.[30] He reflects on the crisis in this manner:

> Thus two conflicting feelings developed among the Arabs: on the one hand recognition of the superiority and progress of the West, and on the other hand fear of western cultural, political and economic shackles. The West thus has infused in us a perpetual internal conflict whose source is western historical domination. We live the West in ourselves, in our inmost depths. The struggle with the West has become the

---

[28]Munīr Shafiq, *Al-Islām wa-Taḥaddiyāt al-Inḥiṭāṭ al-Mu'aṣir* (London: Ta Ha Publishers Ltd., 1983) 28.

[29]Yvonne Haddad, "Islamists and the 'Problem of Israel': The 1967 Awakening," *Middle East Journal* 46, 2 (Spring 1992): 266–85.

[30]Burhān Ghaylūm, Professor of Political Science at the Sorbonne in an interview with Ṣalāh al-Dīn Jouchī, *al-Majalla*, 642 (27 May–2 June 1992) 76.

> struggle with the self. This is the center of the crisis in understanding the other and in understanding ourselves.[31]

North African intellectual Muḥammad Arkūn observes that French colonialists in Algeria brought with them racist attitudes that affirmed the superiority and universality of Western civilization. France came to Algeria not to colonize but to "civilize" the Algerian savages. Arkūn faults the French for projecting their culture as superior to all other cultures, refusing to acknowledge the Arabs or their national languages. Islam, he notes, was marginalized by Christianity, whose missionaries came to Algeria to Christianize the Algerians. Thus several generations of Muslims learned to keep silent; since freedom of speech was not extended to the subjects being ruled they had no right to protest or even talk freely. As the colonial administration began to anticipate its demise, it became increasingly severe and arrogant.[32] From the Islamist perspective, Western colonialists based their actions on a belief in violence and subjugation, *qahr*, at the same time they projected it on the Arabs in order to justify their intrusion and possession. The subjugation continues. The irony is that the "liberal West" has become the oppressor. From this Islamist perspective, there is no question that the world order under the domination of the West has failed to provide justice.[33] In the second half of the twentieth century Europe has been replaced as the primary oppressor by the United States and Israel. Arabs find themselves denied knowledge, wealth, weapons, freedom, and political status.[34]

One context in which Muslims are considering their past is related to how the West sees its own past. They understand that Europe's civilization evolved out of a dialogue with its Greek heritage. Looking to the classical age as a valid source for revival, then, is justifiable not only because of the richness

---

[31]Ghaylūm 76.

[32]Arkūn, *Al-Fikr* 268.

[33]"The sons of the French Revolution were the enemies of liberty, equality and fraternity." Also, "The Leninist-Marxists in the Soviet Union are not only the enemies of social justice, they are also the enemies of freedom and of everything that has human values." See Muḥammad al-Bahī, *Al-Fikr al-Islāmī wa al-Mujtama' al-Mu'aṣir* (Beirut, 1975) 7.

[34]Arkūn *Al-Fikr* 174.

and vitality of the Islamic heritage itself, but it might perhaps be key to an Islamic renaissance, as it was in the West.

For the Muslims, several issues are at stake here. First, the perception by Muslims that European philosophers tend to ground their culture strictly in the authority of the Greek past troubles them. Muslims see in the West's view of its own past and of the history of civilization a deliberate effort to suppress totally the contributions of Islam. They accuse Western thinkers of completely failing to acknowledge that Muslim philosophers, theologians, and historians had access to Greek literature from their first century, and were actually the medium for transmitting Greek philosophical teachings to Europe.

Second, for Muslims, the West's past is pagan in origin and has no relevance to the Muslim worldview, which affirms that all things begin and end with God. Muslim intellectuals during the Middle Ages flirted for several decades with Greek ideas, including their social, political, and economic ramifications, their impact on society, and their relationship to the ruler and to power structures. In the end, any adoption of Greek philosophy was ruled out by orthodoxy, which sought to safeguard society from disintegration. Thus, for some Muslim thinkers, Islam had already explored Greek teachings and found them wanting, opting instead for a just society safeguarded by a code of law as maintained by an independent *ulema* class, preserving society through the enforcement of the ethics of Islam.

Third, Muslims perceive that the power of the clergy in the Catholic church is different from that of the Muslim *ulema* class. This issue, one of the earliest to be highlighted, continues to be stressed. In rejecting the separation of church and state, Muslims emphasize the rational teachings of Islam over against what they see to be the superstitions of Christianity. Even secularists among Muslims have not seen Islam or religion as a source of oppression in their societies. The complete disjuncture seen by Muslim thinkers between the Western model of the political hegemony of the Catholic church and the Islamic system has made it possible to assert that Islam is immune to the problems associated with the division of church and state because the division simply does not exist in Islam. The Muslim *ulema* class play the role of guardians of the faith, upholders of justice safeguarding against possible abuse by the rulers.

From their perspective, then, Muslims are able to say that there is no history of struggle or conflict in Islam between religion and the state. Nor has Greek philosophy left any permanent mark on Islamic orthodoxy. While it is the case that Arabs were responsible for providing translation of the Greek classics, by the time of Ibn-Rushd (Averroës) the influence of Greek philosophy had been rejected by his detractors. To go back to the Western classics therefore would mean a return to an alien heritage found wanting centuries earlier; the past worth resurrecting is their own, a past that not only had created a great world civilization but was itself the vital instrument that gave the impetus to the rise of the West.

The Context of the Islamic Heritage

As a monotheistic religion Islam affirms that God reveals himself through books and prophets. God's final revelation, the Qu'rān, is his unerring word; consequently its teachings are valid for all time and all places and binding on all Muslims for eternity. The Prophet was a perfect man, sinless; his life and works as well as his practice and teachings are guidelines for all life on earth. He established a perfect state in Medina from 622 to 632 *C.E.*, during which time the revelation of God guided every aspect of community life. Thus the Qu'rān as well as the traditions of the Prophet are accepted as the basic corpus of truth made manifest and binding on all Muslims in perpetuity. God is the master of history and therefore the rise and fall of nations are within the orbit of his dominion. Victory and defeat, the power and weakness of nations can be seen as signs from God to his people as well as rewards or punishments for their faithfulness or deviance.[35] Prophetic time is ideal time, and as such Muslims must constantly strive to approximate, if not replicate, its just order.

For Sunnī Muslims, the prophet Muḥammad as the final prophet to humanity brought the clearest and most complete message, making it unnecessary that there be other prophets after him. The onus of the guardianship of the faith was en-

---

[35]Haddad, *Contemporary Islam and the Challenge of History* (Albany, N.Y.: State University of New York Press, 1982).

trusted to the Muslim community. Consequently, the social and political developments within the community as well as the ponderings and articulations of its jurists need to be revitalized periodically in order to accord with the essential teachings of the faith as well as the needs of the age. Muslims believe that every century God sends a *mujaddid*, a renewer of the faith to rid the teachings of Islam of historical accretions, false interpretations, and errant perceptions.[36] This is viewed as a built-in system of renewal and regeneration. Different schools of thought have identified different Muslim jurists, theologians, and at times Ṣūfis as *mujaddids*. For Muslims, therefore, "Islam has the proven capacity to revitalize the society one time after another."[37] The questions persist, however, as to who has the authority to propose renewal, what criteria are to be used in such an endeavor, and what constitutes authentic revitalization.

The authority of the past as prescriptive orthodoxy became a prominent theme in the history of Islam and acquired a venerable position in Islamic thought after the decline in the power of the caliphate. The Sunnī understanding of the history of the world has maintained that there has been an alienation from true Islam since the time of the Umayyad Dynasty (661–750 *C.E.*). The concept of the sanctity of the formative period (which includes the prophetic period as well as that of the four Rightly Guided Caliphs) became firmly institutionalized during the Abbasid period (750–1252 *C.E.*) once jurists ceased to develop the religious law for fear that alien military leaders who had assumed power over the government might seek to impose their values on the society. In the face of growing corruption, the goal of the redemption of society and its preservation from social and moral breakdown were seen as attainable only through the implementation of the *sharī'a*, Islamic law. The survival of the Muslim community, the *umma*, is of paramount importance; hence the necessity of obedience to those in power became the overriding concern.

[36]For a discussion of renewal among the Muslims see: 'Umar Farrūkh, *Al-Tajdīd fī al-Muslimīn lā fī al-Islām* (Beirut, 1981); Abū al-A'lā al-Mawdūdī, *Mūjaz Tārīkh Tajdīd al-Dīn wa-Iḥyā'ihī wa-Waqī' al-Muslimīn wa-Sabīl al-Nuhūḍ bihim* (Cairo, 1968); Muḥammad Ibrāhīm Sharīf, *Ittijāhāt al-Tajdīd fī Tafsīr al-Qu'rān al-Karīm fī Miṣr* (Cairo: 1982).

[37]Shafīq, *Al-Islām* 46.

Even early historians who initially were committed to critical historical writings appear eventually to have sympathized with the jurists that the writing of history should have a utilitarian purpose, specifically that of implanting religious and moral values.[38] This seemed to enhance an already prevalent tendency among the Arabs to dwell on ideal conditions of the past regardless of their approximation of reality. Thus the idealized past—the formative period of Islam—became enshrined as a way of vigilantly censoring any possible deviance, of ensuring a continuing dynamic of rejuvenation from within, and of providing a potential refuge from the unacceptable present.[39]

The sanctity of the formative period has been justified by reference to prophetic teaching. Some Muslims take serious account of several hadīths attributed to Muḥammad that imply that the formative period is in fact ideal time and that succeeding generations are progressively more distant from what should obtain. The Prophet is reported to have said, "The best of centuries is the one in which you live, then that which follows, then that which follows that."[40] For societies from the medieval period on, therefore, plagued by decline, division and dissension, hope could come not in the form of an improvement of present society but only in the end of time. One's recourse was to be patient in the times of suffering, knowing that injustice in the world is a given and will persist until the day of judgment. This gloomy assessment sees the community doomed to destruction.[41]

Another hadīth attributed to the Prophet has been influential in this context. "Islam came as a stranger and will return as a stranger as it began. Blessed are the strangers." Some understood this to mean that Islam is destincd to shrink and weaken and that a Muslim may be permitted to compromise with the evil surrounding him and with the oppressor since decline is inevitable. Others have interpreted it very differently. For the contemporary Egyptian writer

---

[38]Hussein Aḥmad Amīn, *Ḥawl al-Daʿwa ilā Taṭbīq al-Sharīʿa al-Islāmiyya* (Beirut, 1985) 102–4; see also Arkūn, *Al-Fikr* 74–76.

[39]Amīn, *Ḥawl* 106.

[40]Ṭayyib Tizīnī, *Min al-Turāth ilā al-Thawra* (Damascus: Dr Dimshq, 1979) 171.

[41]Muḥammad al-Ghazālī, *Qadhāʾif al-Ḥaqq* ([Kuwait], 1984) 208–9.

Muḥammad al-Ghazālī, it points to the crisis that religion faces and the necessity that it rejuvenate itself and not surrender to cultural and spiritual alienation.[42] Ghazālī points out that there is another hadīth that if combined with the first can solve the dilemma. The Prophet is also reported to have said, "Blessed are the strangers for they shall reform what people after me corrupted of my way." In al-Ghazālī's interpretation, then, to be a stranger does not imply a perpetually negative circumstance. Rather, it is projected as a state of permanent unflinching struggle until bad situations are altered and the condition of the religion is improved.[43]

The Modernization Project

Secularism as a worldview challenged Islam just as it did orthodox Judaism and Christianity. Most early Islamic reflection on secularism led to apologetics by two contending groups, those who advocated radical rejection of Islam or complete commitment to secularization and those who condemned secularism as ungodly. By demonizing the religious "other," secularism became a self-serving self-assurance that was accused by its adversaries of being a demonic force unleashed to destroy Muslim society. This was true despite the fact that most secularist thinkers tended to reject radical secularism, which insists that God is absent from the world or that man's tendency to religiosity is grounded in myth. Rather they emphasized that God has revealed himself to humanity and has charged humans to work at building the world by granting them dominion over it.[44]

Secularization and Westernization of education encouraged by indigenous and foreign modernizers created an alternative system of education whose graduates were rewarded with employment within the colonial bureaucracy. This resulted in two competing bodies of knowledge: one fostered by

[42]al-Ghazālī, *Qadhā'if* 209.

[43]al-Ghazālī, *Qadhā'if* 210.

[44]For discussions of Islam and secularism, see Muḥammad Mahdī Shams al-Dīn, *Al-'Almāniyya* (Beirut, 1980); 'Imād al-Dīn Khalīl, *Tahāfut al-'Almāniyya* (Beirut, n.d.); Anwar al-Jundī, *Suqūṭ al-'Almāniyya* (Beirut [1973]).

the colonial powers and those in the leadership of the government in the hope of catching up with the West, and the other designed to preserve Islamic heritage as a sacred trust and to pass it on to future generations. This bifurcation of knowledge, according to some Islamists, dealt a "mortal blow to Islamic thought as well as the religion itself. It distanced religion from life and life from religion ... and thus a duality came into being which is the essence of the plague. It produced two different mind sets, two kinds of intellectuals educated in different worldviews," the one religious but ancient in its thought, outdated in its methodology, isolationist, not relevant to modern life; the other urban or secular, not religious, rich in reflection, progressive in methodology, relevant to modern life and its problems, in charge of the direction of social and political thought.[45]

The implants of secular-liberal ideas from the West took hold only among the elite Westernized classes. For several reasons, they have not proven capable of providing emancipation (as defined in Western circles) for Muslims. First, the West is seen as insisting that in order to be admitted into the ranks of the emancipated Muslims must renounce their faith. Muslims understand that Western ideas of the separation of church and state are posited on the premise that equality of human beings regardless of race, ethnic origin, language, and race can only be realized in a secular context. Yet the different experience that Muslims themselves have had under what is increasingly being termed Euro-American hegemony has led them to see that the separation of church and state professed by the West is belied in its practice. Not only does racism persist in secular Western states, they note, but that leaders in Europe, the United States, and Israel use religious symbols and idioms in their speech, a custom that appears to raise little concern among the population. When Muslim leaders use such language, however, it is considered a threat. Muslims make generous reference to reports about bishops and cardinals at the forefront of political and military action in Latin America or active in political resistance in the Philippines, in Poland, and the Republic of South Africa. They note that the

---

[45]Muḥammad Mubārak, *al-Fikr al-Islāmī al-Ḥadīth fī Muwājahat al-Afkār al-Gharbiyya*, as quoted by Fahmī al-Huwaidī, *al-Tadayyun al-Manqūṣ* (Cairo, 1987) 14.

queen is the head of the Church of England, that the pope is the head of the Vatican City, and that Archbishop Makarios was the president of Cyprus. They also note that many political parties in Europe use the word Christian in their self-definition. And they wonder why Egyptian, Tunisian, and Algerian Islamists are not allowed to form political parties that have a religious vision.[46]

The second reason why Western secular-liberal ideas cannot lead to emancipation for Muslims is what is perceived as an insidious double standard on the part of the West. Muslims are aware that while Western society continues to celebrate its Judeo-Christian heritage and roots, a reciprocal acknowledgment of Muslim heritage is condemned as reactionary or obscurantist by Western intellectuals. This, they believe, is because the West refuses to acknowledge that Islam shares that Judeo-Christian heritage; Western intellectuals, they say, never include anything Muslim as part of the Western heritage; in fact, they see Islam as a foreign entity that the West has been unable to tolerate.[47]

Most prominent in the discourse concerning this double standard has been the creation and empowerment of the state of Israel. The modernizing project from its inception has been charged by an intense yearning for emancipation and democracy, sentiments made popular at the turn of the century by secularist liberalism. This drive for liberalization has been impeded by the dominant experience during this century, increasingly associated with the symbol of destruction, annihilation, and the rejection of secularism. This has been the experience of Israel. As early as the 1960s Sayyid Quṭb in Egypt had argued that the nation state could not have been created by European intellectuals because they did not believe that religion can be the formative ideology of a state. He argued that it was crafted specifically as a way in which to dismember Muslim nations because of the deep hatred borne by Europeans for Islam. Otherwise, he argued, what could have been the rationale for the creation of a Jewish state in the heart of the Muslim world? What is perceived as the unconditional American support of the state of Israel and its expansionist and racist policies in the area have served as convinc-

---

[46]Huwaidī, *Al-Tadayyun* 79.

[47]Arkūn, *Al-Fikr* 42, 259, 270–71.

ing proof to an increasing number of Muslims of the accuracy of Sayyid Quṭb's observation. The existence of the state of Israel, empowered at the expense of the Palestinian people, and Israeli laws that discriminate against non-Jewish residents based on their religious preference or an accident of birth appear to many Muslims to contradict the West's insistence on the necessity of developing secular nation states.[48] Muslims are increasingly asking why it is acceptable for Jews to be Jewish and establish a state exclusively for Jews, and for Christians to be Christian and establish a state "under God," while it is deemed unacceptable for Muslims to create an Islamic state where Muslims can be Muslim.

The United States is held accountable for Israel's policies, from the original confiscation of Palestine to the establishment of the state to the persistence of its aggression, including the 1967 war and the 1982 Israeli invasion of Lebanon. This is seen in the context of a continuing American duplicity. Muslims cite examples of what they see as a record of undermining Arab countries through internal conspiracies and sponsoring of coups d'état as well as military, political, and economic pressures against the various Islamic countries, robbing them of their oil and dominating their finances. This record is not only against the Arab nations but applies to other Muslim countries such as Iran, Turkey, and Indonesia.[49]

The events associated with Israel in this view include a series of massacres against the civilian population of Palestine: Dayr Yāsīn, Qalqīlya, Khiyām, Ṣabra, and Shatīlā. To many Muslims, these massacres make no sense in a modern world, not even in the professed aims of the Zionist project, but rather seem to be the antithesis of all values preached by the enlightened West, by secularism and liberal-

---

[48]For a study of Israeli laws that apply to the occupied territories, see Raja Shehadeh, *Occupier's Law: Israel and the West Bank* (Washington, D.C.: Institute for Palestine Studies, 1985); Konstantin Obradovic, "Violations of Human Rights in the Palestinian and Other Arab Territories Occupied by Israel," in *Inalienable Rights of the Palestinian People* (London: Outline Books, 1985) 164–204; Naseer H. Aruri, ed., *Occupation: Israel over Palestine* (Belmont, Mass.: Association of Arab-American University Graduates, 1983); Jan Metzger, Martin Orth, and Christian Sterzing, eds., *This Land is Our Land: The West Bank under Israeli Occupation* (London: Zed Press, 1980).

[49]Shafiq, *Al-Islām* 14.

ism. The Israeli invasion of 1982, perceived by many as the last straw in the steady erosion of Arab trust in Western values, created a major crisis for Arab thought. Intellectuals who had been at the forefront of coups d'état and revolutions in the name of socialist or Marxist causes abandoned their schemes and began to operate within the Islamic worldview. For Muslims, an authentic rethinking of the faith cannot take place without cognizance of the reality of what Israel stands for. Radical Judaism as articulated in the teachings of the Gush Emunim and the Jewish Defense League projects an antigentile mentality that is justified by a particular reading of the Torah.[50] Israel's treatment of its religious minorities is seen by Muslims as inconsistent with international regulations that are expected to be observed by nation states. If Israel, touted as "a light unto the nations," is taken as the model of the way in which minorities are to be treated, they say, then dispossession, disenfranchisement, and deportation will become the norm. That the United States is silent concerning Israel's undemocratic practices is deemed proof not only of its duplicity in supporting this dehumanizing endeavor, but also proof of its hypocrisy and the obvious double standard by which it views Europeans and Muslims.

The Jewish people, Muḥammad al-Ghazālī argues, have utilized their religious heritage in justifying a state exclusively for Jews is simple hypocrisy on the part of the West:

---

[50]For studies on the Gush Emunim, see Ian S. Lustick, *For the Land and the Lord: Jewish Fundamentalism in Israel* (New York: Council on Foreign Relations, 1988) 42–71; David J. Biale, "Mysticism and Politics in Modern Israel: The Messianic Ideology of Abraham Ha-Cohen Kook," in Peter H. Merkl and Ninian Smart, eds., *Religion and Politics in the Modern World* (New York: New York University Press, 1983) 191–204; Charles S. Liebman and Eliezer Don-Yehya, *Civil Religion in Israel* (Berkeley: University of California Press, 1983) 200–4. For studies of the Jewish Defense League, see Aviezar Ravitsky, *The Roots of Kahanism: Consciousness and Political Reality* (Jerusalem: Shazar Uriv, 1986); Meir Kahane, *Uncomfortable Questions for Comfortable Jews* (Secaucus, N.J.: Lyle Stuart, 1987); Robert I. Freedman, *The False Prophet: Rabbi Meir Kahane—From FBI Informant to Knesset Member* (Brooklyn, N.Y.: Lawrence Hill Books, 1990); Raphael Mergui and Phillipe Simonnot, *Israel's Ayatollahs: Meir Kahane and the Far Right in Israel* (London: Saqi Books, 1987); Yair Kotler, *Heil Kahane* (New York: Adama Books, 1986).

> The Jews decided to establish a national home for themselves in Palestine. Their religious hopes have been transformed into plans that are laid out carefully and implanted ferociously. They have come in the name of the Torah and the Talmud. Under the slogans of revelation which they consider holy, their ranks have moved from the east and the West towards Palestine.... Palestine when the Jews decided to appropriate it was not an empty land; thousands of Arabs lived there. The meaning of Judaizing the land is the expulsion or eradication of the people who live on it according to the teachings of the Old Testament. Peace under these conditions is surrender to a massacre.... It means the annihilation of Arab existence in the Middle East and through it the attack on the Muslim world.[51]

Islamists are fed up with those who tell them not to grieve over the past and to concentrate realistically on the issues of the present. They wonder at the logic that condemns Muslim efforts to restore Palestinian rights in Palestine by insisting that they should not turn back the clock to what obtained forty years ago. Yet they witness Euro-American recognition of Israel's efforts to reconstitute itself after four thousand years.[52] Al-Ghazālī continues, "The past is condemned when it reflects the glories and guidance of Islam and is used to influence the international scene when Israel is being established and the ideas of the Torah are being revived."[53]

There is despair because of the continued domination of the West and Israel. For Islamists, the menace of the star of David and the cross continue as Israel has wrested Jerusalem from Muslim hands and the United States has helped Israel maintain its control.[54] Many see this as a daily witness to the Western belief that might makes right, that the vision of a new

---

[51]al-Ghazālī, *Qadhā'if* 233.

[52]'Abd al-Ḥalīm Maḥmūd, *Bayt al-Maqdis fī al-Islām* (Cairo, 1969) 49–51; 'Abd al-Laṭīf al-Ṭibāwī, *Al-Quds al-Sharīf fī Tārīkh al-'Arab wa-al-Islām* (Amman, 1981).

[53]al-Ghazālī, *Qadhā'if* 78.

[54]For example, "It is known that the war declared on us is based on religious fanaticism among the Christians, I mean the imperialists among them; resistance will not be successful unless it is driven by a parallel religious sentiment in order to repel this fanatic aggression." See al-Ghazālī, *Qadhā'if* 109.

moral world order based on intrinsic human dignity and the rights of a people to self-determination is a sham and a travesty.[55]

The Arab "Intellectual Crisis"

From the beginning of the modernizing endeavor, there has been a coalition of government officials and intellectuals. The former saw the need for change, not only in military technology but in educational and social and economic patterns in order to preserve the Islamic community in the face of massive external efforts to subvert or destroy it. The intellectuals were encouraged by Arab governments to help create a modern state, and they assumed a role in reinterpreting the past as a means of preserving the future.

During the period of struggle against colonial domination, the governments of Muslim countries projected an image of the intellectual as a committed participant in the movement for national liberation and/or the socialist revolution. Thus the intellectuals themselves were co-opted into becoming voices that denounced imperialist knowledge and preached a return to the Arabic-Islamic heritage. They set out to rewrite history from a magnified perspective, to glorify not only the countries in which they lived but the Arab nation itself. As Muḥammad Arkūn points out, however, in doing so they effectively ignored the fact that they were responding to a state ideology that had reformulated Islam to serve its goals and were in effect building a kind of dogmatic fence around themselves.[56] When the discourse is controlled by political authorities there is no allowance for a serious addressing of the issues. It is necessary rather to resort to ideological slo-

---

[55]Ziyād Abū Ghānima, *Al-Ḥaraka al-Islāmiyya wa-Qaḍiyyat Filasṭīn* (Amman, 1989) 16; Isma'il al-Faruqi, *Islam and the Problem of Israel* (London: Islamic Council of Europe, 1980); Ziyād Maḥmūd 'Alī, *'Idā' al-Yahūd li-al-Ḥaraka al-Islāmiyya* (Amman, 1982).

[56]Arkūn, *Al-Fikr* 16; see also Muḥammad Arkūn, *Tārīkhiyyāt al-Fikr al-'Arabī al-Islāmī*, trans. Hisham Salih (Beirut, 1986).

gans and empty words that talk about development and anti-imperialism.[57]

The issues that have attracted the attention of intellectuals during the twentieth century have ranged over a whole spectrum of political, economic, social, and cultural themes. They have generated lively and intensive debate over the desirability of modernization and renaissance,[58] the tension between authenticity and contemporaneity,[59] the adequacy and efficacy of positive law and the *sharī'a*, the relationship between religion and state, the models for an effective political system, the kind of social and political values that should govern the implementation of change, and the relationship of Islam as an ideology to Western civilization.[60] While it is clear that the same questions continued to haunt Muslims in the 1960s and 1970s the answers these questions engendered were different from those suggested earlier, reflecting a change not only in the Arab mind but one that had first occurred in the Western mind.[61] The ideas were borrowed and derived from an alien context, rather than being "critical, innovative or rejuvenating."[62]

Caught between renaissance and reformation, between the critical study of history and events and the confinement of orthodoxy, the Muslim intellectual found the prevailing atmosphere stifling. There is no freedom of speech in the Arab world because those who assumed the control of the government after independence were a small group of political activ-

---

[57]Arkūn, *Al-Fikr* 22.

[58]Anwar 'Abd al-Malik, *al-Fikr al-'Arabī fī Ma'rakat al-Nahḍa* (Beirut, 1974); Maḥmūd Amīn al-'Alim, *al-Wa'ī wa-al-Wa'ī al-Zā'if fī al-Fikr al-'Arabī al-Mu'aṣir* (Cairo, 1986).

[59]Anwar 'Abd al-Malik, "Al-Khuṣūṣiyya wa-al-Aṣāla," *al-Ādāb* (May 1974) 41–43.

[60]Nabīl 'Abd al-Fattāḥ, *Al-Muṣḥaf wa's-Sayf: Ṣira' al-Dīn wa-al- Dawla fī Miṣr* (Cairo: Maktabat al-Madbuli [1983]) 11. See also Ṣābir 'Abd al-Raḥmān Ṭu'ayma, *Irādat al-Taghyīr fī al-Islām* (Cairo, 1968); 'Abd al-Salām Yāsīn, *Al-Islām bayn al-Da'wa wa-al-Dawla: al-Minhāj al-Nabawī li-Taghyīr al-Insān* (Casablanca, 1392H).

[61]'Ābid al-Jabrī, *Al-Khiṭāb al-'Arabī al-Mu'aṣir* 8; see also Muḥammad 'Ābid al-Jabrī, *Naḥnu wa al-Turāth* (Beirut, 1980); Muḥammad Arkūn, "Al-Turāth wa-al-Mawqif al-Naqdī al-Tasa'ulī," *Mawaqif* 40 (Winter 1981): 40–57.

[62]'Abd al-Fattāḥ, *Al-Muṣḥaf* 14.

ists. While they were the product of the Arab nations, they gained their political knowledge from outside the local culture by acquiring bits and pieces of liberal and socialist ideas. Their ability to hold on to power and to claim legitimacy is based on the fact that they participated in the struggle for liberation from occupation under the banner of revolution or socialism and not in the name of liberal culture. The irony of the situation has been noted by Arkūn: "We could not have achieved liberation through liberalism since it was the ideology of the colonizer."[63]

In the 1970s Muslim intellectuals were caught up with an intense exploration of what constitutes authenticity and what is to be preserved as the true foundation of Islamic civilization.[64] This was in part a reaction to the tendency of Western theorists to generalize from European experience and come up with what they posit as universal laws. Many Muslims found it necessary to reject orientalist theories of history because such theories tend to glorify pre-Islamic history and ignore the achievements of the Arabs and Islam. Muslims accused orientalists of seeking to "scavenge the tombs of the polytheistic civilizations" and falsify Islamic history by glorifying pre-Islamic systems, trying to get people to identify with these preceding non-Islamic civilizations in order to divide and fragment the area.[65] Some have even argued that in certain academic circles in Egypt history is presented as though the Arabs are locusts unleashed on verdant valleys, with nothing recorded about their religious mission. They may be depicted as transmitters of ancient civilization to medieval Europe, but there is no mention of the great achievements of Islamic civilization itself.[66]

The last twenty-five years have seen a growing consensus on the part of many Muslim intellectuals that the present situation is intolerable. They are dissatisfied with the political systems that exist in the various Muslim nations, created

---

[63]Arkūn, *Al-Fikr* 274.

[64]See for example Malek Bennabi, *Mushkilat al-Afkār fī al-'Ālam al-Islāmī* (Cairo, 1971); Ḥasan Ḥanafī, *Al-Turāth wa-al-Tajdīd* (Beirut, 1981); Muḥammad 'Ābed al-Jābrī, *Takwīn al-'Aql al-'Arabī* (Beirut, 1984); and *Naḥnu wa-al-Turāth* (Beirut, 1980).

[65]Shafiq, *Al-Islām* 37.

[66]Ghazālī, *Qadhā'if* 80.

either by European colonialism or by military regimes who came to power after independence. These unpopular governments are perceived to be maintained in power by the West, all considered illegitimate systems since they have not been chosen in a democratic fashion by the people. At present, the quest for democracy increasingly is led by the Islamic movements. Intellectuals are also dissatisfied with current wasteful economic policies that keep Muslim countries dependent and underdeveloped, waste their resources, and continue to invest Arab wealth in Western banks and industry rather than in Arab countries. They are dismayed at the social conditions that prevail, including poverty, ignorance, and disease. Increasingly, many believe that the solutions offered that are based on the emulation of Western models are destructive by definition since they clearly have not worked in less developed countries. More importantly, they have failed in the West itself. Continued emulation of the West can only lead to a moral, cultural, and intellectual bankruptcy and to a replication of its ills, represented, these critics say, by the breakdown of the family, pornography, drugs, and AIDS.[67]

The task of intellectual reflection, especially using the rational methodologies developed in the modern West, is an increasingly problematic business in the Islamic world. For a few self-designated Arab intellectuals, reflection on the problems of the modern world basically means a recasting of Western thought that has already become out of date because of the course of events, that in effect was rendered obsolete before the Arabs even had a chance to test it.[68] They have found themselves therefore in the odd position of theorizing about an alien present that is not theirs, a present that has already become the past.[69]

While the overall number of Arab intellectuals has dramatically increased, they have been caught in a pincer of fear between the politicians, who are suspicious of their endeavors, and the masses, who are not ready for their intellectual

[67]Islamist literature warns readers that emulating the West can only lead to a breakdown in the social order, pornography, promiscuity, and drugs. One book published in Cairo in 1985 bore the title *AIDS: God's Judgement on America.*

[68]'Abdallah al-'Urwī, *Al-Idyōlogiyya al-'Arabiyya al-Mu'āsira* 69.

[69]Adonis, *Al-Thābit wa-al-Mutaḥawwil: Ṣadmat al-Ḥadātha*, vol. 3, 276.

output. Consequently, they are not able to extricate themselves from a discourse that is of necessity defensive and geared to counter the opposition. They avoid addressing taboo topics either as a tactic of self-preservation, out of fear of the reaction it may engender, or because of their ignorance of Islamic history and society.[70] The current regimes therefore have fostered a cadre of thinkers who write on topics that do not threaten the authority of those in power. They function much as did the "palace intellectuals" of classical Islamic days. There is an obvious distinction between those who are committed to free intellectual inquiry and criticism and those who, connected to strategies of the government, provide a justification for its operation.[71] Those intellectuals who do attempt to make use of critical reason in their analyses have become increasingly isolated, especially since 1970. This has led to something resembling a mass exodus of intellectuals from Muslim countries. As Arkūn puts it, "All intellectuals I have had a chance to deal with closely have expressed their desire to leave their nations, or to enter into a period of closed silence."[72] The serious battles for the souls of Muslims, therefore, are taking place away from their homelands in places like Europe and the United States since a large number of intellectuals, whether socialist, Marxist, Islamist or liberal humanists, tend to live in self-imposed exile.

The Authority of the Past

It is possible to identify three phases of or approaches to renewal in the twentieth century. The first, iṣlāḥ ("reformation," "restoration"), was advocated by the modernists as a means of reviving Islam by infusing its teachings with modern thought. This attempt was dominant until the middle of the century when the effort to modernize society was assumed by socialist revolutionaries who assumed political power in various countries. Their agenda became the second kind of renewal, *tajdīd*, the effort toward development and the

---

[70]Arkūn, *Al-Fikr* 18.

[71]Arkūn, *Al-Fikr* 22.

[72]Arkūn, *Al-Fikr* 23.

reinterpretation of Islam and Islamic history as a struggle between leftists and rightists.[73] It became especially prominent after the 1956 Suez crisis. The 1967 Arab-Israeli War and its aftermath initiated a new and third effort by Islamists at revitalizing society, now called ṣaḥwa, the awakening, alertness, and awareness of the bankruptcy of both East and West.[74] With this new effort the question is no more "whether to embrace Islam?" but "when?" and "how?"

During the last fourteen centuries Muslim authors—historians, jurists, philosophers, theologians and exegetes, among others—have left a great legacy of manuscripts defining their understanding of the religion, institutions, and ordinances of Islam. When Muslims today look at the past they find a wealth of options, a rich heritage that provides for different ways of understanding the Qu'ranic text, for multiple and varied examples from the life of the prophet Muḥammad, and for fresh interpretations relevant for life in the modern world. The past becomes not only the treasure chest where the soul of the nation and its path has been preserved, but also the incubator where its future is nurtured into life.

The study of history and the underlying prejudices and values of the historian have received extensive comment. There is a prevailing belief that orientalists and western historians and their surrogates have deliberately distorted Islamic history.[75] Furthermore, Islamists continue to condemn the products of the Nasserite endeavor in the 1960s to rewrite Islamic history from a socialist perspective. Thus the preservation of the past has become crucial as a means of safeguarding authenticity.

---

[73]Salīm 'Alī al-Bahnasāwī, *al-Ghazū al-Fikrī li-al-Tārīkh wa al-Ṣīra: Bayn al-Yamīn wa al-Yasār* (Kuwait, 1985) 47–159; the 1970s saw a debate on whether there were Islamic precedents to "left" and "right." See Aḥmad 'Abbās Ṣāliḥ, *al-Yamīn wa-al-Yasār fi al-Islām* (Beirut, 1972); 'Imād al-Dīn Khalīl, *Lu'bat al-Yamīn wa-al-Yasār* (Beirut, n.d.); Muṣṭafā Maḥmūd, *Ukdhūbat al-Yasār al-Islāmī* (Cairo, 1978).

[74]See Yūsuf al-Qaraḍāwī, *al-Ṣaḥwa al-Islāmiyya* (Cairo, 1984); Anwar al-Jundī, *al-Ṣaḥwa al-Islāmiyya* (Cairo, n.d.); Aḥmad al-Najjar, *Manhaj al- Ṣaḥwa al-Islāmiyya* (n.p. [1977]); see also Anwar al-Jundī, *al-Yaqza al-Islāmiyya* (Cairo, 1978).

[75]'Abd Allah al'Urwī, *al-'Arab wa-al-Fikr al-Tārīkhi* (Beirut, 1973).

Islamist ideology affirms that those who do not study history do not understand the present and inevitably will fail as they move into the future. "The human being is to a certain extent fashioned by history, just as history is fashioned by humans," says Qāsim 'Abduh Qāsim. The past lives in the present because man is part of his past experiences.[76] Munīr Shafīq argues that those who do not fathom the profound impact of religious, intellectual, and psychological aspects of civilization will not be able to know the reality of people's ideas and their present psychology. In order for future projects to be successful and gather the support of the people they have to take history into account.[77] While questions of history and heritage may appear distant from issues of primary concern, that is really an illusion. All one has to do is look beneath the surface of contemporary events and the sense of history and heritage will awake like two giants and impose their existence on the present.[78] From this perspective, history is not only a means of understanding the present, but a social necessity. If a society loses its collective memory, it means somehow that it never existed. It is then stripped of its civilization, dress, arts, literature, scientific knowledge and technology, laws, and ethical values; moreover, it loses its present, most of which is a product of its past.[79] Only by understanding the depth of a people's history can one fathom its potential for the future and how to deal with current problems in order to build that future.[80]

The modernists developed an interpretation of Islam in which change is projected as a foundational principle of the religion. The role of the *mujaddid* itself provides a sanction for change for Sunnī Islam. In their reinterpretation, the *mujaddid* is not only a restorer of pristine Islam but a renewer, one who generates and sanctions change. At the same time, change itself has become important as the dynamic for rescuing society from its decadence. The significant new factor from what was earlier the case, especially under Ṣūfī hegemony, is

---

[76]Qāsim 'Abduh Qāsim, *Ahl al-Dhimma fī Miṣr al-'Uṣūr al-Wuṣṭā* (Cairo, 1979) 7.

[77]Shafīq, *al-Islām* 29.

[78]Shafīq, *al-Islām* 2.

[79]Qāsim, *Ahl al-Dhimma* 9.

[80]Shafīq, *al-Islām* 30.

that while God is still affirmed as being in control of history and human destiny, the onus of change has been assumed as a human responsibility. Muslims are no longer enjoined to wait for God to reach out and save them from oppressive regimes or Western colonialism; now they themselves are understood as having been responsible for their miserable condition. Does not the Qu'rān affirm "God will not alter what is in a people until they alter what is in themselves?"[81] The condition in which Muslims find themselves is of their own doing. That change is necessary is recognized; the question is the content and form of the change. While the future must be progressive, it is still necessary that it be grounded in an Islamic past. The past is the necessary component of the psyche of the community, and that past includes a glorious civilizational achievement under the hegemony of the Islamic faith.

Within the context of this connection with the past and acknowledgment of the ultimate authority of God, the emphasis has shifted to the centrality of human action in shaping the world and creating a civilization that does not despair of God's providence, that does not see God as uncaring because he has not intervened to save the faithful and innocent from the hatred of non-Muslims. Rather, the emphasis is on fulfillment of human responsibility ordained as divine will since creation. Thus passive awaiting for God's deliverance, which prevailed until the last century, is transformed into an active and personal engagement in attempting to bring about change, and human action becomes not only the means for reclaiming the covenant and the promise of God's victory but one of its essential components. Man is created and placed in this world for a purpose, one that unfolds in history, manifesting God's dominion over the world. Historical events are within the scope of that dominion, providing specific significance in the context of an overarching meaning. God's majesty is revealed and manifested in creation. The need for a state that is accountable to ethical principles with a new emphasis on social welfare and education is strongly affirmed, based on belief both in God's faithfulness and abiding will and in human responsibility.[82]

---

[81]Sūra 13:11.

[82]The role of the Muslim human being in the modern world has received a great deal of attention from twentieth century authors. See for example

For Islamists, people are not born into a place in the social order that they have to accept. Rather as God's agents on earth they are charged with the mission of finding their place in God's order and with fashioning a just society. Islam projects a vision of the necessity of creating the fullness of Islamic life in fulfillment of the Islamic mission. In the process of developing this new understanding of human responsibility the focus of the religious quest has shifted from awaiting eternal felicity in the hereafter to the quest for political power and prosperity in this world. Covenant has been given a new meaning as social contract (*bay'a*), and the commission given to the prophet Muḥammad to proclaim the teachings of Islam has been extended to include every Muslim as a *dā'ī*, one who actively participates in commanding the good and forbidding evil in the overall communal effort to maintain the bounds of ethics and morality, a concept that has tapped into a revolutionary dynamic in twentieth-century Arab society.

The jurists of the medieval period, some of whom worked at the discretion of the rulers, censured revolution since it led to chaos in the social order. Muslims were told to put up with unjust rulers in order to safeguard the common good. Revolutionary groups in Islam were judged sectarian and worthy of suppression. In the twentieth century, Islam itself has been projected as a revolution. Some have even talked of it as "revolutionism" unleashed in the world by God for the welfare of humanity. It confronts and devours all that is different from

---

Samīḥ 'Ātif al-Zayn, *Al-Islām wa-Idiolōjiyyāt al-Insān* (Beirut, 1971); 'Abbās Maḥmūd al-'Aqqād *Al-Insān fī al-Qu'rān al-Karīm* (Cairo, 1971); 'Ā'isha 'Abd al-Raḥmān, *Al-Qu'rān wa-Qaḍāyā al-Insān* (Beirut, 1972); Sayyid Aḥmad 'Uthmān, *al-Mas'ūliyya al-Ijtimā'iyya wa-al-Shakhṣiyya al-Muslima*, (Cairo, 1979); Amīna Muḥammad Nāṣir, *Insāniyyat al-Insān fī al-Islām* (Cairo, 1989); Hishām J'aiṭ, *al-Shakhṣiyya al-'Arabiyya al-Islāmiyya wa-al-Maṣīr al-'Arabī* (Beirut, 1984); Bint al-Shāṭi', *Maqāl fī al-Islām* (Cairo, n.d.); Ḥasan Ṣa'b, *al-Islām wa-al-Insān* (Beirut, 1981); Farūq Disūqī, *Ḥurriyat al-Insān fī al-Fikr al-Islāmī* (Alexandria, 1982); 'Abd al-Karīm al-Khaṭīb, *al-Insān fī al-Qu'rān* (Cairo, 1979); Muḥammad al-Sayyid Jalaynād, *Qaḍiyyat al-Khayr wa-al-Sharr fī al-Fikr al-Islāmī* ([Cairo], 1981).

what God ordained.[83] From this perspective, liberation has moved beyond simply addressing the colonial domination of the land to an actual purging of all vestiges of colonialism. It is focused not only on the elimination of the economic stranglehold placed by the colonial powers on the Muslim nations, but also on expunging the alien customs and ideas that had been adopted or indigenized, as well as the rulers who sanctioned or allowed such activity.

Authority of the Past: A Current Debate

All Muslims hope for a better future, although they are not in agreement as to what the future should look like. There are internal conflicts among Muslims about the shape of things to come, what direction they would like society to take and consequently what of the past is worthy of revival and emulation. They all look at the past as a source of pride, of identity, and of authenticity. But they do not share a common vision of what from the past should be emphasized or salvaged for a better future. Thus their interpretation of the past also varies. Nowhere is the dialogue about the efficacy of the past, the means of reviving its potency, and the criteria of measuring what should obtain more prominent than in the current debate about the reinstitution of the *sharī'a* as the constitution of the state in Egypt.

Egyptian Supreme Court Justice Muḥammad Sa'īd al-'Ashmāwī, one of the defenders of the current system, has written articles in several daily and weekly journals insisting that "The Qu'rān does not include any verses that deal with government and the Sunna does not include any system for politics and government," and that the prevailing laws implemented in Egypt are consistent with the Islamic *sharī'a*. Those who want change insist that the demand to amend the constitution is a natural byproduct of the Islamic revival, justified by the failure of the existing system to eradicate crime. They reject the promulgation of Islamic laws under a different name

[83]For a discussion of Islam as revolution, see 'Awn al-Sharīf Qāsim, *al-Islām wa al-Thawra wa al-Ḥaḍāra* (Beirut, 1982); Muḥammad Maḥmūd al-Zubayrī, *al-Islām Dīn wa Thawra* (Beirut, 1982).

in order to avoid controversy, seeing such an equivocation as a dangerous first step in the loss of the spirit of the Islamic system, which would help its enemies to realize their long-range goals of defeating Islam.[84]

While agreeing that Islam should be the source of law in Muslim society, some oppose the immediate implementation of the *sharī'a* in Egypt on the grounds that the present Egyptian society is not an Islamically mature society that has been raised on Islamic principles. Therefore too many people would be penalized, with hands severed and other severe punishments inflicted. They insist that the Muslim community in Medina where the Prophet first implemented Islamic justice was mature and spiritually committed to righteous living and therefore did not need a gradual initiation into the *sharī'a*. Today's society, they say, is far from such righteousness. They also argue that the current legal system is Islamic already since Islam is not a theocracy, and that such an implementation would violate the rights of the large Coptic community of Egypt.[85]

The advocates of implementation, on the other hand, affirm that it is because immorality is so prevalent in Egyptian society that it is necessary to put such a system into place as soon as possible. Furthermore, if Islam is to function in reforming society, they say, its principles have to dominate. In defining punishments, advocates point out that Islam does not punish the thief if he is stealing to feed his hungry family; amputation would affect mostly those who rob the wealth of the community and steal from widows and orphans, among them the present leaders of the government who embezzle the wealth of the state. Furthermore, they point out that Islam does not impose the flogging of the adulterer unless adultery is witnessed by four people. Thus the punishment is not for what people do in their private domain, but for acts of public immorality.

Fahmī Huwaidī, a moderate Islamist, calls for a revision of the jurisprudence. First one must ascertain whether an injunction is authentically from the Prophet, he says. If it is, it must be read in the context that brought it into being in order

[84]Muṣṭafā Farghalī Al-Shuqayrī, *Fī Wajh al-Mū'amara 'alā Ṭaṭbīq al-Sharī'a al-Islāmiyya* (Cairo, 1986) 10.

[85]Al-Shuqayrī, *Fī Wajh* 10.

to ascertain whether it is a commandment by which the believers must abide, or the report of an event for which there was a temporary solution but not a precedent for the future.[86] The painful experience of the present reality "has left a deep imprint on the memory," says Huwaidī. It has led some to claim that Islamic jurisprudence is decreed by God, "whereas jurisprudence continues to be fashioned by history. This has left us with a corpus of jurisprudence, some of which is in need of revision while other sections need deletion either because they do not accord with the spirit of the text of the divine teachings or are the product of a historical moment that has passed and can no more express the need or the spirit of the age."[87]

Aḥmad Kamāl Abū al-Magd, a cabinet member of the Sadat regime who sees himself in the mainstream of the Islamist movement, identifies five groups in society that are seeking Islamization.[88] The first are the conservatives who define themselves as *salafiyya*,[89] those who adhere to what was agreed upon by the forefathers whether as opinions, perspectives, or laws. At times they show flexibility in the choice of what is worthy of highlighting or emphasizing at a particular moment or in a particular circumstance. However, there is no allowance for seeking interpretations outside the accepted corpus of material; anyone who exceeds that is considered an innovator (innovation being an Islamic heresy).

The second group are the Ṣūfis who identify the problem facing society as one pertaining to the heart and not in the area of the rational. For Ṣūfis the corruption and backwardness that exist in the Muslim world are byproducts of the fact that Muslims try to compete with others for the fruits of the earth. Worship and the renunciation of the world are the primary duties of the human being. Reason is to be ridiculed and the supporters are to be directed toward life in the hereafter.

---

[86]Huwaidī, *Al-Tadayyun* 177

[87]Huwaidī, *Al-Tadayyun* 8.

[88]Aḥmad Kamāl Abū al-Magd, *Kiṭāb al-Qawmiyya al-'Arabiyya wa-al-Islām* (Beirut, 1980) 32–33.

[89]Several small groups have assumed the name of salafis and seek to recreate the seventh-century model. See 'Abd al-Raḥmān 'Abd al-Khāliq, *al-Uṣūl al-'Ilmiyya li-al Da'wa al-Salafiyya* (Kuwait, 1402H); and 'Umar Sulaymān Al-Ashqar, *Ma'ālim al-Shakhsiyya al-Islāmiyya* (Kuwait, 1979).

A third group carries the banner of Islam but is in total rebellion against the prevailing Muslim condition. They seek the liberation of Muslim society from all of its heritage and advocate the primacy of reason in solving modern problems. They see no exit out of the bitter condition of Muslims today except by following the West. While they attempt to move beyond Islam, they are nonetheless eager to hang on to Islamic slogans. The fourth group consists of a variety of movements that are raising the banner of Islam. They are consistent in calling for a return of the *sharī'a* as the constitution of the state, insisting that it is crucial to govern by what God has revealed. For them control of political power in society is the most effective way to work for Islam. The majority, the fifth group, Abū al-Magd identifies as moderates. They believe in the use of reason in applying the teachings of Islam as a guide for life. This group is considered to be erring deviants by members of the radical movements who disagree with them.

Secularists as well as Islamists are concerned about those that they feel have become ossified in the past. They have identified them as the *salafis* (the most noted among them are the religious authorities who share power in running Saudi Arabian society) and the radical Islamic groups such as Takfir wa Hijra, Quṭbiyyūn, al-Jihād al-Islāmī, and Shabāb Muḥammad.

There is no agreement on who comprises the salafiyya movement.[90] In some quarters it is used as an epithet to banish one's intellectual enemies to the dustbins of obscurantism. Others wear the title as a badge of honor, authenticity, and faithfulness to the essence of Islam. Neither is there any agreement on what constitutes *salafi* truth. Is it the adherence to the teachings of Ibn Ḥanbal or Ibn Taymiyya, the emulation of life in Saudi Arabia, or following those who restrict themselves to the literal textual reading without allowing room for interpretation? For some, it is defined as an intellectual and emotional view that is bound to the formative period of Islam which was committed to the book of God and the Sunna of his Prophet. They believe that Islam is eternal, a natural and rational religion, and despair of what they see around them

---

[90]Muḥammad Fatḥī 'Uthmān, *Al-Salafiyya fī al-Mujtama'āt al-Mu'āṣira* ([Cairo], [1982]).

propagated in the name of Islam.[91] As Ṭayyib Tīzīnī asks, "What Islam do you call for, that of the Ayatollahs of Iran or the army [generals] of Pakistan, the Islam of the Arab sultans or the Islam of the amīrs, of the militias, or of the extremist movements that have been organized in the dark?"[92]

In general, for the *salafīs* the present constitutes a deviance from what is ordained, what must be realized before prosperity can be regained. Thus change is necessary, but it is change designed to replicate the past. The mujaddid provides an opportunity for a new beginning, a new venture toward right conduct, right belief, right course. The *salafīs* have been criticized as viewing the past not only as the original starting point but also "the goal of every activity.... The past moment becomes the initial as well as the ultimate goal of humanity ... for all ultimate existence."[93] The past for them is the optimal solution for the present and the future. "The *salafī* movement in its essence is a metaphysical and not a dialectical phenomenon. It is afflicted with 'time blindness'.... It is incapable of distinguishing between the whole and the parts, between the forest and the trees," concludes Tīzīnī.[94]

Islamic groups such as al-Jihād al-Islāmī, al-Takfīr wa al-Hijra, al-Quṭbiyyūn, and Shabāb Muḥammad have focused on Sayyid Quṭb's treatise on the duty of the believers to judge others as well as rule by the Qu'rān.[95] They have gone so far as to validate the death of anyone who does not agree with their interpretation of Sūra 5:44 of the Qu'rān which addresses the Christians and the Jews (Who so ever does not rule by what God has revealed, they are unbelievers). Several religious leaders, including Shaykh Gād al-Ḥaqq, 'Alī Gād al-Ḥaqq, rector of al-Azhar, have pointed out that this interpretation is wrong since the verse does not address the Muslims. The word *ḥukm*, he says, is used in reference to Jewish rabbis

---

[91]Huwaidī, *al-Dīn* 262.

[92]Huwaidī, *al-Dīn* 267.

[93]Tīzīnī, *Min al-Turāth* 128.

[94]Tīzīnī, *Min al-Turāth* 129.

[95]For a discussion of the use of the verse on *ḥakimiyya* by Sadat's assassins, see Johannes J.G. Jansen, "Tafsīr, Ijmā' and Modern Muslim Extremism, *Orient* 27 (1968): 642–46; see also J.G. Jansen, *The Neglected Duty: The Creed of Sadat's Assassins* (New York: 1986) 55–56.

and Christian priests, referring therefore to religious opinion and not to government.[96]

Conclusion

It is clear, then, that the need for an investigation of the Islamic past and for a reaffirmation of the crucial task of creating as well as preserving Islamic knowledge has been motivated to a great extent by a profound sense of victimization on the part of Muslims. The very hope of Islamization, therefore, is based on the assurance of ultimate vindication.

Modernization and emancipation as defined by the West and imposed on Muslim cultures through its hegemony challenge the feasibility of the *sharī'a* as divine guidance for all of human life by setting up an alien standard as "the rule of acceptable conduct." The Western claim that its culture and practice are universally valid led to generations of Muslims desperately seeking to emulate the West, wearing Western clothes and buying Western products and at the same time rejecting their own heritage. The perceived failure of Western culture, both Marxist and liberal, in creating the good society and the apparent discrepancy between the ideals proposed by both civilizations and the policies they practiced in the lands they dominated have led to a new crisis. This has resulted in Muslims having to look for answers in the authority of the past.

While glorification of the past has been utilized by Arab nationalists (during the first half of the century) and Arab socialists (in the 1960s and 1970s) as a defensive measure against the disintegration of the society or as a legitimating affirmation of national identity, it appears to have harbored within it an insidious force that undermines the present. The greater the past depicted, the more insignificant the Muslims of the present felt. Thus it became a double-edged sword; while imbuing disenfranchised, dependent Muslims with pride

[96]For other discussions on the topic, see Faruq 'Abd al-Salām, *Azmat al-Ḥukm fi al-'Ālam al-Islāmī* (Cairo, 1981); Muḥammad al-Ghazālī, *Mushkilāt fi Ṭarīq al-Ḥayāt al-Islāmiyya* (Qatar [1982]); Adnan al-Naḥawī, *Dawr al-Minhāj al-Rabbānī fi al-Da'wa al-Islāmiyya* (Cairo, 1979).

in the exploits of their forebears, it highlighted the terrible conditions that prevailed and in the process undermined their confidence.[97]

Islamists provide answers in the context of uncertainty and affirm Truth in a supermarket of truths. They offer insights for the right course and identify the signposts that must guide one's journey as well as simplify the process of making the right decision. Thcy do not eschew learning from the experience of others; rather they are seeking their own answers to their own reality. The Rightly Guided Caliphs themselves based the foundation of the glorious Islamic civilization and heritage on what they found in Persian and Roman civilization. As Muḥammad al-Ghazālī put it, "When I eat foreign food I need, the body that grows is mine and the strength that empowers me is mine. What is important is that I maintain my vision, my principles and all the values I cherish because it is my mission in life."[98]

There appears to be a consensus among Islamists that nationalism, especially its Arab version, is contradictory to Islam since it affirms racial, linguistic, or tribal identity above the bond of religion. Arab and Egyptian nationalists, who at the turn of the century rebelled against the Ottoman Empire in favor of the nation state, are now being condemned for what some perceive to be their role in aiding Western interests of divide and rule. From this perspective, the Ottoman Empire is viewed in a positive light as the true defender of the faith. One author goes as far as to attribute the decline of the Ottoman Empire to the generous treatment of non-Muslims within the empire and to the fact that the state did not try to convert them to Islam.[99]

Islamists have abjured secularism, which in their opinion makes God marginal to the dynamics of history and is a rejection of the Qur'anic message. Nonetheless they preach full human responsibility for the condition of the secular world. The God of Islamism is one who is in control of the world through his surrogates; Muslims are committed to bring the whole world under his dominion. Islamists have rejected secularism, but even though they subsume scientific knowl-

---

[97]Amīn, *Ḥawl* 101.

[98]Ghazālī, *Qadhā'if* 232.

[99]Siddiqi, *Non-Muslims* 62.

edge under the power of God they have in fact become secularized insofar as humanity and the world have become of ultimate significance. Western political and philosophical ideas have penetrated deeper into Islam than is apparent at first glance. The concepts of state, parliament, elections, representation, and democracy have been appropriated and indigenized in the ideologies of many Islamic states, although the structures left behind by colonial powers and maintained by them continue to violate those ideas to protect their own interests.

Thus for Islamists the renaissance is yet to come. It will not be judged by a Western past, present, or future; rather, in order for it to be authentic, it will have to be grounded in Islam. While they affirm a return to a golden age, a return to unfettered faith, the basic concern of the Islamists is for the promise of a future age when the whole world will recognize the universal truth of Islam: "The Islamic people have not begun their renaissance as yet, one that would be an extension of their history and a projection of their personality, or a growth of their principles and an affirmation of their characteristics."[100]

From the Islamist perspective, reclaiming the authority of the past does not mean a denial of the future, a declaration of the end of history, or an affirmation of cyclical repetition. Reclaiming the authority of the past is the restoration of authenticity. The suffering, the tragedy, the division in Muslim ranks are not a punishment per se as much as a consequence of humans' renunciation of their role as God's agents, guardians of the public order, and marshals of justice. Islamist literature affirms that the end of alienation and the rule of justice are to be realized in the here and now and not to be awaited in eschatological time when the Mahdī comes as earlier generations had hoped, or through a denial of the importance of this world as the Ṣūfīs continue to teach. Islamism in the modern world is rather an attempt to liberate Islam from the chains of alienation that keep it from realizing its true identity. This change is contingent on human action and participation, and a willingness to shed the bonds of tradition and restore authentic life. It can be initiated when believers

---

[100]Ghazālī, *Qadhā'if* 232.

proclaim their resolve to struggle to realize a just order in the world.

For the majority of Muslims today, the reconstruction of Islamic thought is a vital existential imperative. Some of those who engage in the endeavor arbitrarily select from the past and try to convince others that what they have selected is Islam. The recovery of the past is both a political activity and a question of scholarship, and that can create problems. Many of those who are rummaging through the legacy of the past have no grounding in classical scholarship. The task of renewal of the faith today appears to have been assumed by lay people who have claimed for themselves true knowledge of the reality of the world and the validity of their interpretations for the revitalization of the Islamic future. Many are engaged in the attempt to revive the faith to make it relevant for the modern world. They are confident that true Islam is to be determined by Muslims themselves, who have been entrusted with the teachings of God and the precedent of the Prophet. The question is what ought to be highlighted, by whom, and for what purpose. In this context, therefore, the real issue for the liberals and secularists is whether the quest for an authentic Islamic life in the modern world can be grounded in any authority but Islam.

For Islamists, therefore, the authority of the past provides a mandate to assume the responsibility for the present and the future. The past acts as the anchor of dignity in the face of violence, coercion, and subjugation. It is the center of authority in a world where values are threatened by new fashions and fads exported by the intrusive Western media. The more the insatiable appetite for technology is indulged, with all its attendant changes, the more desperate the valorization of the past becomes. Grounding in the past provides not only a sense of a unique culture, of distinctiveness, of operating within the parameters of a divinely sanctioned society, but also a sense of distinction. The brilliance of the Islamic heritage endows a sense of self-worth and places the individual on an equal footing with the oppressor; it is the source of defensive mobilization in the face of subjugation, of empowerment in the face of annihilation and disintegration. The past also provides the means of offensive mobilization of the masses for a better future, a way to wean them from reliance on fate or of blaming outside forces for their predicaments and to inspire them to shoulder responsibility to build a better future in which Muslims can be free to define their own values and priorities.

CARVING FOR THE SAINTS

Michael R. Kapetan

Over the past twelve years I have created sculpture for three denominations of the Christian Church: Eastern Orthodox, Roman Catholic, and Presbyterian. My most pressing problem has been to find visual metaphors suitable to the use of theologically similar but iconically diverse religious traditions.

The more I think about the relation between my recent work and the authority of religion, the more I realize that my notion of religion as authority has differed in character depending on which denomination I worked for. So I will not be offering generalizations or definitions about religious authority and the art of sculpture. As an artist, and in deference to the rigors of true scholarship, I take refuge from definitions and typologies in the faith that artists should create problems for scholars to solve.

Authority takes on many guises within a religion. Each of these denominations has a long history of using art in and as its rituals. Because temple architecture represents theology in crystalline form, church buildings manifestly represent the authority of religion as the spatial context to which sculpture must respond. In each case, the architectural settings (and in two cases the architects) were major factors in shaping my thinking about appropriate sculptural form. Each denomination has a storied legacy of theological thought and ritual practice entrusted to the care of its clergy. The architects and I always worked in consultation with each other and the clergy. I carved certain images at the strong suggestion or even direct instruction of a priest or bishop. Each denomination ultimately relies on its community for the moral and financial support to buy art, and all of my work took place within a continuing dialogue with donors or committees in charge of hiring artists.

When I decided to work for these churches, to step out of my role as studio and exhibiting artist, I knew that I would labor within profound confines of site, style, and subject. History produced these limits both in the sense that a particular theology and artistic style evolved in the course of time and in the sense that each religion grounds itself on a notion of the beginnings and nature of time. Cosmological models influence art and vice versa. For example, Byzantine Orthodox style rests on a God-centered Ptolemaic cosmology, and the creators of Byzantine Orthodox images have spent centuries refining a formal language of otherworldly order and grace. Renaissance Italian Catholic art began displacing the Ptolemaic cosmology with the Copernican by embracing the new artistic device of linear perspective.

I took on the work for four reasons. First, to test whether I could find power in a two-thousand-year-old tradition of iconography and infuse it with my vision. Second, to test my abilities as a craftsman against historical standards. Third, I wanted to collaborate with the architects, clergy, and laity. Fourth, I wanted to practice making images of an unmistakably spiritual purpose.

I first went to work for St. Clement Ohridski Eastern Orthodox Church in Dearborn, Michigan as a subcontractor to Suren Pilafian, the architect, who had designed a monumental new iconostas for the church. Domes, the exterior hallmark of Orthodox churches, symbolize the heavenly home of the faithful. The interior hallmark, the iconostas, an image-laden partition linking the congregation to the altar, symbolizes the idea of *theosis*, movement from mortality toward divinity. Pilafian's program called for 140 square feet of wood carving on the iconostas as well as seven pieces of carved ecclesiastical furniture "recognizably Macedonian in character prior to the twentieth Century." It was a very specific command dictated by history, and one lent even more authority by his absolute creative control over the project.

But even Pilafian had to answer to authority. He was acting under instructions from the church's Interior Decoration Committee to follow Old Country tradition and to hire a local wood carver. I carved a sample based on the scant information available in the University of Michigan libraries in 1980 (fig. 1). When I presented it to Pilafian, he said, "I like the carving. The design is very active; the forms are beautiful, and I think that the scale will work in the large space. But tell me, Michael, what is Macedonian about this carving?" Sensing the commission slipping through my fingers, with mingled resignation and quiet desperation, I replied, "Mr. Pilafian, the only thing that I am sure is Macedonian about this carving is

Figure 1. Michael R. Kapetan,
iconostas panel, 1980.

that my grandmother was born there." It turned out that she emigrated to America from the same town, Bitola, as the father of the church's Interior Decoration Committee's chairman. Whether this geographical coincidence superseded my artistic ability in gaining the commission remains a question. (I never asked it.)

So, in April 1983, my wife, Karen, and I went to Greece, Yugoslavia, Bulgaria, and Romania to find out as much as we could about the character of Macedonian carving. Let me share some not so minor treasures of architecture and painting we found along the way. I will discuss three churches, culled from over a dozen, to illustrate not just their high quality of artistic achievement but the elastic contours of the Byzantine style, which encouraged my later innovations.

On Mount Vodno, just above Skopje, Yugoslavia (now Macedonia) stands the tiny monastery church built and dedicated to Sveti Pantelemon in 1164. The form of the building shows a classical Byzantine cross in square plan with a dome rising over the crossing and a narthex added to the west. It inaugurates a Slavic innovation, the four smaller corner domes. The stout, squat proportions and the heavy arches lend a homely air to the building, but the walls have survived two major earthquakes since they were built, one in 1555 and another in 1963. They have preserved frescoes whose dramatic compositions and emotional expressions prefigure the proto-Renaissance images of Cimabue, Duccio, and Giotto (fig. 2).

Figure 2. The Lamentation, fresco, ca. 1164. St. Pantelemon, Skopje, Yugoslavia.

The monastery of Sopocani has stood since 1255 in the mountains above Novi Pazar along the Morava River. Italian architects designed its basilica form and the table corbel decoration in the masonry below the eaves. The frescoes of Sopocani, which survived four centuries open to the elements before the roof was repaired, evidence in their full-bodied volumes a pre-Renaissance era of classicizing in Byzantine art (fig. 3).

Figure 3. The Dormition of the Virgin, fresco, ca. 1255. Sopocani Monastery, Novi Pazar, Yugoslavia.

The Church of the Holy Virgin at Studenica Monastery, built in 1183–1191, reveals in the competing shapes of its walls, pediments, domes, and sculptures a high-volume argument between eastern and western European cultures that to this day rages through the land of the southern Slavs. The patron of this church, Stefan Nemanya, first emperor of Serbia, hired Constantinople's best painters to execute the frescoes. They represent the quintessence of Byzantine art: stylized, reserved, evoking an austere spirituality. Using travel journals written in the 1950s by the British author Cecil Stewart, we planned our itinerary to see these artistic treasures and also to include buildings that house the best of Macedonian wood carving.

In Skopje, we found the tiny church, Sveti Spas, or Church of the Holy Savior. The Ottoman Turks forbade any Christian structure to exceed one story, not much room for the grand treatment that Orthodox Christians like to give to the interiors of their temples. So, in crafty defiance of their oppressor, the people of Skopje built a single-story exterior, then excavated within the completed walls a sanctuary deep enough to erect a two-story icon screen, thus lending new meaning to the term, "cultural substratum." A three-man team from the nearby village of Garje, Makaria Fukovich and the Fillipovich brothers, Petre and Marko, designed and supervised the creation of all this work. With an unknown number of apprentices and assistants, they spent ten years, from 1814–1824 cutting, fitting, and carving the walnut trees of the Vardar River valley into the iconostas, pulpit, and furniture of Sveti Spas.

The simple subject matter—the stories of the gospels, the lives of the saints, and the feasts of the church—are conveyed in a rich, exuberant, and ornate style, which deploys figures, flowers, and birds in three interweaving layers of carving. An analogy to folk music suggests itself because the rhythms and textures, so rich and compelling, almost become audible. If the best folk musicians play the most notes the most clearly and quickly, then the best folk carvers fashion with the fewest cuts the face of a saint, the flight of a bird, or the scroll of a vine. Literally hundreds of deftly carved figures, four to five inches tall, act out the stories of the saints in the wooden frames of the icons. The depiction of Salome dancing the dance of veils typifies the expressiveness of the carving and the penchant of Macedonian artisans to dress biblical villains in Albanian costume. In place of a signature, the craftsmen carved likenesses of themselves at work (fig. 4).

Figure 4. Detail of iconostas, woodcarvers, ca. 1820. St. Spas, Skopje, Yugoslavia.

This signature style of Macedonia bears the name, Debarski, after the town, Debar, which nestles above the westernmost valley of Macedonia overlooking Albania. There, the Monastery of Sveti Jovan Bigorski hired Makaria Fukovich to carve its iconostas. Fukovich spent another decade fashioning work on an even larger scale than that of Sveti Spas. The Byzantine stylizations at the heart of the Debarski style survived as a substratum, because the Ottoman Empire insulated the region from the Renaissance and subsequent western European stylistic developments.

We found the oldest datable carving in the iconostas at the Monastery Church of Sveti Naum, built on the southern shore of Lake Ohrid in the ninth century by St. Naum. He, along with St. Clement studied under Sts. Cyril and Methodi and became among the first generation of priests and monks to preach Christianity to the Slavs. The carving dates from the eighteenth century. While not as complex in depth as the subsequent Debarski style, it nonetheless richly portrays the traditional motifs of the Slavs, an exuberance of birds, vines, and animals celebrating creation. In particular, the motif of the dragon or serpent chained to the service of the cross struck me and would incubate nearly nine years before I used it at St. Clement. The icons at Sveti Naum represent nothing less than masterpieces of the Slavic style. The artist's name is lost to us, and the date is uncertain, but the images show a skilled hand and vivid imagination. The finer proportions and agitated contours differentiate these from Greek icons.

We also met two of the finest wood carvers still working in 1983. In the town of Ohrid, Yugoslavia, the namesake of the very St. Clement Ohridski who employed me in Dearborn, Michigan, not a hundred yards from the shore of Lake Ohrid, we found the home and studio of Dimitri Jovanski. Carvings as rich and as strong as his homemade wine filled his modest living room. We chatted while sitting on handcarved chairs around a handcarved table. We had discovered examples of his work by accident. They hung on the lobby walls of our otherwise nondescript tourist hotel (fig. 5). He had carved Marshall Tito's desk, but the communist Yugoslav government forbade him to carve for churches.

Figure 5. Dimitri Jovanski, decorative carving, Ohrich, Yugoslavia.

In downtown Sophia, Bulgaria, we met Peter Kushlev. The freshly carved components of a new iconostas cluttered his studio. This work belonged to a chip-carving style favored in northeastern Bulgaria. In contrast to Yugoslavia, Bulgaria under communism hired artists and craftsmen like Kushlev to renovate churches as "expressions of the national spirit." Lazar Lazarov, the architect in charge of restoration, introduced us to Kushlev and served as our translator and guide to several other churches with interesting wood carving, including a Debarski-style iconostas in Pazardjik that may have been carved by the Fillipovich brothers.

Kushlev demonstrated his ability to work in a half-dozen regional styles, but he took particular pride in his mastery of the trilayered complexities of the Debarski style (fig. 6).

Figure 6. Peter Kushlev, walnut candle holder, Sophia, Bulgaria.

Both Kushlev and Jovanski welcomed me to their studios and shared all they could, time and language permitting, of their expertise. In these all-too-brief visits, I tried to learn by observation and osmosis as much as I could about how they organized their work space, detailed their shop drawings, blocked and roughed out work in progress, and finished completed work. During my only "apprenticeship" as a carver, I tried to absorb a sense of how their forms came out of their tools and to find my standard of craftsmanship.

Returning home, I treated my commission as a course of study. I had fifty-five bands and panels, ranging in size from three inches by twenty-four to thirty-four inches by twenty-eight to design. I used the thirty narrow bands to teach myself technique and to practice various regional styles. This sort of eclecticism dovetailed with Pilafian's overall plan. His design met the standard requirements of an Orthodox iconostas and then explored new possibilities. He in fact had no choice in placing the icons of Christ and John the Baptist in the first two places to the south of the royal doors at the central opening of the screen, and he had no choice in placing the icons of the Theotokou and St. Clement in the first two spaces to the north. Tradition further dictated placing the icon of the Last Supper above the royal doors.

Beyond these requirements, however, Pilafian broke with the fundamental hierarchy of traditional iconostases, abandoning strict horizontal stratification in favor of a more diagonally interwoven composition. Furthermore, his instructions to me called for making no two panels alike, thus abandoning the strict left-to-right symmetry of past designs. Truthfully, I had some trouble adjusting to this idea. Apart from the additional task of inventing fifty-four designs instead of twenty-seven, I felt that the architecture of the iconostas called for symmetry. Therefore, I always maintained an underlying symmetry of design to lend unity to corresponding panels (figs. 7 and 8), and I made the panels nearer the center ever more symmetrical. The parishioners grew to appreciate the novelty, challenge, and fascination of nonsymmetrical balance.

Pilafian had two closely related goals. First, he wanted to make the overall experience one of awe, which to him meant creating on a grand scale and with visually dramatic contrasts

Figure 7. Michael R. Kapetan, iconostas panel left, 1983. St. Clement Ohridski, Dearborn, Michigan.

of light and depth. Second, he broke with the security of past compositional formulas, consciously adding harmonious strains of modern to ancient voices. Here lay the common ground on which the aging architect and the then still young sculptor could stand together: our confidence that history authorized us as artists to nudge tradition forward and outward. We both felt that no matter how monolithic Byzantine tradition might seem at first glance, upon entering it, we could find variety, feel vitality, and add our individual voices to the choir.

As my work progressed, I gravitated toward a personal variation of the Debarski style. I felt that I owed it to all the Macedonian craftsmen, living and dead, to try it. By the time I came to carve the royal doors, pulpit, and bishop's throne, I felt that I could have worked along side any of them. And, in all modesty, I know that both in concept and technique my work in some ways exceeds theirs.

Figure 8. Michael R. Kapetan, iconostas panel right, 1983. St. Clement Ohridski, Dearborn, Michigan.

Pilafian and I designed the royal doors as a single plane of carving. Five icons occupy their traditional hierarchy—the four evangelists in the body of the doors, and the Annunciation in the surmounting cross—but the doors read as single expanse of wood, four-and-a-half feet wide, seven feet tall and two-and-one-half inches thick. A beveled overlap conceals the central opening, so that the two halves join in a seamless whole. Technically, such an expanse of wood lies beyond Old Country methods. Like good woodworkers everywhere, the Macedonian craftsmen designed their work taking into account the seasonal shrinking and swelling of wood. In Europe, we never saw single panels larger that two feet square. They built up large and complex items like royal doors, furniture, pulpits, and whole iconostases from small panels fitted into larger frames, which allows all the components to shrink and to swell together without splitting. This technical limit fit perfectly with the Eastern Orthodox concept of hierarchical space, in which all images are neatly ordered within a static framework (fig. 9).

Figure 9. Michael R. Kapetan, royal doors, 1984. St. Clement Ohridski, Dearborn, Michigan.

But we capitalized on the availability of tropical woods like mahogany, which do not shrink or swell very much, so that we could more easily conceive of a dramatic single plane to express a distinctly twentieth-century concept of space as a continuum.

With no supervision from the architect or the church, I conceived the symbolism of the royal doors around the metaphor of the cross as the tree of life growing at the center of the new Eden. The doors represent a richly grown arbor of intertwining grape vines, lilies, roses, and oak leaves that carry on their boughs twenty-eight Christian symbols including the crown of martyrdom, the keys to heaven, the scale of judgment, the anchor of hope, and the banner of victory. A detailed examination of the symbols would take too much space for this essay, but in a gesture upholding Macedonian tradition, I signed the doors by carving an image of my tools in the lower left corner of the arbor. As tradition dictates, the doors are completely covered with gold leaf.

In the pulpit, we used another modern material, plywood, for the internal shell of the piece. It is forty-two inches in diameter and built with fourteen plywood staves whose shrinkage is negligible. Around this stable core, I hung a curtain of carved walnut three feet high and nine feet wide. A twenty-seven square foot piece of wood concentric to an underlying form would have given nightmares to a woodworker a century and a half ago. He might have solved it with tools and materials at hand, but he would have had no compelling concept of space to tempt him into it. It proved very difficult in 1989.

Except for the eagle at the pulpit and the cross on the bishop's throne, I received no instruction for the symbolic content of my carvings. Bishop Joseph required the pulpit to have an eagle at the lectern. I made it fly rather than perch as eagles usually do on pulpits. I carved hummingbirds in the pulpit, just because of their lively shape, but thereby unwittingly made this pulpit a New World pulpit, because hummingbirds do not exist east of the Atlantic or west of the Pacific. I carved four angels playing musical instruments to symbolize the four evangelists, who usually have a privileged position on Eastern Orthodox pulpits (fig. 10).

Figure 10. Michael R. Kapetan, pulpit, 1987. St. Clement Ohridski, Dearborn, Michigan.

The bishop sits on the bishop's throne when he visits a parish, usually once a year on the name day of the patron saint. For the rest of the year, the throne stands empty but in eternal readiness for its ultimate occupant. The Greek term for this preparedness is *etoimasia*. Most important, the throne carries the icon of Christ as bishop who presides from the throne throughout the year. Of the seven pieces of liturgical furniture, the throne looks the most traditional, because it consists of carved elements framed by uncarved elements. The composition of the entire throne centers on the icon: the carving on the back, the lions beneath its arms, the dragons supporting the cross at its apex are linked by carved rays emanating from the icon. Visually reversing the actual, I subordinated the framing to the sculpture and the sculpture to the icon. If all the forms develop centrifugally from the icon, then the whole chair should read as the advancing waves of that single event. I wanted to make a sculpted chair, not a chair with sculpture applied to it. Of all the work I have done for St. Clement, this and this alone follows from a text, a phrase in the closing prayer of the divine liturgy of St. John Chrysostom: "For all good gifts and all perfect gifts are from above and come down from you, the Father of Light" (fig. 11). A detailed account of symbolism is beyond the ken of this essay. Suffice it to say that Eastern Orthodox tradition considers painters as artists and carvers as craftsmen. The irony of this distinction between "high art" and "low art" leaves the carvers freer to turn for inspiration to nature and abstraction. Because the painters make images of mighty spiritual beings and sacred events, the church requires them to adhere strictly to prototypes. George Filipakis painted the icons at St. Clement. Born in Crete, he became an apprentice in the Cretan School at age eleven. He undoubtedly underwent a program of training similar to another young Cretan several centuries ago, Domenico Theotokopolous, or El Greco. Unlike El Greco, Filipakis adheres to the ancient style.

The forms of authority for my carvings at St. Thomas à Becket Catholic Church in Canton, Michigan remained the same as at St. Clement: the architect and his building, the clergy and its rituals, and the community and their sense of traditions. But the differences from the Eastern Orthodox in all three required rethinking my whole approach to imagery.

Figure 11. Michael R. Kapetan, bishop's throne, 1990. St. Clement Ohridski, Dearborn, Michigan.

I think it fair to say that since the fifteenth-century invention of perspective, the Roman Catholic church has proved more open to artistic experimentation than the Eastern

Orthodox church. Once the Orthodox get a thing to their liking, they keep it. They have not changed a word of their liturgy since at least the fourth century, when St. John Chrysostom wrote it down. They had settled on an architectural style by about the sixth century, and their iconography has undergone only minor variations since then. Catholic art, on the contrary, not only served as a vehicle for stylistic and cosmological change in the early Italian Renaissance, but the church in this century has welcomed the pioneering artistic efforts of Matisse, Corbusier, Richier, and other certified modernists. Among the Catholics, I encountered a good deal more discussion about form and content.

The architect, David Osler, solved the problem of accommodating a large congregation on a small budget by building a structure with industrial materials into a simple liturgical form. The pyramidal shape, with virtually all of the roof carried on massive laminated beams, proved an economical way to enclose a large volume. However, it evoked a feeling of emptiness, scalelessness, and chill that he sought to overcome by the interior detailing. He set windows at ground level behind an eight foot tall oak curtain wall on three sides of the building to bring warmth and a suitably mysterious light to the sanctuary. Osler wanted my sculpture to join in lending a sense of human scale, human texture, and human warmth to the big, cold building as well as to satisfy a liturgical necessity.

Catholic Church tradition calls for placing an image of the patron saint of the parish, in this case, St. Thomas à Becket, and an image of the Holy Virgin in the sanctuary for the purpose of veneration. The oak curtain wall has two semicircular niches to accommodate the images. The architect and community had decided to use wood sculpture. Osler felt that the use of wood alone would lend a quality of warmth and intimacy. He asked me to look for old wood, weathered and cracked material that already had its own history and character. Near Manchester, Michigan, I found red oak beams from a 120-year-old barn recently flattened by a tornado.

Although Thomas à Becket belonged to a Norman family that had attained position in English society through their allegiance to William the Conqueror, I decided to emulate the understated style of pre-Conquest British sculpture. This

Figures 12 and 13. Michael R. Kapetan, St. Thomas à Becket and St. Mary, 1982. St. Thomas à Becket, Canton, Michigan.

allowed me to keep the carving budget within reason, summarize the anatomy, concentrate on the hands and faces, and integrate the plain forms into the simple geometry of the curtain wall.

I created the character of Becket virtually from scratch (fig. 12). Like a good Eastern Orthodox iconographer, I looked for prototypes, and, indeed, he appears rather nondescriptly in various stained glass and parchment images. From these I learned that he should be bearded and dressed in the miter and chasuble of a bishop. I gave him the stern face of a warrior and the praying hands of a priest. This represents the two contradictory lives that he led, before and after his ordination, and the dilemma that ultimately brought about his martyrdom.

The frontal, open palm gesture of St. Mary represents a commonplace of Catholic art. But this Mary shows an unusual face (fig. 13). She wears no covering on her head, as she had in my original sketch model, and as she has in countless images throughout history. Instead, luxuriant hair falls to her shoulders. This somewhat nontraditional rendition grew out of discussions between myself, the lay committee in charge of the interior, and especially the priest, Father Pocari. He enjoined us all to conceive of St. Mary as human, to make her common, simple, plain, and strong, and, therefore to dispense with religious regalia, uncover her head, and let her womanhood radiate.

The architect had planned to incorporate the stations of the cross in a traditional European manner, engraving at four to five yard intervals along the curtain wall the roman numerals one through fourteen. Could I carve them? Certainly. This satisfied Osler and the priest, but not the laity. They wanted imagery in the stations to educate their children. The numerals, while traditional and concise, elegant and succinct, seemed too abstract, too far removed from experience. Searching for a visual form not only realistic but vivid enough for the minds of children in the last quarter of the twentieth century, I turned to the paradigms of television images: hand-held mini-cams, zoom lenses, on-the-spot news documentaries. I carried on the theme of the statues of Becket and St. Mary by concentrating on hands and faces. I employed a

Figures 14 and 15. Michael R. Kapetan, Stations VII and XI, 1982. St. Thomas à Becket, Canton, Michigan.

realism as photographic as possible within the limits of quarter-inch deep relief carved in one-foot-square panels—small screen television (fig. 14). I dramatically changed the point of view from panel to panel, enhancing the sense of witnessing the events of Good Friday from within the jostling crowd.

After showing them one sample, the priest and parishioners granted me authority to select the particular scenes. In order to design the stations of the cross one must consult the synoptic Gospels and church tradition. The Gospels recount nine of the fourteen episodes, some cursorily, others in great detail. Five are traditional, and I researched them in the history of art from Dürer to Matisse.

The eleventh station is richest in my memory because it developed out of conversations with Percival Price, the man who brought the carillons to Burton Tower on the campus of the University of Michigan (fig. 15). As a young postgraduate, Price traveled to the Holy Land to research early Christian bells. He had secured an audience with the patriarch of Alexandria. Wishing to use his time well, Price asked the archbishop where one could find the earliest Christian bell. He replied that the first bell of Christianity was a hammer striking a nail. I tried to carve the verb, the striking, with the hammer incidental, and the nail out of the scene.

I will discuss one more piece of work because it grew out of the earlier work. The First Presbyterian Church of Ann Arbor, Michigan held a competition to find imagery suitable for the narthex of their building. The program stipulated two requirements. First, it called for an image to add Christian thought and symbolism to the blank wall of the lobby. Second, it should harmonize with the existing architecture. Because the financing came from a memorial donation, two additional requirements arose. The image must serve as a memorial, and the donors would participate in the selection.

Approaching the competition, I heeded only the requirement to harmonize with the architecture because I had already chosen an image to submit, and I had complete confidence that it met the entire program. Of all my work at St. Clement and St. Thomas, the starburst holds a special place in my mind. It possesses a quality of universality that I strive for in my nonsectarian work. I cannot prove it, but I suspect that woodworkers throughout south-central Europe had fashioned similar images long before Christian churches existed to enshrine them. The symbol of the sun as fire and light has primordial roots. I first saw them hanging in the doorways of the iconostas in Pazardjik, Bulgaria, their makers unknown.

I grafted this archaic image to the celtic cross, sized it to fit the narthex wall, and fashioned it of the Church's dominant wood, oak (fig 16). In this image, the primary symbol of the faith stands centermost and foremost, all other forms radiating from it, all forms echoing upon it. For me, it illuminates a text whose author I do not know, "The last day of Revelation will read what the first day of Genesis has writ."

Each of these churches consecrated the images according to their traditions. The Presbyterian church used a prayer recited in unison by the entire congregation. In the Catholic church, Father Pocari asked that I install the stations of the cross during a special recitation of Lenten prayers on Good Friday, 1982 led by Brother Robert of the Dominican Order. The sanctuary sculptures received blessing from Cardinal Szoka during the consecration of the entire church. At St.

Figure 16. Michael R. Kapetan, Genesis, 1991. First Presbyterian Church, Ann Arbor, Michigan.

Clement, Bishop Joseph of New York consecrated the iconostas by anointing it with holy water and oil on St. Clement's Day, 1989. On St. Clement's Day, 1991, Bishop Joseph anointed with holy water the bishop's throne, the donor family, and the wood carver.

All of the imagery produced by my hand is made of wood. Wood comes from trees, the royalty of the plant kingdom. It seems that even as we near the second millennium, people will worship among trees. The fine irony of carving rose petals and oak leaves in wood is not lost on me. Fashioning wood into objects of contemplation, one can hardly avoid contemplating the nature of wood and the claim that it makes on our imagination even before we transform it into imagery. Our human relationship to trees is symbiotic at many levels. We trade the trees carbon dioxide for oxygen. We cultivate trees for their fruits and nuts, saps and medicines, and their sheer ornamental beauty. What have we not made from their wood? Tools, weapons, utensils, musical instruments, clipper ships, canoes, paper, cloth, shoes, furniture, dwellings, temples—and sculpture. We identify with trees, with their trunks, limbs, and crowns as living beings. The sequoias are the largest forms of life on the dry land, and the Joshua trees are the oldest on the surface of the planet. In the past we have identified with them as spiritual entities. Holders of the knowledge of trees were the Druids. We emulate their attributes: durability and trust, treaty and truth are but a few of the words that we derive from the Indo-European source, *deru*, the ancient word for tree. It is no wonder, then, that we entreat our gods from among them, living exemplars of the best qualities of life.

MODERNIZING TRADITION: *Some Catholic Neo-Scholastics and the Genealogy of Natural Rights*

Robert E. Sullivan

Since 1864 the closing anathemas of Pope Pius IX's Syllabus of Errors have fixed an impression of the intransigence of official Catholicism. If the pope of Rome declared that he could not and ought not "reconcile himself and come to terms with progress, with liberalism, and with modern civilization," then presumably neither could his church.[1] For nearly a millennium, after all, the Catholic faith had been ever more closely identified with the ecclesiastical institutions over which the nineteenth-century papacy was consolidating unprecedented authority. A rebarbative image of official Catholicism may be fixed, but like other familiar images its apparent solidity proves on examination to be deceptive. Pio Nono himself began the papacy's fitful movement to reconcile itself and to come to terms with beliefs that have been conventionally linked with progress, liberalism, and modern civilization. Since then, official Catholicism has adapted so much that in recent years it has been for many self-consciously progressive, liberal, and modern people from the Philippines to Czechoslovakia an indispensable if sometimes baffling presence. When adapting to modernity, however, popes and other Catholic dignitaries have seldom trumpeted the latent meaning of their decisions. Official Catholicism has regularly accommodated itself to the present by invoking the authority of the past, by asserting that its contemporary revisions were, if not simple reiterations, at least expressions of a consistent tradition. It was thus that the church came to endorse the idea that private property is a natural right, an idea upon which modern civil society and its liberties depend.[2]

---

[1]Denzinger-Schönmetzer, *Enchiridion Symbolorum definitionum et declarationum de rebus fidei et morum* 2980.

[2]See Richard Tuck, *Natural Rights Theories: Their Origin and Development* (Cambridge: Cambridge University Press, 1979). Since I wrote my essay, Ernest L. Fortin has probed in a style reminiscent of Leo Strauss the nineteenth-century papacy's accommodation of modernity. See "'Sacred and Inviolable': *Rerum Novarum* and Natural Rights," *Theological Studies* 53 (1992): 203–33.

The Catholic adaptation to modernity depended on the assumption that the High Middle Ages were the cultural and institutional meridian not just of Catholicism but also of European civilization. During much of the nineteenth and twentieth centuries Catholics routinely depicted the medieval era, and especially its Scholastic thought, as the epitome of all the achievements of previous ages and the standard for judging the legitimacy of subsequent developments. Cultural medievalism was one of the many luxuriant traditions that were invented during the last century. A modern vogue that official Catholicism would endorse only late and selectively, the renewed enthusiasm for various artifacts of medieval culture neither began with Catholics nor was it ever confined to them.[3] In 1771, Goethe was famously if briefly transported at the sight of Strasbourg Cathedral, whose vivacity seemed to him to highlight the deadliness of eighteenth-century philosophical materialism. In 1868, as the tenth and last volume of the redoubtable secularist connoisseur Eugène-Emmanuel Viollet-le-Duc's *Dictionnaire raisonné de l'architecture française du xie au xvie siècle* appeared, the papacy had yet to mandate the revival of any aspect of medieval culture. In 1913 when Henry Adams finally published a commercial edition of

---

[3]Eric Hobsbawm, "Inventing Traditions," in Eric Hobsbawm and Terence Ranger, eds., *The Invention of Tradition* (Cambridge: Cambridge University Press, 1983) 1–14, established the concept; despite the multiplication of research on cultural medievalism, Gottfried Salomon-Delatur, *Das Mittelalter in der Romantik* (Munich: Drei Masken Verlag, 1922) and Giorgio Falco, *La polemica sul medio evo* (Turin: Fedetto, 1933) have yet to be superseded; Peter Raedts, "De christelijke middeleeuwen als mythe," *Tijdschrift voor Theologie* 30 (1990): 146–58, may be the most analytically sophisticated introduction to the multiple usefulness of cultural medievalism to the Roman Catholic Church; Philip F. Gleason, "American Catholics and the Mythic Middle Ages," in *Keeping the Faith: American Catholicism Past and Present* (Notre Dame: University of Notre Dame Press, 1987) 11–34, evokes a provincial expression of the movement; Brian Stock, "Romantic Attitudes and Academic Medievalism," in *Listening for the Text: On the Uses of the Past* (Baltimore: The Johns Hopkins University Press, 1990) 52–74, provides a subtle retrospective; Norman F. Cantor, *Inventing the Middle Ages: The Lives, Works, and Ideas of the Great Medievalists of the Twentieth Century* (New York: Morrow, 1991), offers a tour, frontstairs and back, of some monuments of academic medievalism—*se non è vero....*

Mont-Saint-Michel and Chartres, the debut of official Catholic cultural medievalism was still a fresh memory.

Early nineteenth-century Catholic dignitaries could sometimes resemble Enlightened historians in the ease with which they dismissed medieval culture. Cardinal Cesar Guillaume de La Luzerne, for example, sought in a book that appeared in 1823 to accommodate received principles of economic morality to current business practices. He scouted the medieval Scholastics who had condemned as usurious all interest-taking. After asserting that they had departed from the Christian tradition, the cardinal portrayed them as the intellectual victims of their own primitive economy and mindless devotion to Aristotle.[4] For ecclesiastics like La Luzerne, the absolute obligation to uphold church teachings from the past extended only to authoritatively defined dogmas. Apart from them there existed latitude for prudent tacking necessary to cope with changing circumstances. During La Luzerne's lifetime, moreover, a spirit of eclecticism reigned among academic theologians. Descartes's shadow, refracted by the eighteenth-century Protestant philosopher Christian Wolff, was perhaps longer in the world of Catholic divinity than that of St. Thomas Aquinas or of any other medieval.[5]

Cardinal La Luzerne and his contemporaries had come of age in a relatively decentralized church whose stubborn variety and particularism declared a basic continuity between the past and the present. Having forgotten little about the Old Regime and still relishing its sweetness, many priests who had been adults in 1789 and managed to survive the dangerous years that followed were immune both to the urge to romanticize the long vanished Middle Ages and to singleminded attempts to establish medieval precedents for Catholic beliefs and practices. Those survivors seem to have instinctively felt that religious traditions are as much the accumulation of living, or at least remembered and restorable, customs as they are an officially sanctioned compend of texts of remote provenance. Among the next generation of European ecclesiastics there were numerous raw men who had never shared the lived

---

[4]John T. Noonan, Jr., *The Scholastic Analysis of Usury* (Cambridge: Harvard University Press, 1957) 383.

[5]Gerald McCool, *Catholic Theology in the Nineteenth Century: The Quest for a Unitary Method* (New York: The Seabury Press, 1977) 28–29.

traditions of the Old Regime. Haunted by a poignant sense of discontinuity and rupture with they knew not quite what, they felt an insistent desire to strike roots in a distant and secure past, roots that ran deep and strong and unhampered, roots unshakable enough to fix even a precarious sense of identity.[6]

For over two generations many such Catholics worked to identify Catholicism with medieval culture. Finally, in 1879 the papacy authoritatively endorsed looking backward to the Middle Ages as a privileged source of guidance in philosophy and theology. That was done by Pope Leo XIII, Pio Nono's successor, in his encyclical letter *Æterni Patris*. In the decades before its publication, Catholic cultural medievalism had acquired various rhetorical uses. If inventing and lionizing a coherent medieval tradition allowed Roman Catholics to defend their church and to indict the failures of contemporary society, they could also legitimate attractive elements of modern culture by grounding them in the medieval tradition and seek to restore "Catholic civilization" by either imitating or faithfully replicating parts of that tradition. A few Catholic cultural medievalists sought merely to deepen knowledge of the Middle Ages by studying them according to the prevailing canons of historical scholarship.

There was nothing uniform about the Catholic cultural medievalists' conclusions or methods. In 1863, Sir John Acton, a stern critic of the papacy, could acclaim "the mediæval Revival [as] the distinctive achievement of the age in which we live." For that liberal Catholic historian, "Its study was not of death, but of life—not of a world of ruins, but of that which is our own. Therefore its lesson was a lesson of continuity, not of sudden restoration or servile copying. It taught respect for the past, encouraged patriotic sentiments, and awakened the memory of hereditary rights."[7] As Acton's tribute suggests, the diverse uses of cultural medievalism served to keep it from severing the virtuous past from the corrupt present. If the major lesson of "the medieval revival" was

---

[6]Austin Gough, *Paris and Rome: The Gallican Church and the Ultramontane Campaign, 1848–1853* (New York: Oxford University Press, 1986), is an exemplary analysis of the warfare between the old and the new fogies in France.

[7]Lord [John E.D.] Acton, "Ultramontanism," in Douglas Woodruff, ed., *Essays on Church and State* (New York: Thomas Y. Crowell, 1968) 67.

one of historical continuity, then the past and the present tended to merge rather than to separate. In practice, the papacy itself gave scant encouragement to a dualistic notion of history. Gregorian chant was the only other artifact of medieval culture besides Scholastic theology that a pope would ever try to impose on his church.

When *Æterni Patris* appeared, Pope Leo was sixty-nine years old and had been reigning for less than eighteen months—an aging man in a hurry. Carefully marshaling testimonials to the wisdom of Thomas Aquinas from nine earlier popes and five ecumenical councils, he offered Thomism as a virtual panacea for the political and social disease that he believed to be ravaging Europe: the confusion of liberty with license.[8] From the Jesuits who had pioneered the Thomist revival at the Roman College during the 1820s—above all from Luigi Taparelli d'Azeglio—the future pope had learned that restoring the metaphysical order of thirteenth-century Scholasticism would permit the church to recover enough of its medieval authority to end modern revolutionary threats.

Young Gioacchino Pecci's teachers had also introduced him to a sweeping historical myth whose austerity, moralism, and endurance suggest the competing nineteenth-century myths of Auguste Comte and Karl Marx. Already before 1800 Catholic counterrevolutionaries had plotted and elaborated an account of the decline of modern Europe. They accepted an idealist theory of historical causality and assumed that culture's forms are invariably society's substance. Because ideas form the base supporting the economic, social, and institutional superstructures of the world, the sincere teaching and reception of correct doctrine would certainly foster public order and prosperity, just as deviations from correct doctrine would certainly foster public disorder and adversity. According to the authors of the myth, every contemporary intellectual and social failure ultimately sprang from Martin Luther. His ruinous theological legacy had been transferred first to philosophy by Descartes and then to politics by Rousseau. In opposition to that long declension stood the Catholic tradition. Its essential theological and institutional coherence was free

---

[8]Pope Leo XIII, *Æterni Patris* in Etienne Gilson, ed., *The Church Speaks to the Modern World: The Social Teachings of Leo XIII* (Garden City, NY: Doubleday Image Books, 1954) 45–46 (nos. 21–22).

not only of discontinuity or rupture but also of tension and ambiguity. Once restored, the Catholic tradition had the power to renew civilization.[9]

On first hearing, the myth sounds like a straightforward romance, in which good battles and eventually overcomes evil.[10] On examination, the myth turns out to have had a comic subplot. Its interpretation by Leo XIII and those who followed his lead allowed for recurrent if partial reconciliations of good and evil, for the virtue of at least those aspects of modern civilization endorsed by the official church—or capable of being used to justify the position of the church. Reactionaries possess less conciliatory instincts. Espying menace everywhere around them, they recoil from every resistible accommodation to modernity. Thus, Pope Gregory XVI in the 1830s had banned railroads from his states with a pun: "Chemin de fer, chemin d'enfer."[11] Gioacchino Pecci, in contrast, once invoked the authority of Benjamin Franklin to illustrate a point. While praising Franklin for "a life spent in the midst of public affairs, and matured by long experience," he ignored Franklin's notorious heterodoxy and insurrectionism.[12]

Pope Leo privileged the Catholic historical myth by embedding it in *Æterni Patris*, whose primary drafter was the neo-Thomist German Jesuit Joseph Kleutgen. In two books that began to appear in the early 1850s, *Die Theologie der Vorzeit* and *Die Philosophie der Vorzeit*, Kleutgen added rich detail to the received narrative of postmedieval philosophical decline. He was perhaps more accurate about his aversions than about his affections. Uncertainly grounded in the texts of the major Scholastics of the Middle Ages, he imagined that modern non-Catholic thought was an accelerating declension

---

[9]Paul Droulers, "Question sociale, état, église dans la 'Civiltà Cattolica' à ses début," in *Cattolicesimo sociale nei secoli XIX e XX: Saggi di storia e sociologia* (Rome: Edizioni di storia e letteratura, 1982) 109–21.

[10]The classifications are Northrop Frye's as filtered through Hayden White, *Metahistory: The Historical Imagination in Nineteenth-Century Europe* (Baltimore: The Johns Hopkins University Press, 1973) 7–11.

[11]P. Negri, "Gregorio XVI e le ferrovie," *Rassegna degli archivi di stato* 28 (1968): 103–26.

[12]Pope Leo XIII, *The Church and Civilization: Pastoral Letters for Lent 1877–1878* (New York, 1878) 102.

from the "unified theology of the Angelic Doctor," Thomas Aquinas, which rested on a perennial philosophy. Participation in that fundamental philosophical unity, Kleutgen believed, dwarfed any disagreements between Thomas and Kleutgen's own master, Francisco de Suarez, an early-modern Spanish expositor of Thomas. To the extent that Kleutgen was able first to construct a philosophical identity for himself that minimized the rifts between Thomas and Suarez on such essentials as the nature of being and the process of knowing and then to secure official endorsement for his own construction, he endowed the neo-Scholastic concept of a perennial philosophy embodied in Catholic theology with a generous vagueness.[13]

The historical myth launched by Catholic counterrevolutionaries and officially sanctioned by Leo XIII would enjoy a long life. Some details necessarily changed. Luther's aberrations would be traced back to the late medieval nominalist theologians, Descartes would be at least partially rehabilitated as a Scholastic epigone, and Kant would be increasingly more harshly indicted. The basic plot of the myth, however, remained unchanged, and it informed papal documents into the reign of Pope Pius XII (1939–1958). As a young man, the future Pope Paul VI wrote the preface to the Italian translation of Jacques Maritain's *Trois réformateurs: Luther, Descartes, Rousseau* (1925), a relic of Maritain's flirtation with the Action Française and one of the most popular twentieth-century renditions of the myth.[14] When during the 1960s official Catholicism adopted a more benign approach toward Protestantism and in consequence muted its vilification of Martin Luther, the myth lost its devil but not its allure. For over a decade Alasdair MacIntyre has mounted an impressive effort to rejuvenate it as an explanation of the present condition of moral philosophy.[15]

---

[13]McCool, *Catholic Theology* 168–69, 209–15, and 228.

[14]Gabriele de Rosa, "La formazione di G.B. Montini," in *Paul VI et la modernité dans l'église*, Collection de l'école française de Rome, 72 (Rome: Ecole française de Rome, 1984) 6.

[15]For example, Alasdair MacIntyre, *Three Rival Versions of Moral Enquiry: Encyclopedia, Genealogy, and Tradition* (Notre Dame: University of Notre Dame Press, 1990) 73–74.

Because Pope Leo was convinced that ideas have material consequences, his design to make Thomism—or what he took to be Thomism—the standard theological system of his church had wide-ranging implications, political, social, and economic, as well as intellectual.[16] He presented Thomas as uniquely competent to teach "the true meaning of liberty ... on the divine origin of all authority, on laws and their force, on the paternal and just rule of princes, on the obedience to the higher powers, on mutual charity one toward another"; he also attributed to Thomas's doctrines "the invincible force to overturn those principles of the new order which are well known to be dangerous to the peaceful order of things and to public safety."[17] Since the stakes were concrete and grave, the pope declared that his "first and most cherished idea" was that the bishops of his church "should all furnish to studious youth a generous and copious supply of those purest streams of wisdom flowing inexhaustibly from the precious fountainhead of the Angelic Doctor [Thomas Aquinas]."[18]

Besides an idealist theory of historical causation, aspirations to make peace with modern civilization informed the pope's Ciceronian endorsement of Thomism. In widely noticed Lenten pastoral letters delivered in 1877 and 1878, Leo, then still Cardinal Gioacchino Pecci of Perugia, had preached the necessity for reconciliation between Catholicism and European culture and insinuated himself to the other cardinals as an attractive successor to the isolated, censorious, and visibly failing Pope Pius IX. While loyally echoing Pio Nono's condemnation of the kind of modern civilization "that *seeks to supplant Christianity*, and ... to destroy every blessing it has brought upon us," Cardinal Pecci had also assumed a more benign attitude toward the prospects of the contemporary world.[19] He admitted that reconciling Catholicism with modern civilization was imperative if the church was to stop "the apostacy [sic] of her children."[20] A rapprochement would serve the purposes of both sides, since "civilization, not only has

[16]See also Pierre Thibault, *Savoir et pouvoir: Philosophie thomiste et politique cléricale au XIXe siecle* (Quebec: Les Presses de l'Université Laval, 1972).

[17]*Æterni Patris* 48–49 (no. 29).

[18]*Æterni Patris* 48 (no. 26).

[19]*Church and Civilization* 57; see also 118–19.

[20]*Church and Civilization* 13–14.

nothing to fear from the Church, but has everything to hope from her and from her co-operation."[21] Cardinal Pecci's conviction that everything worthwhile in modern civilization derived from Catholic, and especially medieval Catholic, sources was unoriginal.[22] As early as 1802, Chateaubriand had presented it in a rhapsodic series of historical vignettes, and forty years later the Catalan theological apologist Jaime Balmes sharpened and broadened it into an interpretation of European cultural history.[23]

Catholic possessiveness of the achievements of modernity held an ironic implication for the authority of the medieval tradition, which Gioacchino Pecci may not have fully appreciated. Throughout his pastoral letters the cause of civilization was in the forefront. He assumed that Roman Catholic apologists must prove that their church is indispensable for the preservation of civilized life, declared that civilization was still enjoying much admirable progress, and identified Catholicism with every aspect of such progress.[24] Whatever the cardinal's intentions, his approach implied that the advance of modern civilization is to some extent a norm that Catholicism must prove that it upholds. Ultimately, Cardinal Pecci's attempt to make modernity safe for Catholicism may have helped to make Catholicism safer for modernity. When, for example, he tried to dissipate fashionable notions of a protracted warfare between science and theology by invoking the example of Galileo as a believer, "to whom experimental philosophy is indebted for so powerful an impetus," the effect was potentially as explosive as what is said to follow after new wine is poured into old bottles.[25]

Similarly ironic was the implication of Cardinal Pecci's effort as pope to renew the achievement of Innocent III, the medieval predecessor on whose reign he modeled his own. Leo XIII's ambition was to recover for the papacy the combination

---

[21] *Church and Civilization* 37.

[22] *Church and Civilization* 7.

[23] See also François René de Chateaubriand, *Génie du christianisme, ou beautés de la religion chrétienne* (Paris, 1802), and Jaime Balmes, *El Protestantismo comparado con el Catolicismo en sus relaciones con las civilización europea*, 3 vols. (Barcelona: 1842–1844).

[24] *Church and Civilization* 7 and 12.

[25] *Church and Civilization* 45.

of undisputed authority over the institutional church and moral ascendancy throughout Western society that it had most fully exercised at the beginning of the thirteenth century.[26] Since church and society had long ago ceased to be one, the costs the papacy sometimes had to pay for increasing its secular influence were concessions to extrinsic values and diminished authority over Catholic opinion. The latent tension between the two objectives surfaced early in Leo's pontificate. In February 1880 the pope accepted an unfavorable compromise with Otto von Bismarck that would have at once blunted the German Empire's campaign of persecution against the Roman Catholic church and strengthened Bismarck's hand in the Reichstag. The parliamentary leader of the Catholic Center party, convinced that he was the victim of collusion between the pope and the chancellor, exclaimed, "Shot! Shot in the face! Shot in the back!" and balked at the scheme.[27] Notwithstanding the double-mindedness of Pope Leo's policy, it has exercised continuing appeal in the Vatican.

Æterni Patris possessed a rich background. It also had a potentially formidable authority. According to the norms that the Vatican insisted upon, Catholics were obliged to give to the doctrinal content of the encyclical their exterior and interior assent and their obedience.[28] Before 1878 the neo-Scholastic theologians had steadily gained ground at the expense of the Catholic eclectics. Pope Leo granted the insurgents what amounted to an official monopoly on the teaching of philosophical divinity, and he was able to impose his policy on the centralizing church he ruled. Personnel changes had begun in the Roman schools months before *Æterni Patris* appeared, and they would continue for years afterward. Yet even in Rome the ascendancy of neo-Thomism took decades to achieve. There were too few competent adherents to Thomism to sustain existing curriculums and too much confusion over the content of historical Thomism. Outside of Rome, the im-

---

[26]See also J. E. Ward, "Leo XIII: The Diplomat Pope," *Review of Politics* 28 (1966): 47–61.

[27]Margaret Lavinia Anderson, *Windthorst: A Political Biography* (Oxford: Oxford University Press, 1981) 284, and generally 273–95.

[28]John P. Boyle, "The Ordinary Magisterium: Towards a History of the Concept," *Heythrop Journal* 20 (1979): 380–98 and 21(1980): 14–29.

plementation of the Leonine program would take a couple of generations.[29]

Even after 1900, the impact of neo-Thomism was diffused by a stubborn imprecision about the actual content of Thomas's thought. It was a house of many mansions, or maybe a gallery of many mirrors, which allowed prelates and divines to cast reflections of their own opinions onto the Common Doctor. Techniques for reading old documents in their historical contexts were available, but most neo-Scholastics were slow to use them. Critical editions of the works of the greatest medieval doctors had yet to be produced, but even if those texts had existed, many theologians, schooled in an essentially unhistorical hermeneutics, would have been hard-pressed to understand how to read them contextually. When they meditated on the psalms every day, they relied on a figural interpretation. When the official church documents they read quoted the Bible, prooftexting was the norm. When they referred to recent commentaries on canon law, they were likely to face a lumping conceptualism that mimicked the European civil codes rather than the splitting categories of historical jurisprudence.[30] When reading Thomas's works, therefore, many of them easily found themselves first lifting a phrase here or an idea there and then developing it more or less according to the reading of some postmedieval expositor.

As long as the content of official Thomism was vague—as long as the often fundamental differences among thinkers as various as Bonaventure and Suarez and Duns Scotus and Cajetan could be ignored, and they could all be joined, as they were in *Æterni Patris*, in a timeless comity of masters teaching according to the mind of St. Thomas—then Thomism could be portrayed as the definitive theology of Catholicism.[31] Such

---

[29]Roger Aubert's "Aspects divers du néo-thomisme sous le pontificat de Léon XIII," in Giuseppe Rossini, ed., *Aspetti della cultura cattolica nell'età di Leone XIII* (Rome: Edizioni lune, 1961) 133–227, and "Le grand tournant de la faculté de théologie du Louvain à la veille de 1900," in André Duval, ed., *Mélanges offerts à M.-D. Chenu, maitre en théologie* (Paris: J. Vrin, 1967) 73–109, remain indispensable guides to the first decades of the Thomist revival.

[30]Stephan Kuttner, "The Code of Canon Law in Historical Perspective," *The Jurist* 28 (1968): 129–48.

[31]Leo XIII, *Æterni Patris* 42–43 (nos. 14–17).

generous vagueness was essential to Leo XIII's strategy. He proposed that the Catholic church should creatively imitate the philosophical divinity of the High Middle Ages rather than try to replicate it exactly.[32] Interpreting medieval theological pluralism as if it offered a pattern of unity permitted some measure of modern theological pluralism. No more could be reasonably demanded in the present than had been demanded in the past. When the content of official Thomism became more precisely determined, however, its serviceability as the universal theology diminished. Greater knowledge of the historical Thomas tended to foster rigid standards of theological correctness that threatened a suicidal proscription of ideas.

In 1914 the Vatican decreed that all Roman Catholic schools offering instruction in philosophy teach twenty-four theses derived from Thomas.[33] The decision raised insuperable difficulties for the largest Catholic teaching order. Most Jesuit philosophers and theologians were Suarezians rather than pure Thomists, and they were unable to teach all the mandated theses. It was as if the entire French professoriat were suddenly commanded to obey every edict on usage promulgated by the Academy and so, with the exception of a handful of purists, be threatened with speechlessness. Two years later a formal query inspired by the Jesuit general led the Vatican to reduce its decree to a recommendation.[34] Within a year the first universal code of canon law bound all who taught Catholic ordinands to follow absolutely "the method, doctrine, and principles of the Angelic Doctor." The canon footnoted an escape clause from its own requirement. Since the mitigating gloss of 1916 was cited as the last source for interpreting the canon, the canon itself had no binding force.[35]

---

[32]Karl F. Morrison, *The Mimetic Tradition of Reform in the West* (Princeton: Princeton University Press, 1982) 351–60, is instructive, though he perhaps works at a higher level of abstraction than the popes whose strategies he analyzes.

[33]Pope Pius X, "Doctoris Angelici," *Acta Apostolicae Sedis* 6 (1914): 336–41.

[34]"Decision of the Sacred Congregation of Seminaries and of University Studies, 7 March 1916," *Acta Apostolicae Sedis* 8 (1916): 156–57.

[35]*Codex Iuris Canonici* (1917), canon 468, n.4; see also canon 6.

Years before that suave maneuver was executed, greater accuracy about the content of Thomas's actual teaching was already inhibiting naive attempts to portray a unified Thomist tradition as the fountain of solutions to urgent modern questions. During 1890–1891 Pope Leo XIII commissioned two neo-Thomist theologians to draft *Rerum Novarum*, an encyclical that was elaborately commemorated last year as the beginning of modern papal social teaching. Charged to produce a document that would combat socialism and address growing social tensions, they found in Aquinas no justification for the modern idea of a natural right to private ownership. In two articles of the *Summa Theologiae*, Thomas considered, first, whether the collective human dominion over external things is natural and, then, whether it is lawful for individuals to possess such things as their own. Mingling quotations from the book of Genesis, Aristotle's *Politics* and Christian antiquity, Thomas allowed that the human race "as regards their use and management ... has a natural dominion over external things." Thereby we are collectively able to realize the reasonable potential of our nature without compromising the "preeminent dominion" over all creation that belongs to God. Having established that humanity's collective possession of things is natural, Thomas went on to assert both that individuals can licitly possess property—indeed that such possession is practically necessary to maintain orderly human life—and that no one "is entitled to manage things merely for himself, [but] he must do so in the interests of all." Thomas was convinced that the "distribution of property," is an instance of the "positive law," a construction put upon the natural law that is decided by human discretion and hence is variable. Elsewhere, Thomas insisted that cases of "urgent and blatant" individual need restore the natural community of goods. Those in misery may "supply [their] own needs out of another's property" and still be innocent of theft.[36]

---

[36]The translation of 2a2ae, 66, is found in Thomas Aquinas, *Summa Theologiae: Latin Text and English Translation*, vol. 38, trans. Marcus Lefébure (New York: McGraw-Hill, 1975) 63–69 and 81–83; see also Anthony Parel, "Aquinas's Theory of Property," in Anthony Parel and Thomas Flanagan, eds., *Theories of Property: Aristotle to the Present* (Waterloo, Ont.: Wilfred Laurier Press, 1979) 88–111. I have not seen Abdon Ma. C Josol, "Property and Natural

In abetting Jean Valjean's expropriation of candlesticks in 1815, Victor Hugo's bishop of Digne showed that he understood Thomas's idea of the basically communitarian nature of property. By the mid-nineteenth century, a number of Catholic theologians had seemingly forgotten the principle. Effectively appropriating John Locke's concept of private property as a natural right, they helped Catholicism to come to terms with the nineteenth-century regime of economic individualism.[37] The weightiest of the revisionists were Pope Leo's old teacher, Taparelli d'Azeglio, and his Jesuit confrere Matteo Liberatore. Both of them wrote influentially on social ethics before they commanded the earlier Catholic literature on the subject. Taparelli issued a treatise on natural law in 1840. Working quickly and with a shaky hold on the major Scholastic texts, he relied on a number of popularizers of Locke's doctrine. Writing a decade later, Liberatore, then an old-fashioned theological eclectic and only superficially acquainted with the pertinent writings of the medieval theologians, facilely annexed many of the modern authorities on whom Taparelli had relied to the "Scholastic tradition."[38]

By 1890 Liberatore, now an octogenarian and a convinced neo-Thomist, knew better.[39] His initial version of *Rerum Novarum* was rejected as insufficient. Whatever Leo XIII's precise objections to the draft, he was immune to the obsession of many European Catholic social theorists: trying to reorganize modern economies according to the allegedly corporative

---

Law in Rerum Novarum and the Summa Theologiae 2–2 66 1, 2, 7" (S.T.D. dissertation, Academia Alfonsiano, Rome, 1985).

[37]Friedrich Beutter, *Die Eigentumsbegründung in der Moraltheologie des 19. Jahrhunderts (1850–1900)*, Abhandlung zur Sozialethik, vol. 3 (Munich: Verlag Ferdinand Schoningh, 1971) 96–106.

[38]Léon de Sousberghe, "Propriété 'de droit naturel', thèse néo-scolastique et tradition scolastique," *Nouvelle revue théologique* 82 (*sic*; 1950): 593 n. 33 and 594 with n. 36.

[39]My account summarizes Ildefonso Camacho, "La propriedad privada en la 'Rerum Novarum.' Processo redaccional y texto definitivo de la encíclica," in *Miscelánea Augusto Segovia*, Biblioteca Teológica Granadina, 21 (Granada: Facultad de Teologia, 1986): 303–42.

guild system of the Middle Ages.[40] He wanted something more up-to-date, a document that could address and be heard by a world in which the provider state was being created and trade unions were organizing and striking. Cardinal Tommaso Zigliara, long a protégé of the pope, was then commissioned to prepare a second version. After ten more drafts that were increasingly closely supervised by the pope, a publishable text finally emerged.

Liberatore and Zigliara offered differing justifications of private property. Clinging to the old agrarian economy, Liberatore virtually identified all property with land. In his version, individual ownership was theoretically derived from the law of nations rather than from the law of nature and had somehow to provide for the common use of goods. Without invoking the *Summa Theologiae*, Liberatore produced a loose but recognizable extrapolation from Thomas's analysis. Elsewhere in his draft, however, he quoted Thomas directly but misinterpreted him as giving priority to individual ownership over the needs of the community. Liberatore seems never to have broken the habit of reading texts by dividing them into bites. A generation younger, Zigliara accepted modern commercial and industrial society and regarded private property as a natural right. His point of view prevailed. Yet like many others since John Locke, Zigliara ignored the split between personal labor and possession and derived the right of individual ownership from the figure of the simple laborer appropriating the fruits of his own work. Liberatore was not without influence, for he secured the deletion from the encyclical of Zigliara's proposed reference to the *Summa Theologiae* that muddled general dominion and individual ownership. No draft of *Rerum Novarum* invoked the ultimate source of its doctrine of private property: sections thirty-two through forty-eight of John Locke's *Second Treatise of Government*.[41] That was impossible. Locke had

---

[40]See also John W. Boyer, *Political Radicalism in Late Imperial Vienna: Origins of the Christian Social Movement* (Chicago: University of Chicago Press, 1981) 166–83.

[41]For a generation the import of Locke's theory of property has been the subject of an intense debate between those who see him as an ideological father of modern capitalist appropriation, such as C. B. MacPherson, *The Political Theory of Possessive Individualism: Hobbes to Locke* (Oxford: Oxford University Press, 1962), and others who link him to earlier, more sociable doctrines of

been a fixture of the Index of Forbidden Books since the 1730s and featured in the Catholic narrative of postmedieval philosophical decline as a contributor to modern materialism.[42]

In the end, the two ghosts produced a document that satisfied the pope. *Rerum Novarum* still seems clear-eyed in both its acceptance of the inevitable role of competing interests in modern economies and its recognition that the church has constructive obligations to modern society but only a limited competence to prescribe technical details of economic organization. Such at least was the judgment of Alcide de Gasperi. Convinced that changing the world requires a clear understanding of the ways of the world, the primary architect of contemporary Italy, while first a prisoner and then an outcast under Mussolini, wrote an intellectual history of the encyclical.[43] The durability of *Rerum Novarum* owes much to its endorsement of the natural right of private property. After decrying harmful novelties including the immiseration of "the majority of the working class," the encyclical marshaled a defense of individual ownership.[44] It asserted that "every man has by nature the right to possess property as his own"; maintained "that private ownership is in accordance with the law of

---

natural law; see James Tully, *A Discourse on Property: John Locke and His Adversaries* (Cambridge: Cambridge University Press, 1980). Since it jars to transpose Locke with either Herbert Spencer or Thomas Aquinas, I find persuasive mediating interpretations that present Locke as endeavoring to balance the competing claims of deserts and needs or private ownership and public stewardship but in the end stressing the rights of the owners of private property to the fruits of their industry. See also John C. Winfrey, "Charity Versus Justice in Locke's Theory of Property," *Journal of the History of Ideas* 42 (1981): 423–38, and Sibyl Schwarzenbach, "Locke's Two Conceptions of Property," *Social Theory and Practice* 14 (1988): 141–72.

[42]See also *Index librorum prohibitorum* (Rome: Typis polyglottis Vaticanis, 1917) 199, and [Cardinal] Zephirin Gonzalez, *Histoire de la philosophie*, trans. G. de Pascal, vol. 3 (Paris, 1891) 341–48.

[43]Mario Zanatta [Alcide De Gasperi], *I Tempi e gli uomini che prepararono la "Rerum Novarum"* (Milan: Vita e pensiero, 1931); see also Elisa A. Carrillo, *Alcide De Gasperi: The Long Apprenticeship* (Notre Dame: University of Notre Dame Press, 1965) 92, 94, and 101–2.

[44]Pope Leo XIII, *Rerum Novarum*, in Gilson, *The Church Speaks* 205–7 (nos. 1 and 3).

nature" because by "the activity of his mind and the strength of his body toward procuring the fruits of nature ... [one] makes his own that portion of nature's field which he cultivates—that portion on which he leaves, as it were, the impress of his personality"; and represented the principle of private ownership as being enshrined in "the common opinion of mankind," "consecrated" by "the practice of all ages," and "confirmed and enforced by the civil laws."[45]

Nowhere in that detailed analysis were the pertinent articles of the *Summa Theologiae* invoked to vindicate the asserted natural right of private property—indeed no authorities from the past are cited there. In any well-trod field, such an omission generally signaled that the papacy was proposing to depart from a traditional teaching. If Thomas or another medieval or ancient Christian authority could have plausibly been invoked to buttress the right of individual ownership, silence would have been inexplicable. Six months before the publication of *Rerum Novarum*, Pope Leo had assembled a pastiche of quotations from his predecessors to support the arguable point that the church had since late antiquity consistently anticipated modern civilized opinion in championing manumission, and in *Rerum Novarum* itself he pointedly contrasted the generosity of the good old days of Christendom with the rapacity of contemporary secular society.[46] By 1891 the official Catholic practice of invoking the authority of the past to legitimate virtually every current belief and practice had been ritualized to an unprecedented extent. The hold of that ritual would prove to be so tenacious that official Catholicism had to struggle for most of the twentieth century to acknowledge that it has been affected by the movement of history which is conventionally termed the development of doctrine.[47]

---

[45]*Rerum Novarum* 207–10 (nos. 6, 9, and 11).

[46]See also *Catholicae Eccelsiae* in [Mary] Claudia Carlen, ed., *The Papal Encyclicals, 1740–1978*, vol. 2 (n.p.: McGrath Publishing Co., 1981) 232–35, and John F. Maxwell, *Slavery and the Catholic Church: The History of Catholic Teaching Concerning the Moral Legitimacy of the Institutions of Slavery* (Chichester: Anti-Slavery Society, 1975) 116–22; *Rerum Novarum* 206–7 and 220 (nos. 3 and 27).

[47]R. Guelluy, "Les Antécédents de l'encyclique 'Humani Generis' dans les sanctions romains de 1942: Chenu, Charlier, Draguel," *Revue d'histoire ec-*

When *Rerum Novarum* appeared, it was not just unthinkable to trumpet a modification of tradition in favor of novelty but necessary somehow to associate contemporary official teaching on a subject with the most respectable earlier opinion. Hence the encyclical eventually cited the *Summa Theologiae* in an effort to identify it with the idea that individual ownership is a natural right. The result is a long, dense paragraph juxtaposing divergent visions of the economic organization of society.[48] The section begins with a warning to the rich that they "should tremble at the threatenings of Jesus Christ." It goes on successively 1) to reassert that "private ownership ... is the natural right of man"; 2) to quote Thomas on the legality and practical necessity of holding private property; 3) to invoke "without hesitation" his words to answer the question, "How must one's possessions be used?"—Thomas is accurately quoted as having written, "Man should not consider his material possessions as his own but as common to all"; 4) to maintain that "no one is commanded to distribute to others" what possessions are required either to meet personal and household needs or "to keep up becomingly [one's] condition in life"; and 5) to associate Thomas's notion of common ownership with almsgiving, which is declared to be "a duty, not of justice (save in extreme cases), but of Christian charity—a duty not enforced by human law."

Rerum Novarum never acknowledged its more radical departure from Thomas's principles. He had not made the institution of private property an element of the natural law, but he believed in the concept of the natural law, a set of obligations to the Creator that are imposed on human beings to enable them to fulfill the imperatives of their nature. Thomas appears, in contrast, to have failed to elaborate a doctrine of unconditional natural rights, a set of inalienable dues like private property to which all human beings are entitled because of their nature. The shift from the concept of law to that of right, from the idea of a natural obligation to the idea of a natural due, is obvious in English because a different word designates each concept. In both Latin and Italian, however, a

---

clésiastique 81(1986): 421–97, is a judicious introduction to a topic more often alluded to than studied.

[48] Leo XIII, *Rerum Novarum* 217–18 (no. 22).

single word can be used indiscriminately for both of them: *ius* in the case of Latin and *diritto* in that of Italian.

Even so, Italians knew the difference between homonyms and synonyms. Pope Gregory XVI had repeatedly demonstrated that he was perfectly aware that laws were one thing and rights quite another. In 1832, for example, he had invoked "the most holy precepts of the Christian religion" to "condemn the detestable insolence and improbity of those who, consumed with the unbridled lust for freedom, are entirely devoted to impairing and destroying all rights of dominion while bringing servitude to the people under the slogan of liberty."[49] That unblushing reactionary was invulnerable to the kind of defensiveness that would occasionally seize later English-speaking apologists when they confronted accusations that their church was hostile to human rights.[50] Neither did Pope Gregory anticipate neo-Scholastic efforts to merge natural law and natural rights doctrines by positing that since humans naturally have God-given duties to perform, God must also have endowed them by nature with the means they need to discharge those duties.[51] Although official Catholicism would develop a coherent doctrine of human rights only in the mid-twentieth century when it finally accepted the normativeness of liberal democracy and complete religious liberty, none of Pope Gregory's successors tried to sustain the full pitch of his tone of defiance. Leo XIII for his part was constitutionally disposed to write more easily about natural human obligations than about natural human rights. With a few exceptions, his treatments of natural rights were hedged with qualifications and restrictions.[52] He nonetheless accepted that many modern rights were undeniable social realities and declared private property to be an effectively inalienable right. More than any earlier pope, Pope Leo officially sanctioned Catholic invocations of human rights.

---

[49]Gregory XVI, *Mirari Vos*, in Carlen, *Papal Encyclicals* 1:239 (no. 19).

[50]For example [A. Young], "Catholicity and Human Rights," *American Catholic Quarterly* 14 (1889): 387–409.

[51][Cardinal] Tommaso Maria Zigliara, *Summa philosophica in usum scholarum*, new ed., vol. 3 (Lyons: 1893) 123–24.

[52]See also Pope Leo XIII, *Libertas Praestantissimum* (1888), in Gilson, *The Church Speaks* 57–85.

The conflation of natural law and natural rights in *Rerum Novarum* seemingly went unnoticed, but there was no escaping its tilt away from medieval communitarianism toward modern individualism. Later commentators on the encyclical had to face two primordial issues of hermeneutics—"whether you *can* make words mean so many different things" and "which is to be master," you or the words. Several presuppositions ordinarily informed Catholic discussions of both issues. Despite the qualifications favored by professional theologians who studied the category of tradition, Catholicism was widely felt to be a completely integrated and largely institutionalized system of practices and beliefs. Its present form had elaborated over 1,900 years with something like syllogistic inexorability, much as a conclusion follows from the earlier premises in which it is implicit. The present, therefore, has always been potential in the past. Hierarchical authority—above all the papacy—is uniquely competent to determine the content of that potential by explaining what the past really meant.[53] Pio Nono probably never declared, "La tradizione son'io," but for nearly a century many Catholic academics, seemingly aspiring to be more papal than the pope, wrote as if they accepted the principle.[54] Whatever a pope officially taught had to be consonant with earlier Catholic teachings—and above all with the teachings of Thomas Aquinas—even if a pope had neglected to assert such consonance.

In the aftermath of *Rerum Novarum*, the habit of identifying the content of the Catholic tradition with the process of its transmission in papal teaching spawned a theological cottage industry. Acting on instinct and without any central direction, many theologians sought to reinterpret the communitarianism of major Christian writers of late antiquity and the Middle Ages so as to make them, if not quite advocates of the natural right of private property, at least antisocialists. Few commentators were as brash as one young American: "None of the Fathers either explicitly or implicitly denied the right of private

---

[53]Notwithstanding a modest subtitle, Yves M.J. Congar, *Tradition and Traditions: An Historical and a Theological Essay*, trans. Michael Naseby and Thomas Rainborough (London: Burns and Oates, 1966) is magisterial; see particularly 177–229.

[54]For Pius's alleged remark, see Roger Aubert, *Le pontificat de Pie IX (1846–1878)*, *Histoire d'église*, vol. 21 (Paris: Bloud & Gay, 1952) 354.

property.... All the doubtful passages can and should be explained in a sense consistent with the belief in private ownership [i.e., with the teaching of Leo XIII]; and ... there are other passages in the writings of these Fathers which show beyond question that such was their belief."[55] There were less ingenuous ways of preserving at least the appearance of a univocal—or at any rate a consistent—Catholic doctrine of property. To lift the words "justice" and "necessity" and "right" from their historical contexts and to group them together as if they were synonymous was to insinuate a fundamental unity of principle between the thirteenth and the nineteenth centuries without having to prove it or even to assert it.[56]

More sophisticated and widespread was the effort to represent Leo XIII's teaching on the right of private property as a homologous development of Thomas's. It depended on an early-modern simplification of Thomas's theory of law. Differentiating the eternal law of nature from the laws that are commonly observed in all nations and the laws of nations from the positive laws that are peculiar to some communities, he presented individual ownership as a matter of positive law. During the late sixteenth century, a number of Spanish thinkers made a clear-cut division between primary and secondary natural laws, which left uncertain the basis of everything that Thomas had included in either the laws of nations or positive law. Francisco Suarez dealt with the uncertainty by classifying the laws common to all the nations as general conclusions of the law of nature, "not absolutely and necessarily but in comparison with the specific determination of civil and private law."[57] Taking a similar line in 1925, a theologian from the Catholic faculty at the University of Tübingen maintained that

---

[55]John A. Ryan, *The Alleged Socialism of the Church Fathers* (St. Louis: Herder 1913) 18.

[56]V. Cathrein, in the *Catholic Encyclopedia* (1911), s.v. "property."

[57]Francisco Suarez, *De legibus*, in Carolo Berton, ed. *Opera omnia*, vol. 5 (Paris: 1866) 169–70 (2, 20, 2; see also 2, 19, 6, and 8). Quentin Skinner, *The Foundations of Modern Political Thought*, vol. 2, *The Reformation* (Cambridge: Cambridge University Press, 1978) 151–54, gives a summary of those developments, which includes the assertion that "the right to hold property had always been treated in the Thomist theory of political society as part of the law of nature"—a useful reminder that Thomas's teaching on property can elude even distinguished non-Catholic scholars.

Thomas had treated private property not as a natural law "in the strictest sense" but rather as one of the laws of nations, which made it a "category" or "institution" of natural law. Once private property was elevated above a mere positive law, Pope Leo could be plausibly depicted as having simply brought fuller clarity to a consistent Catholic teaching about property by developing Thomas's ideas.[58]

By the 1930s a new set of interpretive conventions was becoming necessary. The weakness of earlier readings had become plain, especially when the papacy in response to the apparent meltdown of liberal capitalism embarked on the course that it has thereafter generally pursued: qualifying *Rerum Novarum* by stressing with greater or lesser urgency the priority of social obligations over the individual right to property.[59] Even American Catholic graduate students knew that in Thomas "the emphasis is upon the common good of society," though they discretely avoided contrasts between his teaching and that of *Rerum Novarum*.[60] Senior European academics who had to write about Catholic social ethics could adopt a

[58]Otto Schilling, "Die Eigentumslehre des Hl. Thomas von Aquin und Leos XIII," in Sadoc Szabo, ed., *Xenia Thomistica*, vol. 1 (Rome: Typis polyglottis Vaticanis, 1925) 461–74; on the evidence of J.S. Hickey, *Summula philosophiae scholasticae in usum adolescentium*, 7th ed., vol. 3 (New York: Benzinger, 1934) 447 n.1 and 452–53, such an interpretation was commonplace among neo-Thomists.

[59]Sandor Horvath, *Eigentumsrecht nach den Heiligen Thomas von Aquin* (Graz: Ulrich Mosers Verlag, 1929) raised troubling possibilities and seems to have caused ripples in unlikely places. See also Joseph Biederlack, "Zu P. Horvath's 'Eigentumsrecht nach den Heiligen Thomas von Aquin,'" *Theologisch-Praktische Quartalschrift* 38 (1930): 524–35, and "Accord de la doctrine de S. Thomas et de l'enseignement de Léon XIII," *L'Ami du clergé* 48 (1931): 657–64; Pope Pius XI, *Quadragesimo Anno* (1931), in Terence P. McLaughlin, ed., *The Church and the Reconstruction of the Modern World: The Social Encyclicals of Pius XI* (Garden City, NY: Doubleday Image Books, 1957) 234–35 (nos. 45–48); Jose Maria Díez-Alegría summarizes the twentieth-century history in "Ownership and Labour: The Development of Papal Teaching," in John Coleman and Gregory Baum, eds., *Rerum Novarum: One Hundred Years of Catholic Social Teaching, Concilium* (London: SCM Press, 1991) 18–23.

[60]Casimir J. Czajkowski, "The Theory of Private Property in John Locke's Political Philosophy" (Ph.D. dissertation, University of Notre Dame, 1941) 73 and 102.

similar tactic. They avoided exposing the tension between modern official teaching and medieval ideas. Hence the article on property in the most distinguished Roman Catholic theological encyclopedia of our century begins its treatment of "Traditional Catholic Teaching on the Right of Property" with Pope Leo XIII, as though he had been the first notable Catholic to address the subject.[61] The developments of the interwar years could spur the ingenuity of clerics who wanted to read Thomas Aquinas on property through the shifting lens of papal encyclicals. One priest successively denounced the baleful influence of Locke's economic ideas, hailed Leo for having solved the social question by returning to Thomas, and attributed to Thomas a doctrine of "socialized private property," which managed to avoid "the extremes of selfish possession and violent dispossession."[62] The author would die as a bishop.

Another approach was to indicate the differences between the past and the present without drawing excessive attention to them. At the beginning of fat books, general statements about the acceptance of economic individualism during the Middle Ages could be paraded ("Private ownership was considered to be in accord with the nature of man. Private property is a normal expression of man's right of ownership"); hundreds of pages later nullifying qualifications were introduced (according to Thomas Aquinas, "Each individual man does not have in his nature the right to private ownership, in the sense that strict justice would be violated if he were not an owner").[63] Only in 1950 did a Catholic scholar detail insistently in print the radical divergence between the teaching of *Rerum Novarum* about property and that of Thomas Aquinas and other medieval Scholastics.[64] Theologians bent on reconciling the Leonine and Thomist teachings, on vindicating, if

---

[61]J. Tonneau, in the *Dictionnaire de théologie catholique* (1937), s.v. "propriété."

[62]William J. McDonald, *The Social Value of Property According to St. Thomas Aquinas* (Washington: Catholic University Press, 1939) v, 103–6, 119–26, and 185.

[63]John F. Cronin, *Catholic Social Principles: The Social Teaching of the Catholic Church Applied to American Economic Life* (Milwaukee: Bruce, 1950) 15 and 477.

[64]De Sousberghe, "Propriété de droit naturel" 580–607.

not their essential identity, at least their essential continuity, sought to disregard the revelation that Pope Leo XIII's encyclical proposed a natural right unknown to Thomas.[65] Theirs might seem to have been a twilight exercise. Catholics would after all soon find themselves wrangling over far more crucial matters than the provenance of Pope Leo's endorsement of the natural right of private property. In the event, efforts continue to homogenize the economic teachings of medieval and nineteenth-century churchmen.[66]

Alice and Humpty Dumpty believed that hermeneutics demand an unequivocal choice: "'The question is,' said Alice, 'whether you *can* make words mean so many different things'"; "'the question is,' said Humpty Dumpty, 'which is to be master—that's all.'" Most of us expect less clarity than either the little girl or the talking egg. We admit that both of them had a point. The number of meanings that any word can possess is ultimately limited, but words are never totally self-defining. Hence people must try to master words by pinning down their meanings. In seeking to revive and to impose the authority of Thomas Aquinas, official Catholicism learned the truth of those lessons. To survive in a world gripped by change, an ancient and embattled church not only had to preserve a sense of its basic continuity, it also had in some measure to reconcile itself and to come to terms with modern civilization. In privileging neo-Thomism, Pope Leo XIII believed he had found a living tradition that would allow his church to adapt when necessary but within limits that could be officially determined. He seems to have underestimated the possibility that his desire to accommodate the realities of his own society could exhaust the conceivable meanings of many of the old words he had authorized. Unless some Orwellian memory hole exists to devour words from the past, they retain a life of their own and with it the power to contend for mastery with those who seek to master them. In such a contest, human beings

---

[65] J. Y. Calvez and J. Perrin, *Eglise et société économique: l'enseignement social des Papes de Léon XIII à Pie XII, 1878–1958*, 2d ed. (Paris: Aubier, 1959) 259–68.

[66] For example, Matthew Habiger, *Papal Teaching on Private Property: 1891–1981* (Lanham, Md.: University Press of America, 1990) 39–40, 330–31, and 346.

can resist, fall silent, or look for new words to voice the requisite new meanings.

The vocabulary of Catholic cultural medievalism eventually resisted its human masters and so came to outlive its usefulness to them. By the middle of the twentieth century, official Catholicism was rediscovering what Cardinal La Luzerne had known in the 1820s. Modernity requires adaptation to a variety of realities unimagined in the thirteenth century. At the same time increasingly detailed research into the intellectual history of the High Middle Ages had exposed a world often alien enough to baffle accommodation to modern categories and needs. During the Barcelona Olympic Games we became too familiar with a spectacular monument of the possibilities and limits of Catholic cultural medievalism: the unfinished transept of the church of the Sagrada Familia. Its boldly crenulated spires rise from a staid neo-Gothic portal to remind us that in religion as in art works of manifest originality have often begun as tributes to the authority of the past.

PURITANS IN BABYLON:
The Ancient Near East and the Revolution in Intellectual Life, 1880–1930

Bruce Kuklick

In 1888 the University of Pennsylvania sent out the first United States archæological expedition to the Near East. In the next twelve years the Americans excavated near the biblical Babylon, at Nippur, the religious and educational center of ancient Mesopotamia. During this period they unearthed tens of thousands of cuneiform tablets that since then have given scholars the basic evidence for our knowledge of Sumer, generally regarded as the world's oldest known civilization.

This essay has three connected goals. The first is to tell the story of the dig. My larger purposes, however, are to connect this story to some problems that have occupied intellectual historians of the late nineteenth and early twentieth century. These problems concern the history of the American university and the professionalization of knowledge. That examination in turn will allow me to explore the bases of modern historical thinking and in widest terms the conflict between the sacred and the secular in the last one hundred years. Many different stories have been told about the conflict. I do not mean to claim uniqueness for the one that follows, but I do mean to build out from it to take up in a somewhat different fashion issues that are significant, even if familiar from other stories.

In the 1880s a committee of wealthy Philadelphians contracted with the university to fund an expedition to Iraq—then called Mesopotamia. Pennsylvania itself promised to construct a fireproof building to house any antiquities that were found, aside from the tokens that would go to the financial contributors. The tasks of mounting and staffing an expedition were enormous. It ordinarily took almost two months to make the trip to England, to Germany, through south-central Europe to Constantinople, and then through the Ottoman Empire to Baghdad and then to Nippur. Each leg of the trip was, from the American view, more primitive and time-consuming. Supplies were usually purchased in London and shipped to Baghdad. Although portions of the journey could be abbreviated, stopovers in Constantinople and Baghdad were mandatory, always to placate functionaries of the Turkish government and its representatives, sometimes to secure necessary permits.

Once the explorers got to their destination, disease, loneliness, and the hostility of the locals took their toll. The turnaround time for mail was three months. The diaries and letters of the participants show that they were soon engaged in a war of each against all. On the first dig, for example, each of the five Americans was jealous for the fame a successful venture would bring, and self-promotion and the desire for preferment quickly overcame joint aspirations. Arduous living conditions and ambition exacerbated petty animosities; personal idiosyncrasies flowered in an exotic environment that undermined Victorian decorum.

The Americans had a taste for this kind of adventure, but many soon had their bellies full. Penn waged four campaigns, as they were called, in the desolate surroundings of the buried city. The initial one excavated in the first part of 1889 and ended with a deadly raid by Arab warriors on the retreating caucasians; the second excavated in the first half of 1890; the third for thirty-six months from 1893 to 1896; the last for almost a year in 1899–1900.

The most committed proponent of the first dig, John Peters, dropped out completely after 1890 and instead ministered to an affluent Manhattan church. John Henry Haynes, who was the photographer of the first expedition, was the only person continuously active for the whole period and, indeed, was the sole educated Westerner at the scene for most of the long third trip. He paid a price. Only Haynes's solitary personality made it possible for him to sustain his commitment, but in any event he suffered some kind of mental breakdown toward the end of the dig. His collapse was probably triggered by the fact that, in the middle of this expedition, he hired a young American in Baghdad, Joseph Meyer, as an architect. Haynes was soon on intimate terms with Meyer, but within six months Meyer had died a horrible, lingering death from fever. Soon after, Haynes's letters home began to sound disturbed. When the university later persuaded him to return to Nippur to lead the final campaign, he went only on the condition that his new wife accompany him. Complete with pith helmet, she was carried to Babylon in a sedan chair. In addition to these dramatis personae, many academics and hangers-on taking bit parts came and went, unable or unwilling to stick it out at Nippur.

In deciding to stake a claim in the area, the Americans were complexly motivated. They wanted to give U.S. researchers the opportunity to do original work on long-dead cultures. In particular they wanted to uncover the full history of the lands that were featured in the Old Testament. In general one cannot doubt the intrinsic importance and fascination of the distant past to these nineteenth century men of leisure and learning *and* the way this past had left traces in the present. Nonetheless, they were as much creating as discovering what came to be known as the Ancient Near East. One cannot dissociate archæological triumphs from their connection to Western ideas about progress and civilization that grew up coordinately with the construction and reconstruction of ancient Mesopotamian culture. The remains of scattered cities variously occupied for over two thousand years were used to tell a peculiar story. The narrative showed how a single civilization—that of the Ancient Near East—contributed to that of the early Judeo-Christian world and, consequently, to the linear evolution that led to the urban West.

Accomplishing these partisan goals involved the expenditure of a great deal of money. The costly accumulation of antiquities was necessary to provide evidence for the story. Objects were not only material rewards but also physical signs of the past. University officials were under the spell of the successes of Henry Austen Layard who had dug at Nineveh in the 1840s and brought back to London the great pieces of Assyrian sculpture that helped to make the British Museum the premier place to study the peoples of the Old Testament. The main focus of the American explorers thus became the acquisition of cultural treasures. The Penn archæologists wanted big objects—large works of art; they ultimately had to be satisfied with tens of thousands of inscribed bricks.

Edward Said's 1978 *Orientalism* is hyperbolic in claiming that Orientalism is the highest stage of capitalism, but many other critics of philanthropic imperialism have argued that archæology was another form of Victorian theft from colonial lands. As an easy generalization, this judgment is sound enough. American universities attempted to staff their expeditions with competent people, but they were hard to come by. People with experience were almost nonexistent. Although most were clergymen, there was a chasm between scholars of the ancient languages and people who simply enjoyed adventures in the field. The epigraphers, or "Assyriologists," were not interested in the details of excavation or in the importance of nonlinguistic evidence in the reconstructions of civilizations. They preferred to stay at home and examine the cuneiform tablets shipped back from Mesopotamia. The chief diggers had little ability at translating the old scripts and, in the case of the Penn expedition, were selected mainly because they were adventurous sorts with strong constitutions. Even before the turn of the century architects and photographers served as assistants, the idea being to bring as much expertise to bear on a site as possible, but the level of skill was rudimentary. The result was that early archæologists ripped up the sites of ancient cities with only the vaguest ideas of what they were doing aside from systematically collecting trophies.

If this was theft, however, it was theft of a unique kind. The western European powers and the Americans were assisted in their work by a corrupt Ottoman Empire whose complicity was not merely due to its weakness. In Mesopotamia itself, a distantly governed province of the empire, leaders did not regard the archæologists as thieves. The locals were sometimes upset when they (mistakenly) thought the Americans were carrying off gold or silver or precious jewelry. But for the most part the locals looked upon the Westerners as economic benefactors, employers of labor, and often eagerly went out of their way to sell antiquities to any buyer they could find.

The University of Pennsylvania enterprise is a landmark in archæology. In addition to the recovery of Sumer and the discovery of the tablets—among many other things they contained the Sumerian ancestor of the Babylonian epic *Gilgamesh*—the expeditions made America a competitive archæological force among the Western countries. On the eve of World War I, the Americans participated in the breakdown of Turkish authority in Mesopotamia and shared the struggles of the European imperial powers—mainly Germany and England—for influence with Istanbul. The Penn academics also intrigued with the moribund Ottoman Empire to gain an advantage over other scholars in the United States.

These occurrences were part of the emergence of archæology as an academic discipline, the problem in American history that is my second focus. To sketch the contours of this problem I begin with Penn's German Assyriological connection.

In the nineteenth century, German scholarship was thougnt to be the best in the world; its ideals attracted many American institutions, and they actively competed to secure young German Doktors trained in Berlin seminars. The Germans who came to the United States were a fascinating lot. They were, overall, extremely intelligent and well trained. But they had to be powerfully motivated to uproot their lives and come to a provincial academic culture of second-rate status. The motivation was often a driving desire for recognition coupled with a sense of the impediments that the German system would throw up to them (some were Jewish). The net effect was that these German scholars were successful in academic terms in the United States. They were also, by and large, contemptuous of the culture that had offered them such opportunity and remained ultimately German in their loyalty. Their foreign accents were as noticeable as their Kaiser Wilhelm mustaches.

Penn's contribution to this German-American character type was Herman Hilprecht, who came from Leipzig as the university's first Assyriologist. Hilprecht had little interest in field archæology and was as bad at it as his peers, although he did pontificate about the need for *wissenschaftliche* (scientific) excavation and the obvious inadequacies of those Americans charged with the actual responsibility for the digging. His forte was as a scholar of cuneiform inscription, and he parlayed his gifts into the creation of a monograph series that centered on his transcriptions of Nippur documents. He thus put himself at thc hub of thc publishing empire critical to the development of the field of Assyriology in the United States.

In order to achieve his goal he found himself derogating the achievements of the other members of the expedition, indeed blaming them for all the real (and even imagined) failings of the dig. At the same time he wanted credit for the scholarly successes that became more apparent as more material was shipped back to the United States. Hilprecht's academic personality had been an issue for the Americans from the time he had complained on the first expedition that he had been made to ride an inferior horse on the journey to Babylon. His published complaints about the abilities of his colleagues soon after the end of the dig in the early 1900s led to a bitter dispute over who was the worse exemplar of archæological method, Hilprecht or his foes.

The "Hilprecht controversy" was a major event in American and international archæology from 1903 through 1911. It resulted, at one point, in a mass resignation of archæologists at Penn, and pitted the university against representatives of its semiautonomous museum. The case became a local scandal, involving Penn scholars as well as the Philadelphia social elite; an academic battle affecting learned circles at Harvard, Yale, Johns Hopkins, and Chicago as well as Penn; and an international imbroglio, generally pitting the British and the Americans against the Germans. When it ended, shortly before World War I, Hilprecht was driven out of the university. He returned to Germany with some 2,500 tablets from the dig. For the Americans this theft was a fitting corroboration of their view of Hilprecht in particular and Germans in general.

The Hilprecht controversy typified cultural differences between the United States and Europe and highlighted national academic and social rivalries. German *Wissenschaft* attracted Americans, but many aspects of the German approach repelled them. Historians have heretofore paid no attention to archæology in their many studies of the professoriat in the United States. Yet the field is of special interest. At all institutions the dramatic archæological efforts received wide public recognition. The donations of the wealthy paid for expeditions, and they often relied upon the genius of well-to-do adventurous young men. Institutions of higher learning drew both on mass appeal and on the financial resources of a cultural elite. Universities transformed romantic encounters with the distant past into an academic enterprise that has a popular and social cachet even today.

The Hilprecht controversy was critical in giving shape to this undertaking. During this period Americans crystallized their national identity. They wanted to distinguish themselves from the arrogance of the German approach, which, they thought, led to scholarly dishonesty. Although the differences were more in tone and style than substance, the American archæologists formulated an implicit code of professional behavior, an articulation of their practice.

To put matters in a shorthand familiar to students of intellectual history, archæology became professionalized at a somewhat later date than other academic disciplines in the United States. Specifically, the Hilprecht controversy aided in the building of a hierarchical apprenticeship program with workers serving in a series of roles supervised by a mentor who himself had served an apprenticeship on a dig. A formal division of labor between field archæologists and Assyriologists emerged. The need for other kinds of specialization was accepted. Institutional funding for digs became regularized. A conscious effort was made to distinguish robbery from what went on in the discipline, and careful, standardized digging procedures became the norm. The mistakes of the Penn campaign, which left Nippur a shambles, served as the basis for an altered conception of what archæology was about.

Let me now turn to my third aim, which is paramount. Archæologists played a crucial role in establishing what I call the basis of the modern notion of history.

Intellectual life at the turn of the twentieth century was characterized by increasing secularization, a process of crucial moment in archæology. The deep Christian purpose of many early Near Eastern archæologists is striking—from it comes the title of this essay. Yet the attempts to grasp the shape of the ancient world often led these pious men of knowledge away from religion. The central irony in the growth of the discipline was the manner in which the pursuit of the truth of the Bible allowed for the undermining of its truth.

The history of the negative impact of nineteenth-century historical studies on sacred truths is well known, but the specific role of archæology in this process is unexplored. Digs and their results contributed to a new understanding of the past.

Let me start with an issue that is conceptually easy but that is of enormous substantive significance. The Americans went to the urban sites of Ancient Near Eastern civilization at a time in their own cultural life when intellectuals discovered the closing of the frontier at home and looked abroad at the possibility of an American empire. Although many thinkers were anti-imperialists, they also came to believe that the torch of Western civilization had been passed from Greece and Rome to Britain and now, at the dawn of the new century, to the United States.

The Americans in Mesopotamia hence carried with them an idea of the greatness of their own culture, defined by economic strength, a war making capacity, and enduring political and religious institutions. Indeed, that idea perhaps helped to convince them that Mesopotamian civilization was itself great: the tablets and art showed that it had similar characteristics. But the decay and waste around them also made the Americans at times reflect morbidly about the impermanence of things. They delighted in quoting the biblical prophecies about the destruction that fell on the Assyrians. They knew their Shelley:

> I met a traveller from an antique land
> Who said: "Two vast and trunkless legs of stone
> Stand in the desert ....
> ....
> And on the pedestal these words appear:
> My name is Ozymandias, King of Kings,
> Look on my Works, ye Mighty and despair! ...
> Round the decay
> Of that colossal Wreck, boundless and bare
> The lone and level sands stretch far away."

One source of the interest in Ozymandias, I think, was the desire to contrast the transience of non-Christian spirituality to the eternal truth of the religion of Jesus. But the traces of the seemingly fleeting religious traditions were so dramatic that they experientially contributed to a growing uncertainty about received religious truth. The conception not just of ancient civilizations in the Near East and India but of *the rise and fall* of these civilizations mitigated against any simple religious commitment. As archæologists popularized their discoveries in the twentieth century, comparative civilization or comparative religion became an attractive area of research, and what philosophers have called the speculative philosophy of history developed. Oswald Spengler, H. G. Wells, Arnold Toynbee, Pitirim Sorokin, and Eric Vogelin all depended on archæological knowledge in their writings. They struggled to find meaning within history but within a history that human inventiveness and discovery had enriched. Extrahistorical meaning was diminished.

Most strikingly, supernatural events—miracles—were ruled out. If God did exist, his existence had to be determined by the ordinary processes that defined human life, not by anything outside these processes. Examining the histories of various civilizations sometimes led later generations of scholars to postulate that every culture pursued activities that could be called religious. But the differences among these activities usually precluded the commitment of the impartial investigator to any one religion as "true." At best, even spiritually inclined academics often would end up merely proclaiming a special human need for myth or for nonempirical symbols—a far cry from the robust Protestantism of the first generation of archæologists who set out to "prove" the Old Testament.

Let me turn now to the more interesting conceptual dimension that revolutionized our ideas about the past. I will not take up the direct ways in which archæological knowledge contributed to the assault on Christianity connected to the higher criticism of the Bible. For those interested in this issue, however, it should be mentioned that Old Testament higher criticism came increasingly to depend on archæological research. Made prominent by Julius Wellhausen, this criticism was different from and more complex than the attack that derived from New Testament criticism reflected in the work of David Strauss's *Leben Jesu*. These matters aside, I want to look at the techniques of investigation that emerged in archæology.

The most simple and powerful was that of seriation, of judging deposits lower in a series of deposits as being evidence of something older rather than something higher. Cities built and rebuilt on a site over a long period left traces of themselves in strata of debris. Out of observation of this fact archæology developed a logic of stratigraphy that had its first early perfection in the work of the British Egyptologist Flinders Petrie, who worked out a system of relative dating. In his research different sorts of pottery were placed in an order from earlier to later.

It is plausible to argue that strata are as much interpreted as given, and there has been no dearth of inconclusive argument about the time something occurred, the proximity of different occurrences, and their *order*. Nonetheless, the manner in which archæologists constructed a temporal continuum forced them to confront fundamental problems in the mind's construction of succession in time. At Nippur archæologists reordered and extended their chronology by some two thousand years, disputing all the while. What they did not—indeed could not—dispute was that there *was* a temporal ordering going from earlier to later, from before to after. This they could not think away; the nature of this sort of order only came to clear consciousness in the practice of archæology but it reflected a priori ideas that could not be dispensed with. The chronicle-like history the Assyriologists wrote—one king after another—in part mirrored the fact that they had very little evidence to build a story of Mesopotamian life around. In part, however, chronology was simply crucial to what archæologists found themselves doing. The establishment of dates became a sign of the objectivity of their endeavor.

Place had a similar role as time at Nippur. Hilprecht's contention that he had unearthed certain cuneiform tablets in a certain place in part fueled the controversy. Their position in one hill at Nippur was critical evidence for his discovery of Sumerian literary culture. As I read the documents in this elaborate debate, it is impossible to tell where the tablets came from. It is also likely that were the disputants to have agreed on the original location of the bricks, the location would have ceased to have been the compelling piece of evidence that it was thought to have been: by that time Hilprecht and his enemies hated one another so much that they would have found something else to quarrel about. Nonetheless, all disputants supposed that objects were truly located somewhere. That is, spatial location played a role in their methodological arguments analogous to temporal ordering.

Things existed at certain times. The discovery of such things and the determination of their age were tasks that all agreed could be accomplished. No one disputed that there was one correct answer to each question of where and when. The concentration on the discovery of a fundamental spatio-temporal ordering, I believe, helped give archæology its reputation for objectivity. It is about fundamental, bedrock truths that can literally be excavated.

The coming into being of modern archæology thus had a devastating effect on religion. Scholars were rewarded for establishing precise information of time and place. The rewards universities were able to grant to professors—money, students, personal advancement, leisure time—all prompted displays of selfishness as one individual or another attempted to demonstrate that some bit of knowledge was *his* intellectual property. The focus shifted from the truth of Old Testament narratives and from the truth of the Bible to truths about the changing character of the spatio-temporal world that, although shared by all, were the unique possession of one scholar or another. At the end of the nineteenth century Near Eastern archæology *was* biblical. At the end of the twentieth century, "biblical archæology" is still an area of inquiry in which there is room for Judeo-Christian theological sensibilities, but it is a suspect subfield that has split off from archæology proper. Digging for institutions of higher learning made scholars concentrate not on their Bibles but on the relation of their careers to an ancient framework in space and time that had little to do with religion.

While field archæologists agreed on these basics, epigraphers were engaged in the impressive accomplishment of deciphering the ancient languages. Although many of these achievements antedated Nippur, the discovery of the tablets there hastened and made easier the decipherment of Sumerian cuneiform and the translation of the *Gilgamesh* epic. In looking at the principles that underlie all the translation projects, one finds that they involve bilinguals. A language that is in some measure known helps in the understanding of one that is unknown. In deciphering the languages, the epigraphers say explicitly, or assume, that the meanings of a known language are somehow commensurate with those of an unknown language. In rare cases when the scholars start at all from scratch, they base their work on the premise that the writers of texts think in some critical way as we do. How else could one begin to undertake such a project? What else would one mean in calling what one was concerned with a language in the first place? Or, more controversially: language for the epigraphers embodied meanings or intentions that are similar across time and culture, that are at least potentially shareable.

It need not be the case that what past peoples said about the world had to be true. The center of historical reasoning rested on the view that to grasp the truth the historian had to translate past peoples' ideas into an idiom that was compatible with our best contemporary sense of the way the world is.

This contemporary sense was of a spatio-temporal world, that is, a world whose interactions were causally governed. The main reason for ruling out biblical miracles was that the world as we know it to be did not permit their occurrence; we had to reinterpret what ancient redactors said happened into our best sense of what could have happened given that the world then, as now, was one of objects in space and time. A core philosophical problem of the twentieth century was to justify how it could be that human meaning of any sort was "inscribed" in or onto the world of objects.

F. H. Bradley talked about the new forms in which we understood the past as "the presuppositions of critical history." They became widely accepted among reflective and educated people during much of the twentieth century. There is a world of objects existing in space and time, and it can be ascertained if statements about that world are true or false. The intentions of human beings were etched in some of these objects and what was said about the world in those objects could be recovered.

It may be that these presuppositions are compatible with religious truths. Or it may simply be that the particular religious beliefs that crumbled in the nineteenth century as the presuppositions became clear were limited or provincial. It is still true that the intellectuals who imbibed, adhered to, or promoted the presuppositions of critical history gave up their Protestant, Bible-oriented theism, or relegated it to a secondary place in their lives. That is why I see the dominance of these presuppositions in the twentieth-century intellectual world as the criterion of secularization. The presuppositions are *worldly*, and over succeeding generations those who promulgated them gave up the clerical for the academic profession.

A lot can be said against the presuppositions. Their fruition is linked to some of the nastier developments in Western industrialism. The scholars who were carriers of these presuppositions were often guided not only by self-interest but also by something more like personal aggrandizement. The level of testosterone involved here is quite high. A lot can be said, too, against the institutional bearers of these presuppositions, against the ethos of the Victorian university. Yet these core presuppositions have something to recommend them. They are not theoretical; they came to the fore in scholarly practice and ultimately cost their purveyors cherished religious ideas. As I have tried to suggest in my sketch of the Penn expedition, it was not a tea party at which the discipline was tidily invented; people like Joseph Meyer died wretched deaths on its account.

It may also be that these presuppositions are unreliable. We can, for example, throw out the achievements of the translation projects. One could argue that attempts to *reconstruct* the language of the Assyrians are, for example, some bizarre sort of Western imperial *construction*. But this is a high price to pay. It is less obvious to me that we can dismiss the mode of reasoning that commits us to believe in a spatio-temporal world, where things indisputably exist in a specific place and time, although various pragmatists in the philosophy of science and social constructionists in the humanities imply such a dismissal. From my sense of these developments there is another exorbitant price to pay. Secular reasoning advanced with the decline of religious commitments. If we deny the foundations of secular reasoning, we put ourselves in the position of leaving the way open for the new adoption of religious commitments. The authority of the modern understanding of the past in this sense is thus its secular authority; if we deny it, we may be left with the authority of religion.

The *Gilgamesh* epic is the story of the unhappy and perhaps unstable ruler of Uruk. On an arduous journey of self-discovery he learns that unresolved struggle is intrinsic to our existence, that human beings cannot be immortal. The satisfaction that one can achieve consists in participating in one's culture, in Gilgamesh's case in ruling justly. The narrator of the epic points out as evidence for this good the lasting city that Gilgamesh built. "See its wall.... Look at its brickwork," says the narrator. The immortality that we have is thus living in the memory of our culture and, for Gilgamesh, literary fame. He engraved "on a stone the whole story," and his editor wrote, "I will proclaim to the world the deeds of Gilgamesh."

THE SEARCH FOR AUTHORITY IN TWENTIETH-CENTURY JUDAISM

Arnold Eisen

It is by now a truism that modernity has shattered the modes of religious authority that undergirded Jewish belief and practice for almost two millennia. For Jews modernity carried a double blow. It meant not only enlightenment, with its formidable challenges to traditional faith, but emancipation: the loss of integral community. The walls behind which enlightenment might have been contained, its shocks more successfully absorbed, weakened and then fell. While exclusivist Jewish communities still survive in places such as Boro Park, and while more centrist commitments ranging from modern Orthodoxy to moderate Reform can claim with some justification to constitute a synthesis between "tradition and modernity" rather than a surrender of the former to the latter, the truism with which I began nonetheless holds true. Most Jews in the modern West retain only vestigial ties to Jewish communities and attenuated allegiance at best to the faith of their ancestors. They may continue to profess belief in God. A substantial minority may even appear on the membership rolls of synagogues. But modern Judaism for all that can nonetheless be characterized in large measure as a series of defensive strategies designed to evade or make peace with besieging forces, intellectual and political, which Jews could not actually overcome.

My title is intended not so much to challenge these givens of my field, which I assume are familiar to readers, as to move our discussion past them by pointing to several paradoxes.

The first is that Jewish thinkers in the modern period can usefully be seen, on the model of Pirandello's famous play, as so many characters in search of an Author—if not God, exactly, then some other "god-term" or ultimate authority upon which to base their commitments. The search preoccupies them, to say the least. One is even tempted to say that it defines their thought as it defines the major Jewish religious movements that coalesced a century and a half ago almost entirely around the issue of what Jews are commanded to do and why, and remain divided over that issue today. All theology of whatever period is concerned with the basis of religious authority, of course, aiming to find new or better reasons for existing commitments, and seeking grounding in the ultimate source of Right that obligates human beings to think and act in certain ways and in return confers the precious sense that they are spending their days on earth correctly and meaningfully. In that effort theologians have always offered justifications couched in terms borrowed from outside their traditions. Jewish thought in the modern period, however, has been disproportionately given over to this activity of justification and, as a result, has paid far less attention than ever before to explication of texts and interpretation of rituals. Theology has been directed outward, we might say, far more than inward. Authority, which normally lies beneath all else and is taken for granted as the basis of all else, has been raised to the surface as *a* or *the* leading issue. Questions of content, as a result, have often become secondary.

It was modernity that made this change inevitable. In the nineteenth century, thinkers such as Abraham Geiger, S. R. Hirsch, and Zecharias Frankel needed to justify their departures from inherited patterns of belief and behavior and to deny legitimacy to the stances to their "left" and "right."[1] Authority could not but be uppermost in their minds. Thinkers in the twentieth century such as Hermann Cohen, Franz Rosenzweig, and Martin Buber among the Germans, or Mordecai Kaplan, Abraham Heschel, and Joseph Soloveitchik among the Americans, have devoted a major portion of their work to locating and redefining the authority for Jewish belief and practice *as such.* Consideration of the significance of Judaism had to be put off while they tackled the prior question of why Jewish meaning and behavior of any sort should concern modern Jews, let alone obligate them. The two questions cannot be entirely divorced, of course, but I think the point stands. Rosenzweig's magnum opus, *The Star of Redemption*, is not untypical in the weight that it gives to the justification of theology and faith as opposed to the actual interpretation of Jewish texts or festivals. The latter is quite thin, and for the most part undistinguished.

In sum: the radically new situation in which Jewish thinkers found themselves, and the innovation through which

---

[1]For a lucid introduction to this material, see Joseph Blau, *Modern Varieties of Judaism* (New York: Columbia University Press, 1964).

they sought to cope with that situation, both demanded confrontation with the issue of what made their chosen path right and what right they had to pursue it. "There's no author here," says the Manager in Pirandello's play. "We are not rehearsing a new piece."[2] New pieces require more than good management. They require authority.

The modern Jewish search for authority, however, has as a rule not proved conclusive. Not only have given theologians' resolutions to the quest been unsatisfactory to others, the usual state of affairs, but many theologians have often been unable to come forward with grounds that justify their *own* commitments. The Judaisms that such thinkers have practiced have remained far out in front of their theologies. This in turn suggests the second paradox that I wish to highlight: namely that the relevant authority in modern Jewish faith is not the ultimate grounding always sought and rarely found, but rather the source of obligation that mandates the search in the first place, directs its course, and dictates our judgment of its outcome. Modern believers, like Pirandello's characters, seem to manage quite well without an "author" of their existence all the while their search for absolutes proceeds. The question of authority is thus far more complex than we (or they) might have thought. Again, we should specify carefully what is new in this situation. People of whatever era have taken on or transformed or rejected the norms and customs of their societies and cultures as part of the personal passage to adulthood, meaning that every authority has had to win the loyalties of those subject to it. Conditions have always been subject to change, perspectives have always altered over time, and authority has had to be refined accordingly. Yet modernity remains distinctive for all that. Modern selves pledge their allegiance to multiple and therefore partial authorities. We learn by adulthood to operate without absolute grounding for our beliefs and behaviors. The changes to which we must accommodate occur with overwhelming rapidity. As a result, modern Jewish religious elites—those most knowledgeable in their traditions and most committed to maintaining them—have been forced to engage in a *perpetual* search for compelling raisons d'être. The reasons often enough *never* come. The

---

[2]Luigi Pirandello, *Six Characters in Search of an Author* in *Three Plays* (New York: E. P. Dutton, 1922) 7.

search goes on unceasingly—compelled by something other than the putative authority it seeks. Our consideration of religious authority, then, should include far more than the overarching source or justification of religious commitment: God, revelation, reason, tradition, or whatever. "The drama is in us," exclaims Pirandello's Manager, "and we are the drama. We are impatient to play it. Our inner passion drives us on to this."[3] If we focus our quest for modern Jewish religious authority only on the ultimates sought and not found, we miss the actual, operative authorities, having looked in the wrong place.[4]

Recent study of religious traditions including Judaism suggests that authority has always functioned in a more complex manner than previous generations of scholars or believers allowed. Jews of whatever century are not adequately described by Weber's threefold categorization of traditional, rational, and charismatic authority, however useful that typology remains. This is the third paradox to which my title is meant to point. The search for contemporary authority has opened up the question of where authority actually resided in periods when, unlike the present, its location seemed self-evident; my study belongs in a series bearing titles like "The Search for Authority in Ancient Judaism." As Rosenzweig put it in a famous letter to Buber, "did any Jew prior to [the nineteenth century] really think—without having the question put to him—that he was keeping the Law, and the Law him, only because God imposed it upon Israel at Sinai?" Rosenzweig's rhetorical question leads him to condemn the fact that "from Mendelssohn on," in search of authority for their commitment, "our entire people has subjected itself to the torture of this embarrassing questioning; the Jewishness of every individual has squirmed on the needle point of a 'why.'"[5]

---

[3]Pirandello 10.

[4]Compare Jean-François Lyotard, *The Postmodern Condition: A Report on Knowledge*, trans. Geoff Bennington and Brian Massumi (Minneapolis: University of Minnesota Press, 1984) 27: "Today the problem of legitimation is no longer considered a failing of the language game of science. It would be more accurate to say that it has itself been legitimated as a problem, that is, as a heuristic device."

[5]Franz Rosenzweig, "Teaching and Law" in *Franz Rosenzweig: His Life and Thought*, ed. Nahum Glatzer (New York: Schocken Books, 1962) 238–40.

Rosenzweig, to my mind, went on to squirm as much as anyone, and given the sheer length of *The Star of Redemption* we can say he squirmed more than most. His reflections on religious authority will be a central concern of mine here. But note for the moment that we must reformulate our notion of the problematic of religious authority in our time if we accept Rosenzweig's claim that our situation is far more continuous with past generations than we had thought. I do accept that claim. Easy schema such as Peter Berger's "deductive, reductive, and inductive" theological modes, however helpful, will not do even as ideal types. Most Jewish thinkers since Mendelssohn have simultaneously "reassert[ed] the authority of a religious tradition in the face of modern secularity" (the "deductive option"), "reinterpret[ed] the tradition in terms of modern secularity," ("reductive" in Berger's terms) and "turn[ed] to experience as the ground of all religious affirmations" ("inductive").[6] Moreover, much of our own century's Jewish thought—including very recent efforts by feminists and neomystics—has found authority for its radical innovation in a source not comprehended by Berger's typology: the claim that previous generations, whose authority we do not question, innovated no less and even in the same ways. We are used to the sight of reformers claiming to return their traditions to pristine founding moments and original beliefs uncorrupted by the accretions of centuries. This is the normal procedure. What we have now is reformers claiming that founding moments are less important than previous moments of transformation.[7] Revelation counts less than tradition, and the latter is not the static tradition that Weber portrayed but the dynamic tradition revealed in the scholarship of Gershom Scholem or Jacob Neusner.[8] Change is precisely what sustains tradition, in this reading, not some putative but deaden-

---

[6]Peter Berger, *The Heretical Imperative* (Garden City, N.Y.: Doubleday, 1979) chaps. 3–5.

[7]See my article, "Constructing the Usable Past: The Idea of Tradition in Twentieth Century American Judaism" in *The Uses of Tradition*, ed. Jack Wertheimer (New York: The Jewish Theological Seminary of America, 1992).

[8]See for example Gershom Scholem, *The Messianic Idea in Judaism and Other Essays on Jewish Spirituality* (New York: Schocken, 1971); and Jacob Neusner, *Method and Meaning in Ancient Judaism* (Missoula, Mont.: Scholars Press, 1979).

ing permanence. "That is the proof that I am a man," exclaims the Father in Pirandello's play. "This seeming contradiction [with past character] is the strongest proof that I stand here a live man before you."[9] The authority that counts has become the authority to retain authority while overturning it.

My concern, having noted the paradoxes that drive it, is to ask two questions: what are the various sorts of authority to which Jews in our century have appealed? And what can we say about the authorities to which they have actually been responsive, the commanding voices to which their belief and practice have been obedient? I will begin with Weber because his discussions of modernity and authority have been enormously influential upon recent study of modern Jewish commitment, and have certainly been so in my case. In particular I hope to show the pitfalls and benefits of employing a concept of authority such as Weber's, formulated to describe *political* allegiance, for understanding Jewish religious faith. I will then focus on Rosenzweig, arguably the most influential figure in twentieth-century Jewish theology, in order to illustrate the strengths and weaknesses of his method of searching for religious authority while presuming it. I will conclude with speculation about the authorities underlying searches such as Rosenzweig's—authorities that, while fragmented and uncertain, have allowed Jews to retain allegiances in good faith that Weber, for one, was unable to conceive.

Religious Authority Reconsidered

This is not the place for a detailed reexamination of Weber's well-known classification of authority, but we should look at it long enough to realize that its use in understanding the history of Judaism is fraught with difficulties. Note first that Weber defines the broad concern of sociology in *Economy and Society* as the understanding of human social action—action oriented to the past, present, or expected future behavior

---

[9]Pirandello 18.

of others.[10] Authority is discussed in the context of human association, which, whenever it is not consensual, depends upon some people obeying the will of others. Because it is inefficient and even impossible for rulers to hold a gun to their subjects' heads at every moment, they must accomplish their *Herrschaft*—domination—primarily by means of something other than sheer power or *macht*. Weber labels this alternative method of securing obedience "authority," but his preferred word for it in German is also *Herrschaft*, a clue to his assumption that power lurks somewhere in the shadow of every authority. The dual usage of *Herrschaft* also expresses Weber's difficulty as an observer in distinguishing the conferral of legitimacy by a population from simple lack of overt disobedience. Power shades into authority, and authority can connote either power held to be legitimate or the right to demand obedience without direct application or threat of force. Hence Weber's preference for the ambiguous term *Herrschaft*, defined only as "the probability that certain specific commands (or all commands) will be obeyed by a given group of persons."[11] He knew the lines were hard to draw.

In his classification of the pure types of authority, however, Weber allowed himself the luxury of decisive differences. "The validity of the claims to legitimacy" can be *rational*—resting on "belief in the legality of enacted rules and the right of those elevated to authority" by these rules; it can be *traditional*, resting on "established belief in the sanctity of immemorial traditions" and the right to authority in accord with them; or it can be *charismatic*, "resting on devotion to the exceptional sanctity, heroism, or exemplary character of an individual person, and of the normative patterns or order revealed or ordained by him."[12] In the essay, "Politics as a Vocation," we find a slightly different formulation. There tradition is called the "authority of the 'eternal yesterday,' i.e. of the mores sanctified through the unimaginably ancient recognition and habitual orientation to conform," and charisma is said to be "the extraordinary and personal gift of grace, the

---

[10]Max Weber, *Economy and Society*, ed. Guenther Roth and Claus Wittich (Berkeley: University of California Press, 1978) 22. My discussion draws on all of chap. 1.

[11]Weber 212.

[12]Weber 215–16.

absolutely personal devotion and personal confidence in revelation, heroism, or other qualities of individual leadership."[13] This formulation sharpens Weber's point and also highlights the issues that bear on our own discussion.

First, despite the protest that he intends these only as pure types, and his reiteration that in actual fact "obedience is determined" much of the time "by highly robust motives of fear and hope," the reader of Weber's *Sociology of Religion* (part six of *Economy and Society*) or his studies of world religions cannot help but note that Weber often describes actual historical phenomena as falling into one or another of the three types.[14] He also exhibits a clear and consistent attitude toward them.[15] Weber is respectful but ambivalent toward the rational authority that governs the vast bureaucratic machines of modernity. He is fearful of unpredictable charisma but dependent upon it to release us from rationality's "iron cage" and restore the ultimate meaning lost in the rationalization of our world.[16] He is dismissive of and generally hostile to tradition as what time and again froze behavior, "stereotyped" it, rendering it habitual rather than purposive, and so thwarted innovation carried by rational or charismatic forces.

Recall the fourfold typology of human action that begins *Economy and Society*, where instrumental and "value" rationality stand at the top, the pinnacle of logic, calculation, and purpose, while behavior driven by "affect" stands on the border of purposive action altogether and behavior "determined by ingrained habituation," on or over the edge of purpose, is labeled "traditional."[17] Note too that in the classifi-

---

[13]Hans Gerth and C. Wright Mills, eds., *From Max Weber: Essays in Sociology* (New York: Oxford University Press, 1969) 78–79.

[14]Gerth and Mills 78–79.

[15]See for example Max Weber, *The Sociology of Religion*, trans. Ephraim Fischoff (Boston: Beacon Press, 1963) 77 ("bondage to tradition"), 199 (where rational and traditional are opposed), and 259 (where "inner responsibility" is opposed to traditionalism); or see Max Weber, *Ancient Judaism*, ed. and trans. Hans Gerth and Don Martindale (New York: The Free Press, 1952) 12 (where Bedouin are called "unimaginatively traditional") or 253 (where *tradition* connotes unconditional acceptance and strict observance).

[16]For the "iron cage" see Max Weber, *The Protestant Ethic and the Spirit of Capitalism*, trans. Talcott Parsons (New York: Scribners, 1958) 181.

[17]Weber, *Economy and Society* 24–26.

cation of authority the rational sort refers not to the ground of our judgment, the basis on which we think about legitimacy, but only to "belief in the legality of enacted rules and the right of those elevated to authority under such rules to issue commands," a characterization that holds for traditional authorities and the routinizing successors to charismatic authorities no less than for modern bureaucracies.[18] Weber could not have alerted us better to the need for caution in applying his ideal types.

Shall we regard the prophets of ancient Israel as charismatic authorities, taking their stand because they can do no other, or traditional authorities who articulated a message and played a role long familiar, and—as Weber emphasized—highly rational authorities not only in the universality of their worldview but in the fact that they appealed in large measure to empirical confirmation provided their predictions by history? In short, they engaged Israelites in familiar rules of decision making and judgment that fit the description of rational authority exactly. Shall we squeeze the rabbis who assumed leadership of the Jews after the destruction of the Temple into Weber's "traditional" category? This is to neglect the role played by charisma in their authority. They effected cures, performed minor miracles. They dared to set themselves apart, taking on asceticism and suffering martyrdom. Their principal modus operandi, on the other hand, was quintessentially rational: the spinning out of legal interpretations according to defined rules of exegesis held valid from one end of the Jewish world to the other. Their message was crafted to make sense under difficult circumstances. The order they provided was desperately needed by a people deprived of it through political, economic, and religious catastrophe. I will take the need for due care in applying Weber to any historical case study as a given.

Let me proceed with a second qualification of Weber's classification that, like the first, emerges from Weber himself. Consider for a moment the two categories of "affect" and "habit" to which, after James and Freud, students of religion cannot but give careful attention. Weber himself tended to view religion primarily in cognitive terms—the search for meaning, the containment of suffering and evil—rather than

---

[18]Weber, *Economy and Society* 215.

in emotional terms. When he accounted for disenchantment, as in "Science as a Vocation," he generally did so in terms of the rationalization of the world through science and technology, which effectively banished God to the periphery of human concern.[19] We cannot afford this dichotomy between the cognitive and the affective, I think. For if Geertz and other anthropologists are correct, *ritual* is the primary vehicle by which worldviews are articulated and reinforced, and by which meaning is provided and experienced, just as Durkheim emphasized.[20] I myself would give more weight to patterns of daily activity structured, no less than ritual, by religious norms and codes. Even so, however, we need to pay more attention to ritual than is generally apparent in sociological or historical studies following on Weber, and this demands different tools than the analysis of theologies or legal systems. Drawing upon James, we would investigate the comparative workings of love, anger, fear, compassion, jealousy, and pain; following Freud, we would probe the drives and concerns never brought to expression, even in affect—in other words, the workings of repressions and obsessions. Weber's residual category of habit, which he labeled "traditional behavior," thus returns to prominence in a way that he never intended.

Consider this formulation by Philip Rieff, heavily influenced by Weber and Freud alike. "A culture survives principally, I think, by the power of its institutions to bind and loose men in the conduct of their affairs with reasons which sink so deep into the self that they become commonly and implicitly understood."[21] How religious traditions accomplish the job of sinking reasons deep into the self, and then drawing upon them in obedience or calling them to indirect expression in ritual, becomes one of the most important questions a scholar of religion can ask. The student of modern faith, therefore, must shift focus somewhat: *from* the cognitive plane of enlightenment challenges *to* the decline in ritual's ability to generate and sustain belief, whether because societal transfor-

[19]Gerth and Mills 139.

[20]The major essay in this connection is of course Clifford Geertz, "Religion as a Cultural System," in *The Interpretation of Cultures* (New York: Basic Books, 1973) 87–125.

[21]Philip Rieff, *The Triumph of the Therapeutic* (New York: Harper Torchbooks, 1968) 2.

mations have deprived it of the context required for it to function effectively (Berger's "plausibility structures") or because processes that once occurred beneath consciousness have been raised to consciousness, where under constant examination they cannot work.[22] Rieff cites Harry Stack Sullivan's witticism that if you know you are sublimating, you can't sublimate.[23] Yet modern believers try—and often succeed in giving themselves over to rituals that return the favor by commanding them.

I will turn now to a third relevant feature of Weber's classification of authority: its political character. Let me proceed by way of a brief detour through several rabbinic discussions in which the sages faced up directly to the enormous interpretive responsibility they shouldered. In the first, they took the "eye for eye, tooth for tooth" passage in *Exodus* 23 to mean monetary compensation rather than physical injury.[24] Their discussion demonstrates full awareness of the difficulties in that position—and yet, as students in my Introduction to Judaism class discover each year, the rabbis' case is no more difficult to make than the case for a literal reading of the biblical code. This and a thousand other examples make clear that authority as the rabbis practiced it never meant unquestioned obedience to a putatively unequivocal command. It meant, rather, the acceptance of certain rules of the game, within which innovation was not only possible but demanded. For ordinary Jews, authority was primarily a matter of obedience to the legal system that the rabbis maintained and acceptance of the general worldview that system presumed and reinforced. Theological concerns often did not impinge. God was always there, of course, underpinning all else, but God's role in transactions of authority was indirect or even remote. Belief in "the God of Israel" or "the Torah from Sinai" or "God's covenant" was compatible with many and various interpretations of God's nature as with many and various interpretations of the Torah's commandments. Religious authority was primarily not theological but sociological, political, even pro-

---

[22]On plausibility structures see Peter Berger, *The Sacred Canopy* (Garden City, N.Y.: Doubleday, 1969) 45–47.

[23]Rieff, *Therapeutic* 5.

[24]The discussion can be found, inter alia, in Tractate Baba Kamma of the Babylonian Talmud 83b.

cedural. It turned on the issue of who decided the law and the teaching, according to what hermeneutical rules.

Many Jewish thinkers in the last generation, intent on wrapping themselves in the cloak of the rabbis' traditional interpretive freedom, have cited two *aggadot*—nonlegal rabbinic passages—that reflect upon and seem to justify that freedom. Scholem featured the stories prominently in his essay, "Revelation and Tradition as Religious Categories in Judaism," and subsequent references have been legion, for example in Michael Fishbane's little book titled, after Scholem, *Judaism: Revelation and Traditions*.[25] In the first story Moses is shown the academy of Rabbi Akiba, the archetypical rabbinic figure, and is perplexed because he cannot understand a word of what Akiba and his students are saying. He is comforted only when Akiba declares that the authority for all he says is the Torah given Moses on Sinai. In the second story the rabbis are debating whether a certain oven is or is not susceptible to impurity, and Rabbi Eliezer, against whom all the others argue, invokes the proofs of a stream that flows backward at his request, walls that shake and a tree uprooted forty cubits from its place, "some say two hundred." None of these proofs is allowed. When a voice from heaven attests that Eliezer's is the right interpretation of God's intent the rabbis reply that "it is not in heaven" (see *Deuteronomy* 30:12) and remind God that He has given them sole authority to determine the meaning of His Torah. Their prooftext is *Exodus* 23:2: "One must incline after the majority." What was God's response to the rabbis' brazen independence? According to Rabbi Jeremiah, who heard it from the prophet Elijah, "God smiled and said, 'my children have defeated me.'"

One *aggadah*, to be sure, docs not a rabbinic worldview make. Presumably other voices would have dissented from the tale and not claimed such interpretive latitude in the reading of God's holy Torah. But the text rings true as an insider's view of traditional authority; indeed all of the Talmud, by exposing the thrust and parry of rabbinic argument, rather than simply presenting the outcome of debate, demystifies the rabbis in the same way that the American Supreme Court is demystified if one takes the trouble to read the court's opinions.

---

[25]See Gershom Scholem, "Revelation and Tradition as Religious Categories in Judaism" in Scholem, *The Messianic Idea* 283, 291.

A quick look at *Exodus* 23:2, the concluding prooftext cited by the rabbinic majority in its dispute with Eliezer, reveals that it does not say, "one must incline after the majority," but rather "thou shalt not incline after a majority" to pervert justice. The rabbis knowingly misconstrued the plain meaning of the verse—a daring illustration of the larger and no less daring enterprise that the story and its prooftext come to justify!

This is welcome ammunition to modern Jewish reformers, of course, and they have not hesitated to use it. Indeed, the examples of "eye for eye" read as a metaphor for monetary compensation, Moses not comprehending later readings of his own Torah, and sages disregarding voices from heaven that they themselves took to be authentic, remind us of the *political* character of their interpretive authority. It is political in the two senses that 1) external societal considerations impinge on how the rabbis read and selected among inherited traditions and that 2) their readings were never untouched by contests of power within the interpreters' own institutions. The Jewish search for authority in the modern period has been no less decisively political in both these senses, shaped not only by the new social and political order in which Jews found themselves with emancipation but dominated by the question of who has the right to speak for the Jews and Judaism in that new order, who shall legitimately define and constrain them. Weber therefore did us a great service, on balance, in applying to religious authority a classification originally meant to explain political domination, despite the confusion caused by conceiving of religious authority in terms of overt power, particularly in the modern West where religion has lost that power. It is no coincidence that the prehistory of modern Jewish thought began with Spinoza's *Theologico-Political Treatise*, which sought to end the age-old wars between church and state by redefining both in such a way as to guarantee the loss of religious authority, and undermined Jewish religious authority as a result. Nor is it an accident that the first major work of modern Jewish thought, Moses Mendelssohn's *Jerusalem*, responded to Spinoza with a text divided into two parts: a political discussion of contract theory that denied religion any legitimate power of coercion, and a religious discussion that tried to find persuasive reasons for Jewish observance now that compliance with the Torah would have to come voluntarily or not at all.

In Weber's terms once again, it was not that all authority suddenly became rational, leaving faith founded on charisma and tradition out in the cold. Rather, past linkages in Jewish and general society between political and religious authority had been broken, leaving religious authority of whatever sort unable to back up its claims with the force of arms and the prima facie plausibility that arms confer. In this reading, emancipation and not enlightenment is again the key variable for modern Jewish faith. Authority became the main theological concern instead of merely the prerequisite to other concerns because authority, religious as political, came to rest in the people's voluntary consent to be ruled by it. Civil rights and human rights decisively undermine claims to divine and traditional rights even *before* religious belief and observance have been considered in their own right. If that ground prior to belief and observance is where the battle lies, theologians do well to join it there.

Jewish Authority Sought, Found, and Dispensed With

I am going to focus in this section on Franz Rosenzweig (1886–1929), who sits astride the dividing line between nineteenth-century and contemporary Jewish thought. We will begin with a schematic overview of Rosenzweig's predecessors, the better to understand why he felt obliged to propose a "new thinking" that broke with them. The logical starting point for our discussion, as for most matters pertaining to modern Judaism, is Moses Mendelssohn.[26]

The first thing to note about Mendelssohn's rational theology is that for him God was the least problematic subject to be discussed. Mendelssohn had proven to his own satisfaction that God exists, superintends the world with providence, and rewards us according to our deeds in the world to come. The issue was what God wanted us to do and why. Jews, Mendelssohn affirmed, were bound by a unique set of commandments given their ancestors at a unique revelation which had taken place at Sinai. Yet Mendelssohn also believed that

[26]See my article, "Divine Legislation as 'Ceremonial Script': Mendelssohn on the Commandments" in *AJS Review* 15, 2 (Fall 1990): 239–67.

God guaranteed salvation to everyone and provided everyone with the means needed to know Him and thus secure it. This caught Mendelssohn in an apparent contradiction. If the Jews derived unique advantage from the law, God's justice was in question. If they did not, what was the point of observing the law, particularly when that observance so often seemed onerous? Why not simply be an enlightened Christian? The saving in time and trouble would be enormous. Mendelssohn could not quite get around this conundrum. He reiterated that Sinai did occur, meaning Jews were not free to abrogate their covenant, and attempted to show that the commandments, far from being onerous, were an especially good method of grasping "eternal truth." What is more, they constituted an ingenious "ceremonial script," a set of symbols that allowed individual Jews great latitude in interpreting the meanings that the symbols conveyed. Mendelssohn's argument, if I read it correctly, is sociologically brilliant. On the one hand, the community had always been and would remain united by virtue of common observances rather than common beliefs; on the other, that being the case, individuals were free to endow their observance with personal meaning. At a time when individuals were asserting political rights, Mendelssohn knew, they would not accept religious observance on any other terms, but once having invested themselves in the commandments, they might come to perceive them as entirely rational and desirable. If so, the continuation of the Jewish people and the observance of God's Torah would be secured.

But what if one did not believe that the Torah was God's, given to Moses at Sinai? Suppose God revealed only eternal truths of metaphysics or ethics? Did it not follow, according to Mendelssohn's own logic, that the commandments serving as instruments to apprehend the truth should be observed, while those that did not could justly be forgotten? This was the Reform position. To do it justice we should place emphasis not only on the desire to acculturate to the German milieu newly opened to Jewish participation, no doubt a principal motive for change, but on the relative conservatism—by our standards—of many Reform proponents, especially their chief theoretician, Abraham Geiger. Some departures from accepted practice were striking, particularly in matters labeled as "ritual." However, the Reformers could and did bring the new findings of *Wissenschaft* to bear in order to demonstrate that they were not the first in Jewish history to propose major departures. We should note that they rarely questioned God's existence, revelation, or providence, and reasserted the purpose of Jewish existence—called into question by both emancipation and enlightenment—in the newly central notion of the Jewish people's eternal mission to bring ethical monotheism to all humanity. Belief in God as the creator of humanity and the revealer of ethical reason mandated retention by Jews of some observances and the elimination of others. Who should decide which was which? Those who both used reason well and "controlled" the sources, historical and textual. Orthodox opponents were disqualified on both counts.[27]

Samson Raphael Hirsch, the prototype for subsequent modern Orthodox figures who chose to dispute the challengers on their own turf, so to speak, rather than by retreating to safer, more insular ground, had to demonstrate the rational nature of the commandments (Mendelssohn's enterprise, harking back to medieval philosophy) and the law's suitability to modern life and citizenship. Hirsch explicitly couched his rationale in these terms, urging Jews to trade a degree of social acceptance, and even to risk emancipation if need be, in order to be true to a higher calling that was not only religious but moral, æsthetic, and spiritual. Torah was a regimen of belief and practice designed to develop mature, responsible, ethical human beings protected from the allures of the senses and the instincts. It offered *Bildung*, in a word, superior to anything Christian Germany could provide. To demonstrate this, Hirsch embarked on a voluminous set of essays and commentaries that set forth the reason for every single commandment, not a reason left to the individual as in Mendelssohn but objectively there, in the sources, albeit in a symbolic code that Hirsch now claimed to decipher.[28]

---

[27]On Reform see Blau, *Modern Varieties*, chap. 2; Michael Meyer, *Response to Modernity: A History of the Reform Movement in Judaism* (New York: Oxford University Press, 1988), particularly chap. 2; and Arnold Eisen, "Secularization, 'Spirit,' and the Strategies of Modern Jewish Faith" in *Jewish Spirituality from the Sixteenth Century Revival to the Present*, ed. Arthur Green (New York: Crossroad, 1987) 283–93.

[28]Hirsch's message is conveniently available in his programmatic essay *The Nineteen Letters on Judaism*, trans. Bernard Drachman (New York: Feldheim, 1969).

The Reform and modern Orthodox positions in place, it only remained for the center to coalesce, and it did so in the form of a group of thinkers who gathered at a new seminary at Breslau directed by Zecharias Frankel. Against the Orthodox, including Hirsch, Frankel's "positive, historical Judaism" insisted upon recognition that Judaism had always evolved and always would. Against the Reformers, Frankel argued that the "essence" of Judaism not subject to change with the times lay not in a belief such as ethical monotheism but in observance, the "positive" content that brought belief to expression and bound the Jewish people together. Only those in touch with the will of the people were competent to guide the slow, "organic" transformation of the tradition. This ruled out Reformers such as Geiger. Only those alert to past historical development could have the wisdom to know what should and should not be altered. This left out the Orthodox.[29] Note once again that the argument is not about God, creation, revelation, or redemption. The actual changes at issue in prayer and ritual are by modern standards minimal. The issue is once more proximate authority: who decides what to change and not to change, and on what basis?

We can summarize this overview, with inevitable oversimplification, as follows. Neither the legitimacy of faith as such nor the desirability and obligatory character of Judaism was in question among the nineteenth-century thinkers, except among the left wing of Reform, though all were sensitive to the rising tide of disaffection and apostasy. Kant and Hegel had offered convincing philosophical rationales for religious belief along with challenges to belief as traditionally formulated. Moreover, except for several urban centers in western Europe, traditional Jewish practices and the communities that nurtured them were largely intact. The battle generally involved adjustment of tradition to new tastes, beliefs, and surroundings rather than its radical transformation. By the end of the century, however, the processes of urbanization and industrialization had decisively affected Jews in western Europe and pushed into central Europe as well; even in eastern Europe, enlightenment had become a force propelling and propelled by the unsuccessful drive for emancipation, with the

---

[29]See Meyer, *Response to Modernity* 84–99 and Eisen, "Secularization" 293–96.

resultant growth of secular Jewish movements such as socialism and Zionism. Jewish thought likewise went in new directions. The search for authority changed course.

Rosenzweig justifiably named Hermann Cohen as the key figure in this transition: head of the neo-Kantian school of philosophy at Marburg, lifelong proponent of German culture, defender of the Jews against detractors vulgar and enlightened. Cohen's *Religion of Reason out of the Sources of Judaism*, published posthumously in 1919, bears an unmistakable debt to Kant from the title onward. One can either deplore or admire but not deny the acrobatics Cohen performs in order to fit Judaism into a Kantian mold. But there is more, as Rosenzweig perceived. The book is passionate in its commitment to the Jewish people and its praxis in a way earlier Reformers never were. Cohen not only loves God, that is to say, the idea of God revealed by the religion of reason, he loves the idea of the Jewish people. Jews had suffered grievously for bringing the idea of God into the world and keeping it there.[30] In Cohen's vision they became a collective symbol of the ideal individual self, working through suffering to knowledge of God and the good, a conception of the Jews that utterly captivated Rosenzweig precisely because it seemed at odds with, or at least unsupported by, the universalist religion of reason. He took the split in Cohen to indicate the workings of two authorities who faced one another as equals: reason's insistence that any faith commitment stand before the bar of universal criteria of truth, and a particularist demand to serve the God of Israel as a member of the people of Israel, not only through belief but through ethical and ritual practices developed over the millennia of the tradition.[31]

Rosenzweig took this to mean that philosophy, which had straitjacketed faith in the modern period, needed to be redefined as much as religion. Paradoxically, however, this meant that he and others like him had to devote enormous effort to that redefinition of philosophy, and were in danger of holding the validity of their Jewish commitment hostage to the effort. Earlier thinkers who placed Judaism in the mold of Kant or Hegel could safely assume its right to existence and argue

[30]Hermann Cohen, *Religion of Reason*, trans. Simon Kaplan (New York: Frederick Ungar, 1972) especially chaps. 1, 3, 9, 13.

[31]See Rosenzweig, *Life and Thought* 58–59, 281–82, 351.

about what I've called the proximate authority of the law. Now that Judaism was breaking out of that mold, its justification or lack thereof was exposed to argument and perhaps dismissal.

Several features of Rosenzweig's redefinitions of philosophy and Judaism will engage our attention.

First, his "new thinking" or "speech thinking" or "empiricism" involved a repudiation of "essence" discourse in favor of a return to "sound common sense, which never bothers to ask what a thing 'actually' is." The special butt of Rosenzweig's animus is modern idealism, of course, but in *The Star of Redemption* (1921) his sweep includes virtually every major religion and philosophical system. Put aside the attempt to find the essence of things, he urges; eschew the reduction of God to humanity, as in projection theories, or of God to world, as in materialist theories, or of world to humanity, as in Berkeley's idealism, and just open your eyes in humility to your own experience. Trust the evidence (and ignorance) of your senses, and you come up with three elements: God, humanity, world. No more and no less. Moreover, while we cannot know the "true nature" of any of the three, "humanity" of course included, we do know (because we experience it) that the three are not isolated but interrelated. Human beings alter and are altered by the world. "World" betrays evidence of a creating hand or mind. And—no less so, to Rosenzweig—human life testifies to encounters with God, whether direct religious experiences or the sort of thing Peter Berger would call "signals of transcendence." These lead reasonably to the conclusion that God's work and ours are unfinished. Creation and revelation point to redemption.[32] Much of the *Star of Redemption* is devoted to a brilliant exercise of picking out such allusions to the divine not only in nature but in logic, mathematics, and grammar. It all makes sense, Rosenzweig wants us to exclaim, fantastic, cosmic, logical sense, so that by the end of his architectonic magnum opus, with its three parts and three books within each part, chapter one of part one and its subsections corresponding to chapter one of parts two and three and their subsections, we are prepared for the claim that if the three elements are connected, the points forming an equilateral triangle, and the three relations among

[32] See Rosenzweig, "The New Thinking" in *Life and Thought* 190–208.

them are likewise connected to form a second triangle superimposed upside down on the first, the six-pointed star of David that results is no coincidence but the revelation or appreciation of a fundamental fact of existence. The people of Israel exist eternally as the "fire at the core of the star," its Christian emissaries constituting the star's rays, bringing light to the nations.[33]

Secondly, it should be apparent from even this brief presentation of Rosenzweig's thought that the rhetorical character of the *Star of Redemption* is crucial to Rosenzweig's intentions, a guide to the nature of the authority he claims. I want to review the book's rhetorical structure in order to expose the argument that its rhetoric advances. Rosenzweig begins the *Star* with death—the reality Rosenzweig confronted daily as he wrote the book in the trenches of World War I. "All cognition of the All originates in death, in the fear of death."[34] No essence here, but nasty, brutish, and short existence, human existence, as if we were reading Heidegger or Kierkegaard. The human experience of moving toward death drives us to want to know the All, in order to escape death. But the "philosophy of the All" accomplishes that end by disposing of the self. No trick to avoid mortality by avoiding existence in the first place. Rosenzweig insisted that we restore "man" to our picture of reality because our experience testifies to our own reality no less than to that of God or world. Throughout part one of the book, titled "The Elements, or the Ever-Enduring Proto-Cosmos," Rosenzweig alternates between an account of "commonsense" human experience and the hints of transcendence that experience contains, on the one hand, and summaries of philosophies or religions inadequate to that testimony of experience, on the other. At the end of each of the three chapters in part one we are persuaded that these views of the world are inadequate. We need to look elsewhere. Reason itself points beyond them, to Creation. We turn eagerly to part two for evidence warranting that faith.

What we find there disappoints. "The Course, or The Always-Renewed Cosmos" has the three elements in their interrelation, grasped by humanity in the partial manner in

[33]Franz Rosenzweig, *The Star of Redemption*, trans. William Hallo (Boston: Beacon Press, 1972). See the Table of Contents and 298, 336, 348–49.

[34]Rosenzweig, *Star of Redemption* 3.

which we can and must grasp truth as we stand after creation but before redemption. Part two aims, in other words, to be a statement of revelation as known to reason and faith supplementing one another. "This new theological rationalism ... here adumbrated ... [hopes to demonstrate] that both sides need something which in each case only the other party can supply."[35] Again, however, Rosenzweig must proceed negatively, pointing up the inadequacy of answers other than those he has in mind but cannot actually name, given the partial character of human knowledge before redemption. Islam is the foil in this section—closest to the best statement of the truth we have but oh, so far from it.[36] It will turn out that only Judaism and Christianity meet Rosenzweig's requirements, and the second aspect of his rhetorical strategy in part two is to explicate key texts from the Hebrew Bible they share: *Genesis* in the creation section, the *Song of Songs* for revelation, and *Psalms* for redemption.

Not surprisingly, he does the most with the *Song of Songs*. We have no direct, irrefutable, unequivocal evidence of creation, and a great deal of evidence against the belief in redemption, but we do know love, and have perhaps experienced God's love. Rosenzweig, following the structure of the Jewish prayers for Sabbath morning, wants us to see God's revelation primarily as revelation of the fact of creation, to understand it as a sign of God's love, and to see our obligation to love our fellows as a commandment flowing from that divine love. Only the lover has the right to command the beloved to love, and "love is stronger than death."[37] Rosenzweig is at his best here.

I said that part two disappoints only because in part one Rosenzweig had created the expectation for more than he or anyone else who accepts his premises can possibly deliver. Rosenzweig affirms no specific doctrine of creation, is utterly vague about redemption, and even on revelation affirms only that God somehow communicated with the Israelites of old and communicates still with Jews and Christians today. The biblical reports of God's remarks are entirely a human product, the law as much a human artifice as philosophy. We want certainty from Rosenzweig, and we get only witness. We want

---

[35]Rosenzweig, *Star of Redemption* 104.

[36]Rosenzweig, *Star of Redemption* 116–18.

[37]Rosenzweig, *Star of Redemption* 156, 173–85.

eternity, the defeat of death, and get only the assurance that we are touched by a larger order, participants by way of prayer and ritual in a cosmic drama that will one day end in redemption.

Part three of the *Star*, "The Configuration, or The Eternal Hyper-Cosmos" of course cannot describe the configuration for us, for we cannot know what we cannot know. Rosenzweig if anything says far too much in these sections, speaking at great length when by his own lights he should have kept silent. Nor is his idiosyncratic portrait of the Jews as the "eternal people" terribly convincing. It turns out that Jews gained eternity over the centuries by renouncing time; exiled from their land, using their language only to pray, studying a law that claimed to derive from God, they overcame death at the price of normal life. Moreover, they do not really overcome death so much as experience eternity here and now through the cycle of the Jewish year, which Rosenzweig of course divides somewhat mechanically into festivals of creation, revelation, and redemption, the Sabbath containing all three.[38] The authority of the tradition—its hold on us, its stance before us as the right way to spend our brief years on earth—depends upon the tradition's ability to proffer the experience of eternity. Insofar as we depend upon Rosenzweig to mediate that experience, he fails us, which is perhaps inevitable. Experience at one remove rarely compels; as we would say, "you had to be there." I reach page 424 of the English edition, where the concluding lines are printed with increasing indentation in order to form a star, and come to the concluding exhortation: "To walk humbly with thy God—the words are written over the gate, the gate which leads out of the mysterious-miraculous light of the divine sanctuary in which no man can remain alive. Whither, then, do the wings of the gate open? Thou knowest it not? INTO LIFE." I know I am meant to have my head held high, ready to embrace God as a philosophically sophisticated modern person, and calmly confront my death. But of course I have been offered no new resources for doing so except the testimony of a learned Jewish philosopher, who has found a way, and his promise that if I walk that way I too will find the meaning I need, the synthesis of philosophy and faith that I had lacked heretofore.

---

[38]Rosenzweig, *Star of Redemption* 298–335.

Hence the central function of rhetoric in Rosenzweig's theological strategy. He not only brings us the Word, newly reinterpreted in a way designed to appeal to moderns, but he brings us himself, its witness, bearer of the only authority we can find credible—authentic personal experience. Appropriately, the larger-than-life picture of Rosenzweig as heroic theologian has arguably had a far greater impact than the *Star* itself: the picture of a Jew on the verge of conversion to Christianity who returns to Judaism only because of a Yom Kippur experience in an Orthodox synagogue; of the philosopher writing his magnum opus on postcards sent home to his mother from the front; of a man stricken with paralysis who works on his translation of the Bible with Buber by means of flickers of the eye interpreted by his wife, and in that condition gathers around him the young Jewish intellectuals who would go on to dominate our century's Jewish creativity.[39]

We should note one final contribution made by Rosenzweig to our understanding of the modern Jewish pursuit of authority, which came in a now-famous letter to Buber. Complaining that Buber had unfairly ruled out all observance of Jewish law as coercive, stereotypical behavior that precluded the spontaneity and authenticity of I-Thou relation with God, Rosenzweig argued that Buber had strayed from his own path to Jewish renewal. You have wisely rejected the attempts of nineteenth-century thinkers to pinpoint a Jewish essence and make that the authoritative criterion for observance, he tells Buber. Instead you offered "the concept of inner power ... what you demand when you ask him who learns to stake his whole being for the learning, to make himself a link in the chain of tradition and thus become a chooser, not through his will but through his ability." The question of what one must know as a Jew could not be answered by a syllabus drawn up according to some putative essence. Neither, however, could the question of what one must *do* as a Jew. In this, too, Jews should rely on inner power, responding to what speaks to them with a force they cannot resist. Rosenzweig is aware of the subjectivity of that criterion. But if Judaism is always changing (Orthodoxy was wrong on this), if no essence existed to guide that change (Reform was wrong on this), if history too provided no sure criterion, and the "voice of the people" was no-

---

[39]See Rosenzweig, *Life and Thought* 1–176.

toriously unreliable (the Historical School was wrong on this)— what then could direct the necessary leap from "path" (Judaism as it exists at any moment) to "pathlessness" (future Judaisms as yet unknown)? Only the "laborious and aimless detour through knowable Judaism gives us the certainty that the ultimate leap, from that which we know to that which we need to know at any price, the leap to the teachings, leads to *Jewish* teachings."[40] The teachings will be Jewish not because Jews author or transmit them (this is not enough) or because Jews transmit exactly the Judaism they have received (this is not possible) but because Jews immersed in their tradition, having taken the varieties of the tradition into themselves and selected among them according to "inner power," author and transmit the teachings that have worked through them. This authority for the revised tradition was less than Geiger or Hirsch or Frankel would have wanted, but it was more than Buber could offer. Moreover, according to Rosenzweig, it was all that could be had: not enough, perhaps, to *conclude* the search for authority on which he had embarked in the *Star*, but sufficient to proceed "into life," armed with the rightness and direction of the authorities operative in the search itself.

Indeed, no one has come along subsequently and offered more except in the form of reiterating previous formulations that Rosensweig rejected. In this sense I must agree with Emil Fackenheim that the "pioneering work" that Buber and Rosenzweig "accomplished still waits for adequate successors." Mordecai Kaplan, to cite one prominent example, pinned his authority to reformulate Jewish belief and practice on a pragmatic appeal to "the modern worldview" and a complicated method of "functional revaluation" that will not bear scrutiny.[41] The Orthodox thinker Joseph Soloveitchik, in a welcome contrast to much Jewish thought in our century, wrote explicitly for insiders, usually in Hebrew. He sought to ennoble a commitment to *halakha* (Jewish law) that he assumed on every page, interpreting texts whose importance to his reader he did not bother to argue. In Soloveitchik's essays non-Jew-

---

[40]Rosenzweig, *Life and Thought* 234–42.

[41]On Kaplan see his major work, *Judaism as a Civilization* (Philadelphia: Jewish Publication Society, 1981), particularly chap. 26; and Arnold Eisen, *The Chosen People in America* (Bloomington: Indiana University Press, 1983) chap. 4.

ish thinkers from Pythagoras to Barth are brought in profusion into Jewish discourse, thereby accomplishing rhetorically the synthesis that, he thereby assures his committed audience, could with no greater difficulty be achieved in fact.[42] Abraham Heschel stood somewhere in between the two, rejecting Kaplan's pragmatism and his emphasis upon Jewish peoplehood rather than faith, but responding time and again to biblical criticism and other modern challenges that Soloveitchik dismissed as of no concern. Heschel, like Rosenzweig, began with experience—this time transcendence, wonder, awe—and tried to move his reader to the recognition that only God satisfactorily answered the questions that their wonder aroused. Reason, he argued eloquently, should not be permitted to dissipate that hard-won faith. It must not be allowed to trespass on sacred ground. Wonder must be protected, along with the faith to which it leads, and we will then require a "pattern for living" suited to God's presence in our world. For Jews this pattern was the commandments, passed down to us by prophets who intuited God's will and put it into words and then by two millennia of interpreters who put those words into other words, guided by reason, tradition, and experience.[43]

Heschel is as traditional a thinker as one finds in the twentieth-century modern Jewish corpus—and, in some ways, as radical a thinker as one finds. This is precisely my point. His justification of the commandments by way of a complex and highly mystical theory of revelation is unsatisfactory. The leap from wonder to God is problematic. Yet the thought is rich, and not uncompelling. In Kaplan, as in Rosenzweig, the authority for faith itself is still questionable, while Soloveitchik's putative synthesis of Judaism with philosophy, rather than bringing the latter safely into Judaism as he pretends, calls such attention to the problems raised by philosophy that the sleep of the faithful reader cannot but be dis-

---

[42]Soloveitchik's two best-known essays available in English are *Halakhic Man*, trans. Lawrence Kaplan (Philadelphia: Jewish Publication Society, 1983) and "The Lonely Man of Faith" in *Tradition* 7 (Summer 1965): 5–67.

[43]On Heschel see especially his *Man is Not Alone* (New York: Harper Torchbooks, 1966); *God in Search of Man* (New York: Harper Torchbooks, 1966); and Arnold Eisen, "Re-reading Heschel on the Commandments" in *Modern Judaism* 9, 1 (February 1989): 1–33.

turbed. All these thinkers, moreover, presume like Rosenzweig the need for and validity of Jewish commitment to a substantial level of belief and practice. Even Kaplan, despite his professed pragmatic rationalism, falls back when pressed for justification of Judaism upon a prerational, nonpragmatic and romantic "Jewish will to live" as a Jew.

We have returned to our starting point. It is time to speculate on the authority that commands Kaplan, Fackenheim, and others like them to pursue commitments that even their own elaborate arguments were unable to justify. I want, in other words, to probe the "Jewish will to live," translating it into warrants and obligations more open to our scrutiny if not our proof.

Authority in Theory and Practice

Because space is limited, and my project now highly speculative—no reliable data exists about Jewish belief and practice in contemporary America, let alone in nineteenth-century Germany—I will once again proceed schematically. Drawing upon the examinations of Weber and Rosenzweig just conducted, I propose to enumerate five sources of authority that I believe are at work among religiously observant Jews in the modern West, theologians and laity alike. These authorities, I repeat, precede and impel the search for authority, and operate while that search—usually interminable—proceeds.

1. *Socially constructed reality*, religious and secular. It seems to me that we are driven by historical research concerning Jewish modernity and by the thinkers I have surveyed to adopt Peter Berger's understanding of modernity as the multiplication of options and the consequent weakening of religious "plausibility structures." God is not refuted but rendered more and more peripheral to the explanation of nature and history. Yet even that is less important than the fragmentation or actual disappearance of the integral communities in which faith had previously been situated. The principal authority for any belief, according to this analysis, is social. It lies in the claim to describe reality, and so rests upon repeated confirmations: political, societal, familial, linguistic, architectural.

One has only to read a historical study such as Roger Chartier's recent book, *The Cultural Origins of the French Revolution*, to realize once again how much church and king relied upon one another during the *ancien régime*, or how much the sheer variety of new reading that became available in the course of the eighteenth century undermined the claim by any one view of things to be authoritative.[44] Conversely, if religion has not disappeared in our day, and all surveys confirm that it certainly has not, it is in large measure because churches and synagogues have managed to create social realities strong enough to withstand secularizing pressures. They have created communities and intellectual resources enabling believers to counter the "massive" reality all around them, and even to interpret the latter in the terms of their traditions. Jews, as we will see, have done this successfully for religious elites and the more active members of the laity, in no small measure thanks to Zionism and the state of Israel. In Boro Park, as in separatist communities of whatever faith, the job is that much easier. Outside such communities, faith must be couched in terms that are credible in light of the accepted social reality in which we all live. This works itself out, philosophically, in the deference paid to Kant by virtually every modern Jewish thinker, including Rosenzweig; the task is to seize hold of the space left to faith by Kant and the secular world, and there nourish a sense of rightness that modernity can neither provide nor preclude.

2. *Religious experience.* However, the need for societal "plausibility structures" to confer prima facie credibility on religious belief shows how precarious is Berger's reliance—or Rosenzweig's, or Heschel's—upon the "inductive" authority of experience. For the latter does not reach us uninterpreted, and given the "social construction of reality" dominant in the modern West, it is a wonder that religious experience remains available at all. Buber had his formative experiences with the "God of Abraham, Isaac, and Jacob" while living as a child among Hasidic communities in central Europe. Rosenzweig had his climactic encounter in an Orthodox service on Yom Kippur, after intellectual preparation provided by cousins who took faith so seriously they converted to Christianity. Heschel

---

[44]Roger Chartier, *The Cultural Origins of the French Revolution*, trans. Lydia Cochrane (Durham: Duke University Press, 1991) especially chaps. 1, 5–6.

and Soloveitchik both grew up in eastern Europe, heirs to long lineages of pietism and yeshiva learning respectively, and then managed, by way of a Kantian division of realms, to safeguard their faith (suitably adapted) from the philosophy they studied in Berlin. For the thinkers themselves, these religious experiences no doubt were authoritative. I read the dramatic ninth chapter of Heschel's *Man is Not Alone*, where encounter with God is described, as undoubtedly autobiographical. But what can this testimony do for the average Jew who has not had such experiences or has not interpreted them as religious, which amounts to the same thing? What authority can experience possess, secondhand?

My guess is that it does have a vestigial authority that would not be enough to undergird faith in and of itself, but is sufficient to motivate or strengthen religious commitment when working in concert with the social reality discussed earlier and other factors to be enumerated in a moment. Berger seems on the mark: modern believers have hints of transcendence that they can either dismiss, or follow to fuller faith, or hold fast, neither rejecting nor accepting their import. A child emerges from the womb. A close friend dies of cancer. A spectacular sunset pierces one's complacent schema of perception. The extraordinary holds out the same promise it always has, even if unable to deliver on that promise as it once did. The presence of the sacred, the hint of transcendence, the promise of larger meaning, is sufficient for the modicum of commitment that is retained.

3. *Meaning*. I have suggested above, building on Weber, that meaning possesses its own charisma in the modern period. Charisma, like value, grows with scarcity. One clings to any ground one can, once the void has opened up in the near distance. Meaning can be received cognitively or affectively or, most likely, through both faculties together. It may reside in a text written by people of an earlier age for whom meaning was assured. We may lack such assurance but respond to its authentic articulation nonetheless. Meaning may also be found in a ritual, despite the fact that one cannot assent in literal terms to the propositions (for example, blessings) featured in the ritual, and despite the loss of context for the ritual that I mentioned earlier. Congregational singing or parading or bowing carries a different significance and weight when one does not sing or bow or parade outside the congregation.

Indeed, communal activity as such may be exceptional. What is rendered problematic, however, may also be rendered that much more attractive. It confers a sort of "religious virtuosity" and partakes in "innerworldly asceticism," to borrow Weber's terms. "Ordinary" believers by definition become extraordinary if the rest of their social reality is determinedly secular. The meaning thus transmitted and adopted will carry substantial authority.

4. *Community* too has its magnetic appeal, its authority, both because we still experience communal activity and belief as intrinsically more compelling than individual experience or conviction, and because moderns deprived of integral community and reveling in individual autonomy may find themselves drawn to self-selected communities and be willing, or even eager, to have those communities obligate them. The authority of community grows the more we find ourselves without community. Durkheim's model of faith as *conscience collective* may paradoxically be more apt in this time of anomie than Weber's paradigm of a highly individualist search for meaning.

For modern Jews, community is both horizontal and vertical: horizontal, encompassing the Jewish people, as it exists in Israel and the diaspora, having survived the Holocaust; and vertical, the chain that "links the generations one to another." Attachment to that community carries with it the enlargement of self, the anchor of meaning, the "pleasure of agreement," the sense of more-than-subjective rightness and the appeal of immortality—recall Rosenzweig's quest—all of which comprise its hold. Severance of that attachment carries enormous guilt—all the more so given the recent slaughter of millions killed because they had not broken the chain. One cannot overestimate the authority that rests in the mystery of Jewish survival over the millennia despite numerous attempts to separate them from their faith or from life.

5. *Ancestors*. The "vertical community" has yet another hold on Jews, I believe. If we pay serious attention to the near synonymous usage of "tradition" and "the fathers" or "the ancestors" in much contemporary Jewish thought, we realize that loyalties and ambivalences deep inside the self operate in the acceptance and rejection of religious authority. The more I study twentieth-century Jewish thought, with its ever increasing weight upon "tradition," this despite the awareness that

"tradition" is not a given but a construct, the more I conclude that Judaism remains a faith of the ancestors. Jews live, as the tradition would have it, by the grace or merits of Abraham and his immediate descendants. The character of Michael Steadman on the recent television show "thirtysomething" agonizes over whether to circumcise his son and is finally convinced by the argument that he cannot take upon himself the responsibility and guilt of breaking a chain stretching back several millennia. Why not? A clue is provided by the impact of Emil Fackenheim's notions of a "commanding voice of Auschwitz," of a "614th commandment" in addition to the traditional 613: "Thou shalt not grant Hitler posthumous victories." Fackenheim's claim is that Jews owe it to those who perished not to abandon the commitment, or even the passive identity, for which they were murdered.[45]

This obligation would seem to rest upon a prior sense of obligation to the ancestors and their faith left unexamined. I would argue that it, like Michael Steadman's obligation to his past, stems directly from the family. Most Jews receive Jewish faith or identity in childhood and then reject or reaffirm it as adults. Their decision concerning faith, like their ambivalence concerning Judaism, forms part of the larger process of identity formation through which they become the children of their parents, indebted but separate. Because Judaism, like Christianity, is permeated with imagery of fathers (and, increasingly, mothers) and children, because one cannot hear "chosen people" or similar phrases without the love of a parent coming to mind, the link is all the stronger. One does not face up to it in dispassionate neutrality. The issue is charged with the most fundamental of passions. One breaks the link binding generations at some cost. I say this not in reductive "explanation" of Jewish faith but simply to note a factor in Jewish commitment to which scholars have paid far too little attention.

Jews who have felt the impact of these five factors may well find modern faith a tenable or even compelling option, despite the secularizing forces we have discussed and the dearth of coherent theological justifications for their commitments. I have tried to show why the inability to offer such rationales

---

[45]Emil Fackenheim, *God's Presence in History* (New York: Harper Torchbooks, 1970) 84–98.

has not proven fatal, and to suggest what authorities may be operating before, during, and after the unsuccessful or only partially successful attempt to locate more absolute or ultimate grounds for faith.

Let me note one final paradox in conclusion. It may well be that the metaphor of unending search is itself authoritative for many modern believers, who would be forced by intellectual integrity to distrust any surer resolution to their doubts and to rebel against any less equivocal directive of their actions. The self-identity of the searcher for authority confers and protects a precious sense of authenticity and truth. It is ideally suited for voluntarist observance in a democratic and highly individualist social context. "Searching" thereby assists believers mightily in withstanding the very challenges to faith that have made the other sort of authority so difficult to attain. That authority remains absent, but I wonder how much it is really missed.

SEEKING THE MERIDIAN: The Reconstitution of Space and Audience in the Poetry of Paul Celan and Dan Pagis[*]

Sidra DeKoven Ezrahi

Paul Celan may prove to be the last of the great German-Jewish poets, last player in the endgame of German-Jewish literature that stretches from Heinrich Heine to Karl Kraus, Franz Kafka, Franz Werfel, and Nelly Sachs. Celan was born Paul Antschel in 1920 in the town of Czernowitz, capital of the Bukovina section of Romania, a cultural borderland divided by vestiges of the Austro-Hungarian Empire, traces of Yiddish culture and Hasidism, as well as Jewish cultural assimilationism and the burgeonings of Romanian nationalism and Russian expansionism. While German may have been his native tongue, it was but one of several languages in which he was at home in that polyglot society, so that his emergence as a German poet under the circumstances in which his poetic identity was forged was a choice among different minority discourses.

As a young man growing up in interbellum Europe, Paul Antschel studied medicine and literature, returning home to Czernowitz on holiday in 1939. And that is where the "normal" biography ends and the life informed by—and interpreted through—the cataclysms of modern Jewish history begins. Antschel's parents were deported in 1942 to a Nazi internment camp in Transnistria where they both died (his mother's death by shooting, reported to him in 1943, becomes a haunting presence in his poetry). Although Antschel spent some time in a Romanian labor camp, he managed to avoid the death camps and to return to Czernowitz before the end of the war; in 1944 or early 1945 he wrote the poem "*Todesfuge*" that would establish his reputation and generate a debate, over the nature and status of writing in extremis, that continues to this day.

[*]I wish to thank Thomas Pavel for his probing and valuable comments.

Todesfuge

Schwarze Milch der Frühe wir trinken sie abends
wir trinken sie mittags und morgens wir trinken sie nachts
wir trinken und trinken
wir schaufeln ein Grab in den Lüften da liegt man nicht eng
Ein Mann wohnt im Haus der spielt mit den Schlangen der schreibt
der schreibt wenn es dunkelt nach Deutschland dein goldenes Haar Margarete
er schreibt es und tritt vor das Haus und es blitzen die Sterne er pfeift seine Rüden herbei
er pfeift seine Juden hervor läßt schaufeln ein Grab in der Erde
er befiehlt uns spielt auf nun zum Tanz

Schwarze Milch der Frühe wir trinken dich nachts
wir trinken dich morgens und mittags wir trinken dich abends
wir trinken und trinken
Ein Mann wohnt im Haus der spielt mit den Schlangen der schreibt
der schreibt wenn es dunkelt nach Deutschland dein goldenes Haar Margarete
Dein aschenes Haar Sulamith wir schaufeln ein Grab in den Lüften da liegt man nicht eng

Er ruft stecht tiefer ins Erdreich ihr einen ihr andern singet und spielt
er greift nach dem Eisen im Gurt er schwingts seine Augen sind blau
stecht tiefer die Spaten ihr einen ihr andern spielt weiter zum Tanz auf

Schwarze Milch der Frühe wir trinken dich nachts
wir trinken dich mittags und morgens wir trinken dich abends
wir trinken und trinken

Deathsfugue

Black milk of daybreak we drink it at evening
we drink it at midday and morning we drink it at night
we drink and we drink
we shovel a grave in the air there you won't lie too cramped
A man lives in the house he plays with his vipers he writes
he writes when it grow dark to Deustchland your golden hair Marguerite
he writes it and steps out of doors and the stars are all sparkling he whistles his hounds to come close
he whistles his Jews into rows has them shovel a grave in the ground
he orders us strike up and play for the dance

Black milk of daybreak we drink you at night
we drink you at morning and midday we drink you at evening
we drink and we drink
A man lives in the house he plays with his vipers he writes
he writes when it grows dark to Deutschland your golden hair Marguerite
your ashen hair Shulamith we shovel a grave in the air there you won't lie too cramped

He shouts jab the earth deeper you there you others sing up and play
he grabs for the rod in his belt he swings it his eyes are blue
jab your spades deeper you there you others play on for the dancing

Black milk of daybreak we drink you at night
we drink you at midday and morning we drink you at evening
we drink and we drink

ein Mann wohnt im Haus dein goldenes Haar Margarete
dein aschenes Haar Sulamith er spielt mit den Schlangen
Er ruft spielt süßer den Tod der Tod ist ein Meister aus Deutschland
er ruft streicht dunkler die Geigen dann steigt ihr als Rauch in die Luft
dann habt ihr ein Grab in den Wolken da liegt man nicht eng

Schwarze Milch der Frühe wir trinken dich nachts
wir trinken dich mittags der Tod ist ein Meister aus Deutschland
wir trinken dich abends und morgens wir trinken und trinken
der Tod ist ein Meister aus Deutschland sein Auge ist blau
er trifft dich mit bleierner Kugel er trifft dich genau
ein Mann wohnt im Haus dein goldenes Haar Margarete
er hetzt seine Rüden auf uns er schenkt uns ein Grab in der Luft
er spielt mit den Schlangen und träumet der Tod ist ein Meister aus Deutschland

dein goldenes Haar Margarete
dein aschenes Haar Sulamith

a man lives in the house your goldenes Haar Marguerite
your aschenes Haar Shulamith he plays with his vipers
He shouts play death more sweetly Death is a master from
Deutschland
he shouts scrape your strings darker you'll rise then in
smoke to the sky
you'll have a grave then in the clouds there you won't lie too
cramped

Black milk of daybreak we drink you at night
we drink you at midday Death is a master aus Deutschland
we drink at evening and morning we drink and we drink
this Death is ein Meister aus Deutschland his eye it is blue
he shoots you with shot made of lead shoots you level and
true
a man lives in the house your goldenes Haar Margarete
he looses his hounds on us grants us a grave in the air
he plays with his vipers and daydreams der Tod ist ein
Meister aus Deutschland

dein goldenes Haar Margarete
dein aschenes Haar Sulamith

Trans. John Felstiner

After a few years in Bucharest and then in Vienna, the poet whose name had become anagrammatized as Paul *Celan* settled in Paris where he continued to live as writer, translator, and professor of German literature until his suicide in 1970. His later poetry is so encoded, so highly private and opaque that it has give rise to competing schools of criticism—roughly divided between those who read a Celan poem as an esoteric, encrusted or buried text that can only be deciphered by a laborious unearthing of every shard of biographical, empirical material, and those for whom the obscurity of the writing is a barrier to be confronted—and respected—within the confines of the poem itself as a texture woven of patterns of internal referentiality. Whereas these competing hermeneutic strategies are hardly unique in twentieth-century criticism, I want to argue that in Celan's case, different principles of reading reflect a presumption of access that is not unlike the differential access of initiated or uninitiated persons to sacred space, that defines levels of intimacy through a kind of devotional attitude or attention. ("Attention," Celan wrote, quoting Malebranche, is the "natural prayer of the soul."[1]) Paul Celan, deterritorialized by radical separation from and total eradication of the cultures of his youth, clings to his native German, living and writing in the severed connection between language, primary audience and ground of reference, and spending a lifetime seeking his readers. The poet's native ground had become a grave, but only set loose, ungrounded—only as a "grave in the air"—could it become truly portable: the locus of a poetry that hovers over the earth, that frees (or *compels*) the survivor to become a wanderer.[2]

Taking his language with him into exile, Celan was performing a profoundly Jewish act. It was, however, not the only Jewish option available to a young survivor of Hitler's scourge in the middle of the fifth decade of this century. The poet Dan Pagis, compatriot and younger contemporary of Paul Celan, made his way to Palestine after the war, where he relinquished his native German and acquired a language that was defining its own territory and audience and articulating the epic story of a collective homecoming. I would go so far as to claim that in adopting Hebrew as the language of his poetry, Pagis may have actually blocked the return route to his own, private past, while Celan became, with the years, increasingly locked

---

[1]Cited in Michael Hamburger's Introduction, *Poems of Paul Celan* (New York: Persea Books, 1988) 31. Hamburger belongs to that primary group of readers and translators who claim a "special kind of attention and perhaps a special kind of faith in the authenticity of what [such poetry] enacts. Without the same attention, it could not have been written, for the risk is shared by writer and reader" (31). See also the debate between Hans-Georg Gadamer and Peter Szondi on the issue of access and interpretation as reviewed by Amy Colin in *Paul Celan: Holograms of Darkness* (Bloomington: Indiana University Press, 1991) xxiv.

[2]I would distinguish here between Celan, the survivor-poet as wanderer, and the "nomadic" condition of the "deterritorialized" writer defined and privileged by Deleuze and Guattari in universalistic-Marxist terms and by Jabès in more ethnically specific terms—as well as the "cultural mobility of late twentieth century Europe and America" celebrated by such writers as Stephen Greenblatt in his *Marvelous Possessions: The Wonder of the New World* (Chicago: University of Chicago Press, 1992) 25.

in a self-referential, autonomous, "hermetic" universe. I want to consider Paul Celan and Dan Pagis, then, in terms of the cultural options each represents within the global conversation among Jewish writers or between Jewish writers and their audiences in their different roles as authors—and authorizers—of the past.

In 1969, in what was to be one of his last major ventures before suicide, Paul Celan visited Israel and addressed the Hebrew Writers' Association. He spoke about the greening of the land and of the language: "Here," he said, "in your outer and inner landscape, I find much of the compulsion toward truth, much of the self-evidence, much of the world-open uniqueness of great poetry."[3] The world-embracing possibility that emanates from a reclaimed landscape, the self-evidence that allows public surfaces to speak, are remarkable concessions to the idea of repatriation on the part of this poet of private depths and unhinged languages. In that address, in that visit, and in the Hebrew words scattered throughout the poetry of his last years, he entered tentatively into a cultural space in which his own "Jewish loneliness"[4] might have found a different resolution.

But in fact Celan and the Hebrew writers he was addressing remained embedded in two distinct universes of discourse. For Celan, one might even say, the universe is bounded by discourse itself, the place instantiated in the poetry. The landscape of his native Bukovina exists utterly in its pastness, as the place of origin, the point of departure ever sought but retrievable only in the precincts of the imagination; "I am searching for my own place of origin ... on a child's map," Celan said in a speech in 1960. "None of these places can be found. They do not exist. But I know where they ought to exist ... and I find something else ... something ... which, via both poles, rejoins itself and on the way serenely crosses even the

[3]"Und ich finde hier, in dieser ausseren und inneren Landschaft, viel von den Wahrheitszwangen, der Selbstevidenz und der weltoffenen Einmaligkeit grosser Poesie." "Ansprache vor dem hebraischen schriftstellerverband," Tel Aviv, October 14, 1969, in *Paul Celan: Gesammelte Werke*, vol. III (Frankfurt am Main: Suhrkamp Verlag, 1983) 203. Translated by Rosmarie Waldrop in *Paul Celan: Collected Prose* (New York: The Sheep Meadow Press, 1986) 57.

[4]Paul Celan, *Collected Prose* 57.

tropics: I find a meridian." Poetry becomes, for him, a "sort of homecoming"—but this homecoming is a *process*, not a place—a tropological rather than a topographical quest; a yearning for a "meridian" or a "u-topia," which is the "no-place" of the displaced soul. The "poem is lonely. It is lonely and *en route*," he added in what became known as the "Meridian speech."[5] In the Hebrew lexicon, these words—utopia, homecoming—configurate as political, topographical possibility, *destination* as well as destiny, a real place on the map of the present.[6]

Celan's u-topia, the irretrievable point of departure to be projected onto an endlessly deferred future, authorizes a very different version of the past from the utopia located within the contained boundaries of a redemptive narrative and a preexistent vocabulary of catastrophe, martyrdom, and national resurrection such as one encounters in modern Hebrew culture. Many of the critical issues that focus on "*Todesfuge*" and have informed readings of postholocaust poetry in America and Europe are absent from discussions of the holocaust in Israel, as I hope to show below.

But no consideration of the poetry of Paul Celan is possible, it seems, without reference to certain questions regarding the authenticity of poetic language and debates over its mimetic function and its soteriological possibilities. The controversy traces back to Theodor Adorno's dictum that "to write poetry after Auschwitz is barbaric."[7] While generally invoked in discussions of writers or texts that seem to challenge implicit æsthetic or moral norms, Adorno's statement, said to have been originally occasioned by a reading of Celan's "*Todesfuge*," has become explicitly linked in the public mind with that poem so that the two have become as intertwined as a Talmudic commentary and its biblical source. Rarely, however, does one find any discussion of the complexity of Adorno's statement within the context of his philosophy of æs-

[5]"The Meridian," in *Paul Celan: Collected Prose* 49, 53–55.

[6]See also Celan's poems "Heimkehr" (in *Sprachgitter*, 1959) and "Was Geschah?" (in *Atemwende*, 1967) with *home* ("*heimkehr*" and "*heimatlich*"—"homecoming" and "homelandly" in Michael Hamburger's rendering) as an adverbial or verbal construction struggling, noun-*like*, for substantiation.

[7]"Cultural Criticism and Society," *Prisms*, trans. Samuel and Shierry Weber (London: Neville Spearman, 1967) 34.

thetics or the dynamics of his own rereadings of Celan. Rarely is it acknowledged that Adorno returned to "Auschwitz" again and again, refining and restating and qualifying his original statement in subsequent essays, probing but never quite resolving the paradox at the heart of his argument that "the abundance of real suffering tolerates no forgetting ... [that] this suffering ... demands the continued existence of art [even as] ... it prohibits it. It is now virtually in art alone that suffering can still find its own voice, consolation, without immediately being betrayed by it. The most important artists of the age have realized this."[8] As Adorno's dictum has been appropriated unreflectively since his death in 1969 by the very "culture industry" he so vigorously attacked in his lifetime, one is tempted to ask how, within the terms of his own critical theory, distinctions might be drawn between "barbarity," which is by definition outside the civilized discourse, and liminality, which is not?

When examined more closely, the critical norms that have their origins in (mis)readings of Adorno relate not only to the so-called "barbarity" or betrayal but to a widespread if unarticulated sense of the *propriety* of the symbolic language that faces Auschwitz. Since the "scorched earth," which is the locus of this language, cannot generate a natural audience for it, the issue of naturalization becomes crucial. Where, in our symbolic geography, do we locate Auschwitz or the Warsaw ghetto: In Poland? In Nazi-occupied Europe? In the vast resonant spaces of Jewish memory? Or as the metonymic limit of Western civilization? The disruption between this place and its signs is greater than the common disjunctions between referents and their signifiers—and the controversy over nominative and metaphoric language settles in that great divide. Is Celan's "*Grab in den Lüften*," after all, an open space with no boundaries? Or do certain images belong to specific symbolic worlds from which they are detached at considerable peril to both writer and reader? Are there holocaust symbols or topoi

---

[8]The "most important artists of the age" include such modernists as Kafka, Beckett and Celan. See Ernst Bloch, Georg Lukács, Bertold Brecht, Walter Benjamin, Theodor Adorno, *Æsthetics and Politics*, trans. and ed. Ronald Taylor (London: NLB, 1977) 188; Adorno, *Æsthetic Theory*, trans. C. Lenhardt (London: Routledge & Kegan Paul, 1970) 352–54, 443–44; Adorno, *Prisms* 245–71.

so overdetermined that they cannot enter other existential universes without being either disruptive or presumptuous—violating an unspoken principle of incommensurability?[9] Or is that which takes "Auschwitz" as its sign in fact so *underdetermined*, in Jean-François Lyotard's terms so "dissipated" by the premise of extermination that it elides into a kind of phraseless space?[10] What we are probing here are both the limits or boundaries of representation and the limits or boundaries of the metaphors that mediate the past.

Like the survivors themselves, a displaced poetic language may move randomly from one cultural realm to another, seeking a home. In spite of attempts to limit the polysemous potential of certain symbolic vocabularies, images that are so decontextualized as to be considered illegitimate may actually become acts of cultural disruption in the most radical poetic sense: ungrounded and migrant, they may be disruptive without being constitutive of alternative worlds. Even—or especially—in the wake of catastrophe, a "redemptive æsthetic" emerges along with public acts of commemoration to create regenerative spaces. With reference to the idealizing function of art, Leo Bersani has written, "a crucial assumption in the

---

[9]See, for example, Sylvia Plath's poems in *Ariel*, William Styron's *Sophie's Choice*, D. M. Thomas's *The White Hotel*, and Fassbinder's *Lili Marlene*—and the controversies, which attended their appearance, over the displacement of images or figures relating to the Nazi genocide.

[10]See Jean-François Lyotard, *The Differend: Phrases in Dispute*, trans. Georges Van Den Abbeele (Minneapolis: University of Minnesota Press, 1988) 13, 56–57:

> The differend is the unstable state and instant of language wherein something which must be able to be put into phrases cannot yet be.... The silence that surrounds the phrase, *Auschwitz was the extermination camp* is ... the sign that something remains to be phrased which is not, something which is not determined.... The indetermination of meanings left in abeyance [*en souffrance*], the extermination of what would allow them to be determined, the shadow of negation hollowing out reality to the point of making it dissipate, in a word, the wrong done to the victims that condemns them to silence—it is this ... which calls upon unknown phrases to link onto the name of Auschwitz.

In suggesting incommensurability or inarticulability or excess, the "dissipation" that comes of extermination, "*le différend*" may actually reinforce the idea of the propriety or the limits of symbolic as well as referential language.

culture of redemption, is that a certain type of repetition of experience in art repairs inherently damaged or valueless experience.... The catastrophes of history matter much less if they are somehow compensated for in art, and art itself gets reduced to a kind of superior patching function, is enslaved to those very materials to which it presumably imparts value; the redemptive æsthetic asks us to consider art as a correction of life."[11] Yet cultures that attempt to appropriate the dislocated languages of the exiles may never succeed in domesticating the fragments of their broken worlds or in defending against the acidity of an irredeemable vision—a vision that not only resists corrective idealizing but positively exemplifies, through a series of defamiliarizing procedures, the irretrievability and irreparability of the loss, constituting a counteræsthetics of loss and catastrophe. Perhaps the only version of utopianism that is compatible with the most unregenerate responses to cataclysm is that reformulated by Adorno in the postwar years. Resisting the totalizing philosophies that lead to fascism while affirming the potential of the most radical art forms to provide a "prefiguration of reconciled life" by which to measure flawed realities, Adorno managed—though not without some messianic hyperbole of his own—to rescue some of the utopian longings from the devastation of the war and of a failed Marxist orthodoxy: "The only philosophy which can be responsibly practised in face of despair is the attempt to contemplate all things as they would present themselves from the standpoint of redemption.... Perspectives must be fashioned that displace and estrange the world, reveal it to be, with its rifts and crevices, as indigent and distorted as it will appear one day in the messianic light."[12]

One of the most striking examples of a "displaced," defamiliarized or "estranged" image in postholocaust poetry is

---

[11]Leo Bersani, *The Culture of Redemption* (Cambridge, Mass.: Harvard University Press, 1990) 1–2.

[12]Adorno, *Minima Moralia: Reflections from Damaged Life* (London: NLB, 1974) 247. Utopia becomes then not only the irretrievable place of origin but the light from an unborn star that illumines the fragments of a broken reality. For a discussion of utopianism in Adorno's thought, see Martin Jay, *Adorno* (Cambridge, Mass.: Harvard University Press, 1984) 20 and Richard Wolin, "Utopia, Mimesis, and Reconciliation: A Redemptive Critique of Adorno's *Æsthetic Theory*," *Representations* 32 (Fall 1990): 37.

the "black milk" that opens Celan's "*Todesfuge*" and provides its incantatory refrain. The "black milk" has become as much an icon of the holocaust as the photograph of the little boy with his hands raised in the Warsaw ghetto.[13] But the oxymoron, no less palpable in our imagination for being an "impossible" image, is not only the rhetorical correlative of liminal reality; as the trope of ultimate contradiction that does not correct but defies the laws of both experience and logic, it relinquishes its compensatory function. That is, what may be so disruptive in such imagery is not its æsthetic properties per se but its defiance of a "redemptive æsthetic."

Yet the public status of "*Todesfuge*" would seem to belie its presumably subversive impact. It was the poem chosen to be recited in the Bundestag in 1988 to commemorate the fiftieth anniversary of Kristallnacht; it is frequently quoted in film, in art, in dance, in music, and is a fixed item in the secondary school curriculum, suggesting that it has actually become central to the official ritual of remembrance in Germany. It would appear, then, that the black milk and the ghetto child have become, in equal measure, constitutive texts in the regenerative semantic of their respective cultures. But consider further. This poem, which is a kind of litmus test of the public attempt to come to terms with or to "master" the past—the *Vergangenheitsbewältigung*—yet remains somehow extraneous to the cultural conversations taking place in Germany. In the classrooms where it is taught as compulsory reading, the poem is read almost universally as *poésie pure*, read for its prosody or for its fugal structure with little regard for its content or for the complex dynamic between form and content. Even more curious is the fact that this poem, which has achieved, after all, the status of a canonical text, has lent itself to charges of plagiarism. The accusation, launched by the widow of Franco-German poet Yvan Goll, that Celan borrowed his black milk from her husband's poetry is in itself less significant—poets with Celan's visibility are not infrequently beset by claims that would impugn their originality (and, like many of his poems, "*Todesfuge*" is replete with citations and allusions)—than the receptivity of sectors of the German pub-

[13]The photograph, taken during the Warsaw ghetto uprising, is prominently displayed in an enormous blowup in the Yad Vashem holocaust museum in Jerusalem. See the "Stroop Report," Nuremberg Documents P.S. 1061.

lic to such insinuations and the defensiveness of Celan's own response.[14] There is an implicit connection, I would submit, between the dis-location of the text and both its legitimating function and its own provisional legitimacy within the society.

One point of departure for probing these questions could be a comparison of the textbook "misreadings" of "*Todesfuge*" in Germany with the simple intertextual acts practiced by certain writers. Allusions to the "grave in the air" in an essay by Jean Améry and in a novel and a poem by Primo Levi—and Levi's disarming admission, when asked how conscious his borrowing had been, that his "stealth" (sic!) was not really plagiarism but "homage"[15]—illustrate not only the fine line between plagiarism and allusion or quotation but the status of other survivors such as Améry and Levi as a natural primary reading community for Celan's poem—or as authoritative agents in the construction of an ethics of reading. The search for such a community is the compelling force that shapes the writing of nearly every displaced writer. Primo Levi struggled to overcome his own "Jewish loneliness" by regrounding himself not only in his native tongue and native soil, but also in the positivistic principle of the transparent or correlative status of language vis à vis experience. The clarity of language relates here to the attempt to "objectify" experience as a property of culture, to rescue it from the irredeemably unique and therefore incommunicable. In Levi's view, the urge to communicate, the mandate of lucidity and the subordination of language to the writer's "message" are betrayed in Celan's more obscure verses:

---

[14]On this charge and other questions of "literary provenance" see John Felstiner, "Translating Paul Celan's *Todesfuge*" in Saul Friedlander, ed., *Probing the Limits of Representation: Nazism and the Final Solution* (Cambridge, Mass.: Harvard University Press, 1992) 243–44 and "Paul Celan's '*Todesfuge*,'" *Holocaust and Genocide Studies* 1, 2 (1986): 262–63. See also the work of other poets, such as Immanuel Weissglas, who raised similar questions of poetic affinity.

[15]See Felstiner, "Translating Paul Celan's *Todesfuge*" 244. See also "Gedale's Song," by Primo Levi: "Our brothers have risen to the sky/ Through the ovens of Sobibor and Treblinka/ They have dug themselves a grave in the air." Trans. Ruth Feldman, *Tikkun* 5, 5 (September/October 1990): inside cover.

> If [Celan's writing] is a message, it gets lost in the background noise: it is not a communication, it is not a language, or at most it is a dark and truncated language precisely like that of a person who is about to die and is alone, as we all will be at the point of death. But since we the living are not alone, we must not write as if we were alone. As long as we live we have a responsibility. We must answer for what we write, word by word, and make sure that every word reaches its target.... [Celan's] destiny [as a suicide] makes one think about the obscurity of [his] poetry as a pre-suicide, a not-wanting-to-be, a flight from the world, of which the intentional death was the crown.[16]

The life urge is equated here with responsibility (i.e., lucidity or communicability) and the death wish with inaccessibility. Yet what Levi is in fact demonstrating in his encounter with Celan's text, and in his own privileged access to that text, is the primacy of acts of devotion over acts of interpretation and the presumption not so much of an interpretive community as of a community of secret sharers. ("I believe that Celan the poet should be meditated upon and pitied rather than imitated," he says.)[17] Even when Levi takes issue with Celan's more opaque poetry, he identifies himself as the initiated reader whom Celan is seeking: Celan's writing, he admits, is "truly ... a reflection of the obscurity of his fate and his generation, and it grows ever denser around the reader, gripping him as in an ice-cold iron vise."[18] So stricken, Levi reveals himself to be the worthy if reluctant recipient of the kind of literary assault defined by Kafka as piercing the "frozen sea within us."[19]

---

[16]Levi, "On Obscure Writing," *Other People's Trades*, trans. Raymond Rosenthal (New York: Summit Books, 1989) 173–74.

[17]Levi 173.

[18]Levi 173. See Celan's comment on the "obscurity" of poetry in his Meridian speech: "This obscurity, if it is not congenital, has been bestowed on poetry by strangeness and distance (perhaps of its own making) and for the sake of an encounter" (46).

[19]The inherent loneliness of the literary process is embraced by Kafka in the same terms in which it is denied by Levi, withdrawal or separation being equated by both with a presuicidal condition: "What we need are books ... that make us feel as though we had been banished to the woods, far from any hu-

Levi's response to Celan dramatizes the perceived links between the survivor's personal, existential strategies and his authorial choices. Whether or not we regard Levi's own (apparent) suicide in 1987 as a sign of his failure to find in the Italian language and soil adequate reflections of the inner and outer landscapes of his imagination, we know from his very first book how desperate was his search for a language and an audience.[20] If we read his own death back into his life retrospectively, as he bids us do with Celan, his equation of life and "responsibility" would render his suicide, regardless of the circumstances that might have induced it, an admission of the failure to meet that responsibility.[21] I would add as an aside that I am here applying Levi's own strategy heuristically, without endorsing the critical approach that regards the suicide of a poet as an exegetical key to be incorporated into the poetry. Literary suicides—and even more dramatically, the suicides of holocaust survivors—pose challenging and profoundly disturbing questions to readers; the temptation to regard self-inflicted death as somehow a fitting (the more terrible) closure to a life whose formative years were spent in or under the shadow of a concentration camp often obscures both the boundaries between the writer and the work and the life-af-

---

man presence, like a suicide. A book must be the ax for the frozen sea within us." Quoted in Ernst Pawel, *The Nightmare of Reason* (New York: Farrar, Straus & Giroux) 158.

[20]See, for example, Levi's admission that the first edition of *Survival in Auschwitz* sold only 2,500 copies, and the somewhat disingenuous remark that after its publication "I hardly thought about this solitary little book any more," followed by: "even if sometimes I burned to believe that the descent into hell had given me, as to Coleridge's Ancient Mariner, a 'strange power of speech.'" "Beyond Survival" in *Prooftexts* 4, 1 (January 1984): 15. Levi's bid for an objective position as purveyor of the reality of Auschwitz is generally taken at face value and he is widely regarded as the quintessential "witness." See Irving Howe, "Introduction," Levi, *If Not Now, When?* trans. William Weaver (New York: Summit Books, 1982) 9.

[21]An alternative interpretation of both Levi's suicide and his last book is offered by Cynthia Ozick in "The Suicide Note," *The New Republic*, 21 March 1988, 33–35. Lingering doubts persist among Levi scholars as to whether his death really was a suicide.

firming and life-preserving nature of the act of creation.[22] Paul Celan lived as fully in poetry as any poet in our century.[23] In terms of a poetics of survival, Celan may be seen as truly Primo Levi's foil, reflecting the attempt to integrate life with the inherent *irresponsibility* of a poetry surviving in a world whose symbolic geography has been convulsed, constituting a place "where," as Celan said in his Meridian speech, "all tropes and metaphors want to be led *ad absurdum*."[24] Levi's insistence on the writer as witness and communicator retains some coherent vision or blueprint of the human order and a designated relationship between history and art; it places the self in a specific, delineated position at a controlled distance from both that which has been survived and the tribunal to which the testimony is being addressed.

The image of a tribunal can be carried further. Read as *evidence*, this literature, its writers, and its readers seem to resemble nothing so much as presences in a judicial court. While Celan's allusions and citations penetrate into the deepest layers of several centuries of German literature and reach across several languages, he is also held to another accounting—one that relates to the representational or historical status of his poetry. In delineating audiences, conversations, and the very nature of the communicative act, the postmodernist discourse has significantly redefined the role of citation and quotation (plagiarism's *legitimate* siblings).[25] Yet debates over those "Holocaust texts" indicted for having transgressed

---

[22]"When a life ends badly," writes Katha Pollitt in her review of Diane Wood Middlebrook's biography of Anne Sexton, "the great temptation is to construe it as a long, inevitable journey to ruin. But the death is not the life.... 'Suicide is, after all, the opposite of the poem,'" Sexton wrote in a memoir of Sylvia Plath. "The Death is Not the Life," *New York Times Book Review*, 18 August 1991, 22.

[23]Peter Szondi, a close friend whose own suicide followed hard on Celan's, went so far, in his claim for poetry as a form of substantiation, as to write that Celan's poetry "ceases to be *mimesis*, representation: it becomes reality." See "*Lecture de Strette*," in *Poésies et Poétiques de la Modernité*, ed. Mayotte Bollack (Presses Universitaires de Lille, 1981) 169.

[24]Paul Celan, "The Meridian" 51.

[25]See, for example, Jean-François Lyotard, "Defining the Postmodern" in *Postmodernism: ICA Documents*, ed. Lisa Appignanesi (London: Free Association Books, 1989) 7–10.

the limits tend to presume a unique decorum or protocol in regard to embedded citation or documentation. Consider, for example, the controversy that ensued over D.M. Thomas's alleged plagiarism of the Babi Yar sequence in *The White Hotel*. Far more memorable than the novel itself was Thomas's defense of his literary practice of borrowing passages from Anatoli Kuznetsov's documentary novel, *Babi Yar*, in order to let history speak, unmediated by the imagination, as it were.[26]

Needless to say, the charges of plagiarism directed at a writer like D.M. Thomas are of a different order from those suffered by Celan and only serve to underscore the differential weight of survivors as authenticating presences in the culture. Thomas's author-ity is, admittedly, located in historical documents or texts with a "documentary" valence; Celan's lies within his own person. And yet the weight of the written historical record, of recorded facts that would be admissible in some hypothetical court of law, often turns even the most abstract poetry into testimony. Rather than simply dismissing as irrelevant the accusations of plagiarism that were directed at "*Todesfuge*," critics like John Felstiner have suggested that "'black milk' may have been no metaphor at all but the very term camp inmates used to describe a liquid they were

---

[26]The fact that Thomas lifted those passages from the *English* translation of a *Russian* documentary *novel* with its own complicated publishing history—not to mention the highly interventionist act of pinioning his heroine through the genitals in order to confer symbolic coherence at the moment of death—all this only underscores the tension between the urgency of the truth-claim and the dislocation of the frames of language and experience without which it cannot be upheld. As one who is not only not a survivor of the Nazi genocide but is far removed from the culture about which he writes, Thomas's "borrowings" are highly conventionalized: he seeks access not to the reports of the atrocities, but to a specific genre of documentary narrative. On the "documentary novel" and the publishing history of *Babi Yar*, see my *By Words Alone: The Holocaust in Literature* (Chicago: The University of Chicago Press, 1980) 28–30. For a glimpse at the debate that ensued over the charge that D. M. Thomas had plagiarized from *Babi Yar* in sections of *The White Hotel*, see "Letters to the Editor" in *Times Literary Supplement*, 2 and 9 April 1982, and the symposium on "Plagiarism" vs. literary *influence*, with the participation of Harold Bloom and others, in the 9 April edition. See also James E. Young, *Writing and Rewriting the Holocaust: Narrative and the Consequences of Interpretation* (Bloomington: Indiana University Press, 1988) 53–59.

given"—citing Celan's own declaration that "what counts for me is truth, not euphony."[27] Celan's insistence on the veracity of the image or of the poem as a whole reflects more than the defensive posture of a poet vis à vis perceived misreadings of his work, just as the critical interest in his ongoing response reflects more than questions of intentionality. It is the survivor's unmediated access to experience, the survivor as ultimate reference, that is being affirmed here as part of a struggle over the cultural status rather than the "correct" interpretation of the poem. Celan's authenticating role as survivor could only, then, be contained or undermined by public charges of plagiarism. We should hardly be surprised, given the stakes in this ongoing debate, to discover that, as recently as 1988 (that is, forty-four years after its composition), "*Todesfuge*" was said, in a *New York Times* article, to have been composed in a concentration camp;[28] such an error actually *elevates* the poem to the status of an artifact, a "document" from the camps. That is, after all, one possible answer to the charge of plagiarism. Those texts, no matter how highly crafted, which appear to be "stolen" (or found) claim a valence that is essentially historical and documentary; in themselves they provide—or constitute—the citation or quotation that establishes authenticity. Their authorizing presence gives the ultimate lie to the charge of excessive æstheticization. Salient and indigestible, they remain appropriated but not fully naturalized into the conversation of the cultures in which they appear. There is an implicit assumption here that accords the "reified text" an existence somehow separate from the artistic or æsthetic domain, yet not fully outside it—presupposing a poetic language of ethereal or surreal images that became incarnated in and validated by experience, and conversely, experience that, through art, can reproduce itself as document.

---

[27]John Felstiner, "Translating Paul Celan's '*Todesfuge*'" 250. Felstiner argues elsewhere that Celan himself, in response to æstheticized readings of "*Todesfuge*," attempted in his later poetry to concretize images that might otherwise be unmoored from their referential base. See Felstiner, "Paul Celan's '*Todesfuge*'" 254.

[28]See Mark Rosenthal, *Anselm Kiefer* (Chicago: Art Institute of Chicago, and Philadelphia: Philadelphia Museum of Art, 1987) 95; and Paul Taylor, "Painter of the Apocalypse," *New York Times Magazine*, 16 October 1988, 49.

This may be even more perceptible in the realm of the visual arts. For the last decade or so, contemporary German artist Anselm Kiefer has engaged the dual figures of Shulamith and Margarete from "*Todesfuge*" in a series of paintings that bear their names. And yet a close examination of those paintings reveals the extent to which they stand out as both text and image, not fully quoted or absorbed into the canvas.

Nazism, which in Lyotard's terms marks the end of moral struggle in that the subject—or the subject's right to "phrase"—has been effaced and reciprocity preempted,[29] allows Shulamith and Margarete (the ultimate symbols of Jewish and German womanhood, respectively) to survive in the imagination as remainders of a mutual recognition that has become an annihilation of one by the other. In the canvas entitled "*Dein goldenes Haar, Margarethe*" (fig. 1), the hair could be the metonymic expression of that process of remaindering; Margarete's hair, straw embossed on an oil and emulsion painting of scorched fields, still retains its integral place in the rural landscape while Shulamith's—a black curve that echoes the shape of Margarete's—is a sign of ruination and blight (fig. 2).[30] As in many of Kiefer's other paintings, the text ("dein goldenes Haar, Margarete") overlays and literalizes the nonliteral, nonfigurative painting and fixes the metaphoric field. The presence of figures in mourning or of memorial candles in other paintings in the Shulamith/Margarete series (see cover illustration) as well as the commemorative, ritualistic performances of "*Todesfuge*" throughout Germany suggest, I would argue, that there is nothing left to *do*. Other Kiefer paintings that engage the Nazi past, such as the photographic series "Occupations" (1969) or the paintings "To the Unknown Painter" (1980–1983) are far more ambiguous, leaving more room for interpretation, for the unresolved moral

---

[29]Lyotard, *The Differend* 97–106. See also Sande Cohen's discussion of his argument in "Between Image and Phrase: Progressive History and the Final Solution as Dispossession," in Friedlander, ed., *Probing the Limits of Representation* 177–82.

[30]See also the hair as metonymy of the murdered Jewish woman in "Shulamith" (1990) in *Books of Anselm Kiefer*, ed. Gotz Adriani and trans. Bruni Mayor (New York: George Braziller, 1991) 290–331.

Figure 1. Anselm Kiefer, *Dein goldenes Haar, Margarethe,* 1981. Collection Sanders, Amsterdam. Courtesy of the artist.

Figure 2. Anselm Kiefer, *Dein aschenes Haar, Sulamit,* 1981. Private Collection. Courtesy of the artist.

struggle, evoking as well as ironizing the heroic, mythic images of the past. Unlike the "Occupations" series—in which the painter appearing in various "sieg heil" poses activates his audience to a wide range of possible, and very contradictory, responses to the invoked past, from celebration to revulsion[31]—the Shulamith/Margarete series implies a kind of self-limiting or self-chastising in regard to the images and lines from "*Todesfuge*" that remain superimposed on the canvas—both as material and as text—suggesting, perhaps, the extent to which Celan's text remains superimposed upon German culture and resistant to being coopted into a more open, organic, intertextual dynamic or moral struggle. We confront once again the issue of the "propriety" as well as the overdetermined quality of certain tropes, their resistance to the ironizing or decontextualizing efforts of the artist, and the complex cultural responses to them.

Actually, however, as I have already indicated, while the substance remains recalcitrant, the metrical and musical *forms* of "*Todesfuge*" have been absorbed into an ongoing discourse on æsthetic forms in Germany. Even Celan is reported to have distanced himself from the poem of his youth and to have shared the perception that the focus on form may have preempted an assimilation of the poem's content; ironically, this admission also serves to support the argument attributed to Adorno that the more poetically crafted a text, the more inherently estranged from the reality it is meant to represent. While most readers continue to treat "*Todesfuge*" itself with deference, it has become the prooftext for the "danger" that form will betray content, that any deviation from the strict historical account, any mitigation of the encounter with the documentary dimension, poses a threat to its representational status. In "*Todesfuge*," writes German playwright Rolf Hochhuth in 1963, the "gassing of Jews is entirely translated

---

[31]Andreas Huyssen explores the spectrum of responses to these paintings in "Anselm Kiefer: The Terror of History, the Temptation of Myth," *October* 48 (Spring, 1989): 25–45. Kiefer's more recent sculpture, "Mohn und Gedächtnis" (Poppy and Memory) refers to Celan's first book of poems with greater allusive depth and ambiguity. See Huyssen's essay on "Kiefer in Berlin," which explores the status of myth—classical and modern—in Kiefer's later work and its critical reception in Germany and America respectively, in *October* 62 (Fall 1992): 85–101.

into metaphors.... The impression of unreality it produces conspires with our natural strong tendency to treat the matter as a legend, as an incredible apocalyptic fable."[32]

It can be argued, however, that at some subliminal level the Germans have come to *know* the poem the way a people knows its anthems and its liturgies, learning the words at such an early age and on such ceremonial occasions that it has become an incantational procedure rather than an attended text. The "performative" function of "*Todesfuge*"—what it does as distinguished from what it more strictly means—reflects the specific nature of the dialogue between this exiled writer and the culture he is addressing.[33] What has been understood as a formidable denial of the contents of the poem may also be, for two generations of Germans at least, a particular form of knowing. We may be perceiving here a subtle reversal in the relations between æsthetic form and moral content. Rather than betraying the historical matter or obscuring its moral import, the performed poem may actually be the only possible conduit to what cannot be faced without mediation. To understand the fate of "*Todesfuge*" in Germany as the cooptation of art into the precincts of ceremony is, I think, to trace a thrust back from theater to ritual that would reabsorb the subversive nature of the poetry. Ritual, in Turner's and Schechner's terms, presupposes a noncritical, consensual "congregation ... to affirm the theological or cosmological order, explicit or implicit, which all hold in common, to actualize

---

[32]Hochhuth, in his stage directions for act 5 of *The Deputy*, asserts that although in "*Todesfuge*" the "gassing of Jews is entirely translated into metaphors," it is a "masterly" poem; nevertheless, it cannot serve as a model for imaginative interpretation of that period, "for despite the tremendous force of suggestion emanating from sound and sense, metaphors still screen the infernal cynicism of what really took place—a reality so enormous and grotesque that even today [1963] ... the impression of unreality it produces conspires with our natural strong tendency to treat the matter as a legend, as an incredible apocalyptic fable." See *The Deputy*, trans. Richard and Clara Winston (New York: Grove, 1964) 223. For a discussion of *The Deputy* and this issue, see my *By Words Alone* 42–45.

[33]For a range of discussions on the authority of performance, see "Special Topic: Performance," *PMLA* 107, 3 (May 1992): 434–607.

it periodically for themselves and inculcate the basic tenets of that order into their younger members."[34]

Beyond the impact of "*Todesfuge*," the fact that the insularity or incommunicability of Celan's mature verses has so absorbed the critical agenda could be a response not only to their inherent obscurity but also to their continued restless presence in the culture. The presumed impenetrability of neologisms and "hermetic" verses provides a defense against texts that are footloose, uncontained. It is in this sense perhaps that Celan's poetry becomes truly "barbaric," that the poet himself, the last of the Jewish poets in German literature, remains the original "barbarian" as foreigner or outlander—the one outside the community of selves, the one who in Germany most embodies an effaced otherness or nonidentity.

Although Celan himself insisted that he was "'ganz und gar nicht hermetisch,' absolutely not hermetic,"[35] we can find in this characterization more than a defensive strategy of reading; much of this poetry does appear uncontained in that it is *self*-contained, possibly even enclosing within itself the conversation usually transacted between text and reader. In Celan's poem "In Eins," four languages—German, Hebrew, French, and Spanish—populate the first four lines: "*Dreizehnter Feber. Im Herzmund/ erwachtes Schibboleth. Mit dir,/ Peuple/ de Paris. No pasarán.*"[36] Jacques Derrida finds in this and related poems a "multiplicity and migration of lan-

[34]Victor Turner, *From Ritual to Theatre: The Human Seriousness of Play* (New York: Performing Arts Journal Publications, 1982) 112.

[35]Quoted from a statement made by Celan to his translator Michael Hamburger, in Katharine Washburn's introduction to *Paul Celan: Last Poems*, ed. and trans. Washburn and Margret Guillemin (San Francisco: North Point Press, 1986) vi. Adorno, who described the "hermetic procedure" that allows art to "maintain its integrity only by refusing to go along with communication," was, of course, not the only critic to characterize Celan's poetry as hermetic. See *Æsthetic Theory*, Appendix I, 443. See also Amy Colin, "Paul Celan's Poetics of Destruction," in *Argumentum e Silentio: International Paul Celan Symposium*, ed. Amy D. Colin (Berlin: Walter de Gruyter, 1987) 177–8; and Alan Udoff, "On Poetic Dwelling: Situating Celan and the Holocaust," in Colin 321–51.

[36]Paul Celan, *Die Niemandsrose* (1963), from *Sprachgitter; Die Niemandsrose: Gedichte* (Frankfurt am Main: S. Fischer Verlag, 1986) 132.

guages ... within the uniqueness of the poetic inscription."[37] The languages that crowd Celan's poems provide, in a sense, both the speakers and their audience.[38]

For most of Celan's German readers, only one of these languages remains truly inscrutable: the Hebrew words scattered throughout. Like the small empty niches on the doorposts of formerly Jewish homes all over eastern and central Europe, Celan's Hebrew is a marker not only of the absent (and therefore indecipherable) Jewish culture but also of the absent reader. Recovering its status here as the language of origins, the primordial language, it remains uncorrupted, untried.[39] Translators and theorists have grappled with the untranslatability of the foreign phrases in Celan's verse; unique even within the polyphony of his verses, the Hebrew letters and words from a scriptural or liturgical vocabulary—"*Ziv*," "*Hachnissini*," "*Kumi ori*," "*Kaddish*," "*Ashrei*," "*Yizkor*," "*Tekiah*"—remain as salient and unassimilated in his poetry as his poems are in German culture. The Hebrew words per-

---

[37]"Schibboleth," in *Argumentum e Silentio* 22, 24. In Derrida's analysis of the poem "*In Eins*," the incomplete dating (13 February without a specific year) seems to establish historicity not as a limiting fact but as the status and symbolic complexity of reality, past and future. The multiplicity of possible witnesses and the indeterminate nature of this hour or this appointed time, which can encapsulate the Spanish Civil War, the French-Algerian War and of course the unmentioned war, make this both an urgent and an openended poem.

[38]The poem is bound by no single linguistic code or convention, place or situation. Evan Watkin constructs a "counter-theory of lyric ... at the point of missed connections between poet-self *and audience....* That would mean ... [that one could] offer Celan's lyrics, his peculiarly social languages, as a not quite familiar but still responsive audience ... an audience who *does* listen, the multiple languages which crowd his poems a moment of expectancy." See "Lyric Poetry as Social Language," in *Argumentum e Silentio* 270. Celan's poetic transactions included translations from English, Hebrew, Russian, and German.

[39]Hebrew is referred to as the "*wahr gebliebene, wahr gewordene*," the language that has remained true, that has therefore become true. Felstiner, "'*Ziv*, that light': Translation and Tradition in Paul Celan," in *New Literary History* 18 (1986–1987): 630. See also his "Langue maternelle, langue éternelle: La présence de l'hebreu" in *Contre-Jour: Etudes sur Paul Celan*, ed. Martine Broda (Paris: Les Editions du Cerf, 1986) 65–84.

sist, then, unexamined, maintaining the status of a document, a relic, a ritual—or an incomplete memory.

It can be argued, further, that it is not only the languages that constitute multiple interlocutors within the poem but the addressed others ("*mit dir,/ peuple de Paris*") who render Celan's poetry autonomous as an act that incorporates its own recipient. What is the status of the "you" (*du*) so often summoned in Celan's verses? While a number of the later poems especially appear to be firmly located in the conventional lyrical address to a specific beloved, the less-focused dialogical quest is thwarted in some of those texts in which it is most explicitly invoked. "The poem becomes conversation—often desperate conversation," Celan declares in his "Meridian" speech; "only the space of this conversation can establish what is addressed, can gather it into a 'you' around the naming and speaking I."[40] It is this *ars poetica* that informs the reading not only of his poetry but of his much-interpreted prose parable "*Gespräch im Gebirg*" (Conversation in the Mountain). The journey, which is both a parody and a recuperation of the romantic quest, begins, according to Stéphane Moses, as a search for a true dialogue. But as the voice in the mountain echoes back upon itself, it becomes a kind of interior dialogue "of a single voice divided," and the search for otherness issues in a nostalgic gesture—an "encounter with an other who has not come."[41] This failed dialogic, this desperate search for the other that becomes rather a form of endless self-proliferation can be related perhaps to the yearning of the exile to return to some native ground, some original landscape in which he could be repatriated;[42] yet the passage transpires within a primordial mountainous landscape so generic, so nonspecific and elemental, that it becomes the ground of legend.[43]

---

[40]"The Meridian" 50.

[41]Stéphane Moses, "Quand le langage se fait voix: Paul Celan: Entretien dans la montagne" in *Contre-Jour* 125–26.

[42] See Moses 126.

[43]"Lamb's Lettuce and *Dianthus superbus*, the gillyflower, is not far away. But they, the first cousins, they have (it cries out to heaven) no eyes." See *Paul Celan: Last Poems* 208. Blindness to the specific flora, which calls attention parodically to the Jew's insulation from nature, serves also to reinforce the generic, legendary quality of the landscape.

The Bukovina region of Romania was native ground to two German-speaking Jews who survived the war to become major writers elsewhere: Paul Celan and Dan Pagis.[44] The first remained lost at sea, as it were, or stranded on a desert island, positing his poetry as a message sent out in a bottle[45]—potentially consequential but hardly hopeful of destination; the second washed ashore, in Palestine, on a language and a clearly defined audience engaged in a collective act of repatriation. In "Conversation in the Mountain," Celan recapitulates not only the legendary landscape but the conventional rhetoric of the wandering Jew: "One evening, when the sun had set and not only the sun, the Jew—Jew and son of a Jew—went off, left his house and went off ... went under clouds, went in the shadow, his own and not his own—because the Jew, you know, what does he have that is really his own."[46] The other poet from Bukovina struggles with the allure—and the claustrophobia—of homecoming. Pagis invites the kind of comparison with Celan that would illuminate the provenance of each discourse, its poetic, existential, and cultural boundaries.

Born in Radautz near Czernowitz in 1930, Pagis lost his mother to disease and his father through emigration to Palestine in 1934; he survived Transnistria's concentration camps and arrived in Palestine in 1946. He became Israel's foremost scholar of medieval Hebrew poetry and one of its most important poets. He died—of natural causes—in 1986. Strikingly similar in many respects, the poetry of these two men from Bukovina can be distinguished primarily, I believe, by the presumed absence or presence of a targeted reader and a specific gravitational force. Celan's neologisms are radical acts performed on the most primary lexemes of language; his later poems in particular are an assault upon the rules of syn-

[44]For a discussion of other poets from Bukovina who continued to write after the war, see Colin, *Paul Celan* chap. 1. Aharon Appelfeld is another compatriot who survived the war years to become one of Israel's leading novelists.

[45]"Speech on the Occasion of Receiving the Literature Prize of the Free Hanseatic City of Bremen," in *Paul Celan: Collected Prose* 35. See also Celan's poem "*Inselhin*" ("Isleward" in Hamburger's translation) in *Poems of Paul Celan* 100–1.

[46]"Conversation in the Mountain" in *Paul Celan: Collected Prose* 17.

tax and a disarticulation of the integrity of the individual word; as his exile deepens, his German becomes a restless idiolect—bringing him as close as any modern Jewish poet has come to enacting the notion of *parole* as a free, individual utterance. Celan has in a most profound sense legislated himself out of the rhetorical context. Pagis, on the other hand, enters the Hebrew language in its most interactive social manifestations, engaging in a wide range of "speech genres," specific utterances within relatively stable spheres or fields of discourse. There is almost a sermonic (or antisermonic) quality to some of Pagis's poems, which subvert, dismantle, deconstruct, but always remain in dialogue with, the codes and the clichés of Israeli culture; his assaults are always performed within the larger unit of the social syntax.

Since the language of discourse is Hebrew, there is no area in Pagis's linguistic universe comparable to the sacred space inhabited by the Hebrew words in Celan's—no unexamined, opaque, or totemic images. The riddle structure at the heart of much of Pagis's later poetry presupposes encoded meaning that is, ultimately, accessible and public. Unlike Celan's, Pagis's personal exile is embedded within the noisy semantic of a collective homecoming.[47] The conversation is entirely a social one between reader and text that presupposes a *community* of readers. There are no lyrical subjects or objects, no significant addresses to an other within the poems themselves (the "you" who appears in an occasional poem tends to be an impersonal pronominal stand-in for both the integrity of the self and a significant other),[48] no real search for the dialogic moment—but there is, on the other hand, an implied audience as recipient of what becomes at times an urgent message. The appeal to an extratextual reader presupposes natural intralinguistic acts practiced by a living community. Pagis's "*Katuv b'iparon bakaron hehatum*" ("Written in Pencil in the Sealed Railway Car") is one of the shortest poems in modern Hebrew; it is also, possibly, the most resonant, as

---

[47]See my "Dan Pagis—Out of Line: A Poetics of Decomposition" in *Prooftexts* 10 (1990): 335–63; and "Shattering Memories," *The New Republic*, 25 February 1991, 35–39.

[48]See, for example, "How To" in Dan Pagis, *Variable Directions*, trans. Stephen Mitchell (San Francisco: North Point Press, 1989) 117.

canonic in its status in the Hebrew-speaking community as "*Todesfuge*" is in the German:

> here in this carload
> i am eve
> with abel my son
> if you see my other son
> cain son of man
> tell him that i [49]

The "you" addressed here is in second person plural ("*im tiru ... tagidu*"), encompassing the grammatic potential of both male and female witnesses (which a second-person singular construct in the gender-tagged Hebrew would not have been able to accommodate). The reader summoned to perform a speech act ("tell him that i") is absolutely necessary to complete this most "nonhermetic" of poems.

Although it poses as a "found" text, naming its place of composition, suspended, in its lack of closure, as an interrupted inscription, this poem does not perform either an authenticating or a delegitimating role in the culture analogous to other "found" or "stolen" texts we have considered. It is, rather, the transmission of an unspoken but intuited message, *paideia* as a primary communal act, that is invoked here. Celan's "performed poem" finds its counterecho in Pagis's poem-as-performance, which retains the full shock of its theatricality in the ritual community to which it is addressed—never becoming domesticated into the rituals of commemoration.

I have suggested that within the realm of Hebrew literature some of the primary critical questions change. Whereas "i"-witness accounts have acquired over the years a narrow privilege in a community in which the historical and personal terms of existence compete with and are subsumed into the mythical constructs of collective memory, there has been essentially no ongoing argument over symbolic language as a betrayal of the ground of historical memory comparable to the controversy that has focused on "*Todesfuge.*" The collective narrative with its implicit moral consensus relieves the

---

[49]Pagis, *Points of Departure*, trans. Stephen Mitchell, with an introduction by Robert Alter (Philadelphia: Jewish Publication Society, 1981) 23.

Hebrew writer of any historiographical responsibility, thereby conferring a kind of natural autonomy on the tropic discourse. Pagis writes against this backdrop of an explicitly referential, sequential, and coherent *histoire*. One can argue that because the holocaust narrative has itself become a convention, conforming more or less to contours drawn by writers like Primo Levi, both Pagis and Celan defamiliarize it in ways that invoke the uncanniness of primary memory. Both poets speak in codes, burying the referential layer deep within the poetic texture. But an essential difference lies in the status of the "master narrative" as primary reference for the Israeli writer. A critic like Berel Lang may be overlooking that difference when he claims that the poetry of Celan demonstrates the terms of a conflict that appears also in the poetry of (Israeli poets) Avraham Sutzkever, Abba Kovner, and Dan Pagis: "On the one hand, it seems evident that even if in the reading of his poems all knowledge of Celan's biography were put to one side, his imaginative power and the coercive horror of his subject would be recognized. On the other hand, it is far from certain that if the poems were read under a "veil of ignorance" apart from his biography readers would associate the poems with the subject of the Nazi genocide, or (more strongly) that they would require this association in order to experience the force of the poems."[50] Even were one to accept the extreme terms of

---

[50]Lang then brings Celan's "Aspen Tree" as evidence that "poetic reference to specific historical settings becomes increasingly attenuated as the text is more fully realized poetically":

> Aspen tree your leaves glance white into the dark.
> My mother's hair was never white.
> Dandelion, so green is the Ukraine.
> My yellow-haired mother did not come home.
> Rain cloud, above the well do you hover?
> My quiet mother weeps for everyone.
> Round star, you wind the golden loop.
> My mother's heart was ripped by lead.
> Oaken door, who lifted you off your hinges?
> My gentle mother cannot return.

Lang's argument, it would be, quite simply, impossible for Pagis's primary audience to read his verses under a "veil of ignorance."

Through a series of temporal disjunctions, the poetry of Dan Pagis undermines the ideological, theological continuum that brings the past into a meaningful present. Through a series of spatial disruptions, the diffused self, whose most common element in a Pagis poem is air and whose most common thrust is centrifugal enacts, in a way, the afterlife of one consigned to a "grave in the air": "I am nine years old. Beyond the door begins the interstellar space which I'm ready for."[51] Yet unlike Celan's speaker, this poet's response is not only to the claustrophobia and confinement of the concentration camp (or to the scorched ground of childhood) but also to the groundedness, the gravitational force of the collective homecoming.[52] Through juxtaposition or substitution that presupposes a semantic of destruction and regeneration, Pagis recasts the vocabulary of martyrdom. In the poem "Written in Pencil ... " as elsewhere, he replaces the archetypal victim, Isaac, with a composite figure, a fraternity of murder, Cain *and* Abel. The universal resonance of this poem only enhances its impact in the interpretive, "covenantal" community to which it is primarily addressed. Unlike the coupling of Margarete and Shulamith in Celan's "*Todesfuge*," in which, as we have seen, the presence of the one in effect annihilates the other, or in

---

Celan provides here, Lang argues, "only two indefinite clues concerning the circumstances of the death of the mother of the person in whose voice the poem is expressed: the reader learns that she was shot and that this occurred in the Ukraine." See Berel Lang, *Act and Idea in the Nazi Genocide* (Chicago: University of Chicago Press, 1990) 138–139. Yet this poem is actually far more confessional and less opaque than Pagis's "Written in Pencil...." Like "Aspen Tree," Pagis's poem has only two circumstantial markers that locate it historically: "sealed boxcar" and "carload" (*karon ḥatum, mishloaḥ*)—and even these are not exclusive or unambiguous historical references.

[51]"Point of Departure" in *Points of Departure* 41.

[52]See "Footprints" in *Points of Departure* 28–37. For a broader discussion of this subject in Israeli literature, see my "Revisioning the Past: The Changing Legacy of the Holocaust in Hebrew Literature," *Salmagundi*, 68–69 (Fall 1986): 245–70 and "Aharon Appelfeld: the Search for a Language," in *Studies in Contemporary Jewry* 1 (1984): 366–80.

Kiefer's paintings, where they are fixed in memorial space—that is, cultural space largely devoid of moral tension—the brothers in the Cain and Abel poems remain moral alternatives; although invoking a history of Jewish martyrdom in which the identity of the Jew as victim is clear and absolute, they address a society in which the intimation of a possible interchange of identities (in another poem "Cain dreams that he is Abel"[53]) suggests an ongoing moral struggle. It should come as no surprise, then, that Pagis's poems are not read on memorial occasions, that they have not been granted a static, ceremonial presence within Israeli culture.

It may be that George Steiner, consistent with his lifelong argument for the Jewish text as homeland and the Jew as housed in many languages, overstates the cleansing force in Celan's writing. In *After Babel*, he claims that Celan wrote German as if it were a foreign language: "All of Celan's own poetry is translated into German. It becomes a 'meta-language' cleansed of historical political dirt and thus, alone, usable by a profoundly Jewish voice after the Holocaust."[54] One can argue, of course, as many critics have, that the "historical political dirt" is never fully eradicated, that the poet "intends to make readers aware" of just those absences within his language.[55] But just who *are* these readers? The survivors, I have suggested, form an inclusive and safe category of readers across all cultures and languages. But, notwithstanding their mediating presence, the exiled German writer has no more "chosen" them than the Hebrew audience he addressed in 1969. While his fellow survivors and friends like Peter Szondi, who became self-selected readers and explicators of his work, to be joined by a host of contemporary critics, form a kind of cult of the initiated and constitute a protective buffer around him, the open borders of Celan's larger reading community may correspond to the degree of insularity in his language. In the mountain, the Jew remains a wanderer and a stranger; the conversation in the mountain is a conversation in an echo-

[53]"Brothers," *Points of Departure* 5. The translation I have given here is more literal than Mitchell's.

[54]Steiner, *After Babel: Aspects of Language and Translation* (London: Oxford Press, 1975) 389. Quoted in Colin, "Paul Celan's Poetics of Destruction" in *Argumentum e Silentio* 172.

[55]Colin, "Paul Celan's Poetics of Destruction" 172.

chamber. Whether we read Celan's last verses as "hermetic" in the sense of self-contained, autonomous, as the incorporation of text *and* audience—protected by a thick shield from the slings and arrows of outrageous readings—or as a gradual withdrawal into a private, impenetrable, and indecipherable universe, to which suicide was a logical sequel, his self-inflicted death becomes the ultimate cipher of the fate of the survivor-writer with a phantom audience.

Ultimately, though, his "host of invulnerable signs"[56] could signify a withdrawal into a private space that may prove to be a unique form of inviolability. While the reader of Pagis's poetry tears off the public masks one by one, until the hollow contours of the skull appear where the self might have been, the reader of Celan's poetry constructs a profile out of the irreducible sounds that never quite enter public speech. The less mimetic and the more personal or idiosyncratic the inscription, then, the more immune it is meant to be to both the debasement of metaphor and its reification in history. Finally, the grave in the air is the locus of a poetry that hovers over the earth, seeking readers and refusing all forms of containment and closure.

---

[56]Katharine Washburn, "Introduction," *Celan's Last Poems* xxxv.

EPILOGUE: Nietzsche's Lion

Tobin Siebers

To historicize the authority of religion—to inscribe the power of belief within a genealogical model—would seem to define the modern project, and yet Nietzsche, one of the founders of both modernity and the genealogical method, was not concerned solely with reducing belief to historical contingencies. Nietzsche was also impassioned by an unhistorical project that he called the revaluation of values: an attempt to confront the power wielded by belief in the age of skepticism. *Religion and the Authority of the Past* partakes of the modern project and its desire to explain the authority of religion in genealogy. Many of its contributors have employed the historicist methodology familiar to the modern period. And yet there breathes in these essays another spirit that Nietzsche would have understood—one long-banished but still familiar enough to have some meaning. It is a perspective on the authority of religion that attempts to represent both the horror of and longing for belief without losing the knowledge of its value. This perspective tries and fails to account for the authority of religion in terms of historical contingencies and then finds a strange comfort in the failure.

Nietzsche's unhistorical vision of religion and authority is rarely discussed today, and yet it is arguably the main idea of his favorite work. *Thus Spake Zarathustra* assumes that narrative, not history, holds the power to instill belief. Nietzsche's model of history, if it can be called such, takes the form of an allegory about belief called "On the Three Metamorphoses."[1] Nietzsche imagines the first metamorphosis of belief as a camel who lives like a hermit in the desert, diligently bearing the weight of others and exulting in its own strength and suffering. It goes where it is driven on faith. The camel changes into a lion, however, when its thoughts turn to rebellion and freedom. The lion wants to conquer freedom and to become the master of the desert, but to accomplish its desires, it must annihilate everything that it knows. Thus the lion, the great

[1] *The Portable Nietzsche*, ed. and trans. Walter Kaufmann (New York: Penguin Books, 1976) 137–39.

leaper, bounds after its master to defeat him. "Thou shalt," commands the master, whom Nietzsche pictures as a dragon whose values, thousands of years old, shine on its scales. But the lion roars back, "I will." The lion creates freedom for itself by annihilating the authority of the dragon, but the lion cannot create new values for itself. For that the lion must become a child, for only the child understands forgetting and innocence. The child transforms the lion's negative freedom into what Nietzsche, meaning what he says, calls the "sacred Yes." Thus the child rediscovers faith and returns to the world.

We may easily conceive how a hermit becomes a nihilist. How does a nihilist become a believer? Is the leap required to become a child of faith a jump forward or backward in time? Once the lion has succumbed to forgetfulness—and we with it—how are we to tell whether we have found new values or turned upon ourselves to embrace old ones? What matters for Nietzsche is that we choose to believe, even though we cannot make the choice and still retain our reason. Of course choice is not a part of rationality for Nietzsche; choice is an impossible contortion in which the self goes under its own leap of faith.

The leap of faith from belief, to nihilism, to belief again defines the acrobatics of the modern condition. It may also hold the secret to why a parental metaphor subtends all authority, since authority requires belief. As children become parents to their children, the child within them resurfaces, and they rediscover the will to believe. All of the essays in this volume, as Wendy Doniger insightfully observes, are about the will to believe and its acrobatics. In the poetry of Dan Pagis, according to Sidra DeKoven Erzahi, the leap of faith becomes a game of leap frog: one set of beliefs, shorn from the poet, is replaced by another set, which may in turn fall victim to skepticism and require one more leap of faith. For Celan, on the contrary, poetic language embodies both the loss of and longing for belief. Rather than mending belief with the faulty cloth of the latest value, Celan preserves the ugly hole torn in belief by skepticism, testifying to our inability to repair or to replace true belief. Do we choose Dan Pagis's path and overthrow old values for the newest value of the newest moment? Or do we retreat with Celan to the desert island of the heart, not as the camel would, but as the child—the child who, although discontented with the island, longingly sets sail letter-less bottles and dreams of forgetfulness and innocence?

The return to the desert itself holds the power to make belief in an age of skepticism. Perhaps, it is because the will to believe incorporates the loss of belief within itself. There would be no need to will belief, of course, if unbelief were not the rule of the day. Our forms of belief thus require the perception that the leap of faith takes place over an immense chasm that threatens each act of faith with a potential fall. Our lion never completely metamorphoses into a child. Rather, the emblem of our faith is a child sitting astride a lion, provoking by its form thoughts of mythological half-beasts—neither human nor animal, neither innocent nor predatory—divided against themselves in action and belief. Bruce Kuklick, for example, tells how the burgeoning skepticism of the University of Pennsylvania "Puritans" compelled them to forge into the desert to uncover the foundations of their own beliefs in the ruins of the ancient Near East. But the holes that they dug in these foundations only served to aggravate their loss of belief. Remarkably, however, this art of digging became itself the basis for a new religiosity, the secular belief in archæological science, thus demonstrating that the truism—to fill a hole one must dig another hole—fails to account for the fact that filling holes makes holes less noticeable and our losses less cruel. Is it unfair to ask whether archæology, that exquisite science of finding things, did not require a sense of loss to be born and for the world to accept it as a necessary form of human knowledge? Belief, whether secular or religious, seems to require that we have a vision of loss, that we see something like a desert, a hole, or a chasm. The chasm assures us of the necessity of both leaps of faith and falling, for falling, too, has a role in belief.

The people living currently in the Middle and Near East have a similar experience of the desert. That they live in the desert only means that they must find their deserts elsewhere. Yvonne Yazbeck Haddad explains that Arab intellectuals voyage to the West as budding skeptics, hoping to be converted to Western secularism, but they end by returning to Islam with the fervent desire to reestablish their faith and to prevent the westernization of their countries. Here zeal finds encouragement in the emptiness of secularism, despite the modern belief that only faith is barren and that its barrenness always guarantees the superiority of secular understanding. The West is baffled by Islam because it cannot understand, first, how anyone who stops believing might rediscover belief through more unbelief and, second, how anyone could reject Western civilization once they have seen it. That Islam does both terrifies the West. The idea of "fundamentalism" itself defines this terror. Fundamentalism is for the West the other of the will to believe; like Nietzsche's camel, it takes its faith on faith, dispensing with the necessity of repeated acts of willing. The will to believe, on the contrary, incorporates unbelief into itself: to preserve our own unique brand of faith, we require ourselves to believe while simultaneously protecting ourselves against belief; it is as if we renew our faith at each moment of our life through an act of will, thus cleansing ourselves of the terror of belief but believing more truly at the same time.

Whenever power corrupts belief, Nietzsche philosophized, we catch a glimpse of the heresy at the heart of belief: power is for Nietzsche a form of make-believe, a dazzling and deceptive fiction, designed to capture authority by crushing and enslaving others. Many of the essays in this volume describe the heresy of belief in precisely these terms. Robert E. Sullivan traces how the Catholic Church worked to save itself from internal heresy when confronted by the increasing need to recognize private property as a natural right. Its scholars plumbed the depths of its tradition to discover ideas that would permit private property to be valued and that would reconfigure the tradition itself so that it could be preserved from the forces represented by private property. Similarly, Garth Fowden explains that heresy always jeopardizes belief, especially when belief is joined to the desire for empire. The division within Byzantium between Chalcedonians and Monophysites as well as the fragmentation of the Islamic empire along confessional and political lines arise from the meshing of imperialism and missionary monotheism, and the heresies that attend such fusions. Finally, Judith Laikin Elkin illustrates how heresy may become a component of religious authority when it is placed in the service of empire building. The Catholic Church in the New World incorporated its experience with trying to convert the Jews into its mission to convert the Indians. Faced with the idolatry of Native Americans, the church redefined the heresy of the Jews as idolatry and burned them to teach a lesson to the Indians. The auto-da-fé became the ultimate parable designed to instruct potential converts and to rewrite history: the conversion of the Indians would retell the story of old-world conversion with a happier ending.

The will to believe thrives, then, in the most adverse conditions, these conditions being best defined by the world in which we currently live. It is an irony that modernity and its desire for expansion offered the greatest threat to religion but that beliefs akin to religious faith were required to establish the authority of modern, secular powers. Nietzsche authored the most powerful formulation of this insight, redefining heresy as too much self-consciousness about belief and its contradictions. Rather than directing his critique against modern secularism by exposing its similarity to religious belief, however, he attacked religion, accusing it of being too much like empire building. It was a remarkable achievement, but it ruined Nietzsche because he lost his ability to reason his way toward what he most desired, which was to believe. While Nietzsche tried to sidestep his own nihilism by preaching forgetfulness, it did not prove to be a credible strategy for the revaluation of values. For the desire to revalue values only reintroduces the forms of self-consciousness that originated Nietzsche's loss of belief. To desire to revalue values admits that human beings create values, but it is difficult for human beings to have faith in beliefs of mere human making. In Nietzsche, the will to power leapt into the breach created by doubt, introducing such frenzied action that only the birth of a new dæmon could explain it, and so out of the hollow tomb of God arose the will to power itself.

Once we attain the insight that belief is abusive, how can any kind of belief survive? The fact that belief does survive and that Nietzsche wanted it to survive shows that it cannot be reduced wholly to the lust for power. Nietzsche's insight about the genealogy of belief reveals him at his most iconoclastic, but it also shows him to be at a loss. Only belief can heal this loss. It is part of the miracle of belief that it can take so many different forms—forms that we desire and that become our saving grace. Empire does not always compromise religious belief, and neither politics nor religion is of one kind. Rather, belief is as diverse as it is necessary. David N. Keightley, for example, describes the differences between ancient China and Greece to illustrate alternative conceptions of what it means to hold individual authority in society. In Homer's poetry, the quest for particular details is an odyssey toward heroism in which human beings attain strong senses of themselves by learning how to represent their own particular characteristics. For the ancient Chinese, however, individuality was not compatible with the strong desire for social harmony. For Keightley, the distinction between Greek heroics and Chinese social harmony is useful in questioning how different representations of reality give authority to various definitions of individuality and community. It is also useful to illustrate just how diverse forms of belief and authority can be. Similarly, Barbara Stoler Miller finds an alternative conception of religious authority in the heterogeneous traditions of Hinduism. Miller argues that the worlds of the *Mahābhārata* and *Rāmāyaṇa* defy conventional ideas of authority, resonating with what modern mathematicians call chaos. As the countries of South Asia struggle to establish their national identities in the postcolonial era, the heterogeneity of the Hindu epics has been invaluable: communal factions in the region have frequently appealed to their transgressive force to authenticate claims to cultural and political independence. The unbounded texts of the epics thus provide modern readers with the freedom to define their own communities.

How one believes is as important as the authority of belief. The nature of faith does not lie in the end or in the beginning of belief, as Nietzsche's genealogy wrongly explains. If belief could be reduced to cause and effect or to historical contingencies, we would be able to understand leaps of faith. While the genealogical hypothesis is powerful, no one has ever been able to apply it with sufficient conviction to surmount the skepticism encouraged by the hypothesis itself. Secularists, too, know when something is believable, and although their methods are supposed to be credible, they are not always able to summon their own conviction. This is because the will to believe makes little sense if one does not believe, and it is unnecessary, if one does believe. The will to believe can be justified only on faith, and given this fact, it becomes difficult to distinguish the faith of believers from the faith of individuals who only wish to believe.

Arnold Eisen comes to similar conclusions in his reading of modern Judaism. Jewish thinkers in this century, he explains, have tried to undergird their religious commitments in some kind of authority, but they have been remarkably unsuccessful. And yet they have not given up the quest; their will to believe has become their faith. In fact, the writings of Franz Rosenzweig reveal that the unending character and means of this quest are themselves authoritative for many modern believers. The quest for authority not only proceeds for modern Jews; it proceeds in highly defined directions according to widely shared ideas and practices, suggesting that the relevant grounding for them may not be an ultimate authority forever sought and rarely found. Rather, the ideas and practices that define the search of Jews for the ultimate authority guarantee the authenticity of their religious commitments: the daily observances of Jewish law and ritual transfigure everyday life and objects, making them into emblems of more than their mundane shapes can carry. Believers carve the extraordinary out of the ordinary, bearing witness to visitations of holiness in things of no importance. Belief appears in the strangest of places: in a cup, on a plate, in the arrangement of food and drink and the hours of the day.

Perhaps we are all in some way, as Michael R. Kapetan puts it, carving for the saints. Kapetan voyages long distances between places with similar names to remember the links between past and present. He looks to our past for the authority in our future, and for old values to revalue and to make his own. Thus the world is transfigured in his hands and before our eyes. Kapetan's essay has a lesson about authority and belief to teach to the age of skepticism. Although our skepticism tells us that we will never be able to see the forest through the trees, we find in the trees the value of the whole, and at the moment when the whole is least likely to make itself known to us. There in the individual tree lies the truth, trust, and durability that we seek. And yet, despite the fact that these values are there, we find them only if we believe that they are there and take the trouble to hew their likenesses out of rougher shapes. In such complex forms of making, we discover more than human beings can make and more than they can believe, although neither discovery is able to destroy the will to believe.

I think, in the final analysis, that Yvonne Yazbeck Haddad told the exemplary anecdote about the character of belief and skepticism in the modern world—the story that in one form or another all of the essays in this volume are trying to tell. Her story describes how the will to believe sometimes exceeds our ability to disbelieve by creating such vertiginous patterns that it summons our faith. She recounts how a friend rebelled against her strict, church-going mother by raising her own children in an unusual way. Not wanting her own children to be like her mother, the woman forced her children into devotion to the church, hoping that they would grow to detest religion as much as she. Such desire to unhinge belief through belief is exposed for what it is by the dizzying thought that her unbelieving children might choose to continue family tradition by accompanying their children to church and that this family tradition itself might well have been passed down to Haddad's friend, who only thought that she had invented it.

My own version of this story returns to Nietzsche's lion or, perhaps, to a facsimile thereof—if indeed the difference between original and facsimile still matters. I offer it by way of conclusion so that readers might consider not how difficult it is to keep faith in the modern world but how painful it is not to believe in something when we are threatened by loss, which is, of course, the perpetual state of the human condition. A few years ago, the wire services carried a story from Kenya about a revenge-minded Masai tribesman whose brother had been killed by a lion and who attacked a stuffed lion in a glass cage at the Tourist Ministry in Nairobi.[2] Friends had told him that the ministry kept a live lion. He burst into the downtown office on a Saturday, broke the glass with his bare hands, and began strangling the lion. When the authorities asked him why he did it, he said that his brother had been killed by a lion and he had sworn that one day he would kill a lion with his bare hands.

Nietzsche's lion exemplifies the figure of modern unbelief. What if his lion is also stuffed? Does it really matter? What is the difference between the stuffed and unstuffed when it comes to keeping faith? All that matters are the promises that we make to ourselves and to others, and that we find reason to keep faith with them without going crazy or hurting someone.

---

[2]"Wrath Vented on Stuffed Lion," *Detroit Free Press*, 14 February 1983, 4A. See my discussion of this story in *Morals and Stories* (New York: Columbia University Press, 1992) 194–95.

Notes on Contributors

Wendy Doniger has an Arab horse, two large dogs, and a son in college. Under the names of Wendy Doniger O'Flaherty and Wendy Doniger, her writings range from translations of Sanskrit poems and Hindu myths to books about hallucinogenic mushrooms, phallic worship, evil, karma, women, dreams, folklore, horses, and myths. She is the Mircea Eliade Professor of History of Religions at the University of Chicago.

Arnold Eisen is Associate Professor of Religious Studies at Stanford University and author of *The Chosen People in America* and *Galut: Modern Jewish Reflection on Homelessness and Homecoming.* He is currently at work on a project entitled "Rethinking Modern Judaism: Ritual, Commandment, Community."

Judith Laikin Elkin is a Research Scientist with the Frankel Center for Judaic Studies at the University of Michigan and founding president of the Latin American Jewish Studies Association. She is the author of *Jews of the Latin American Republics* (University of North Carolina Press 1980) and *Latin American Jewish Studies: An Annotated Guide to the Literature* (Greenwood Press 1990).

Sidra DeKoven Ezrahi, Fellow at the Institute for the Humanities at the University of Michigan in 1991, spent the 1992–1993 year as a Visiting Fellow at Princeton University. She is Associate Professor of Comparative Jewish Literature at the Hebrew University of Jerusalem and is completing a book on "Reterritorializing the Jewish Imagination: Exile and Homecoming in Modern Jewish Literature."

Garth Fowden is a research associate at the Center for Greek and Roman Antiquity, National Research Foundation, Athens. He is the author of *The Egyptian Hermes. A Historical Approach To The Late Pagan Mind* (Cambridge University Press 1986; paperback edition: Princeton University Press 1993) and *Empire to Commonwealth. Consequences of Monotheism in Late Antiquity* (Princeton University Press 1993).

Yvonne Yazbeck Haddad is Professor of Islamic History at the University of Massachusetts at Amherst. She is the author of many books and articles on Islam and Islamic revival in the twentieth century, the Muslims of the United States, and women in Islam. She is past president of the Middle East Studies Association and former editor of *Muslim World.*

Michael R. Kapetan, a sculptor, is a lecturer in the School of Art at the University of Michigan. His work shows a rare combination of art-historical training and technical sculptural skills.

David N. Keightley is Professor of History at the University of California, Berkeley. He is the author of *Sources of Shang History: The Oracle-Bone Inscriptions of Bronze Age China* (1978) and editor of *The Origins of Chinese Civilization* (1983). One of the editors and founders of the journal, *Early China*, he is currently at work on a book called "Divination and Kingship in Late Shang China."

Bruce Kuklick is Killebrew Professor of History at the University of Pennsylvania, where he teaches American history. He has written several books on the history of American philosophy and theology, and is now at work on a study of archæology and its role in historical reasoning. His essay is a preliminary survey of his findings.

Barbara Stoler Miller was Milbank Professor and Chair of Oriental Studies at Barnard College, Columbia University. Her published works include *Love Song of the Dark Lord, The Hermit and the Love-Thief, Theater of Memory,* and a new translation of the *Bhagavad Gita.* At the time of her death in Spring 1993, she had just completed a book on the yoga-sutra to appear next year. She was president of the Association of Asian Studies and consultant to Peter Brook on his film, *The Mahabharata.*

Robert E. Sullivan teaches Church History at Saint John's Seminary in Brighton, Massachusetts. He is the author of *John Toland and the Deist Controversy* and is at work on a history of Catholic cultural medievalism.